Hiking
California's Trinity Alps Wilderness

Dennis Lewon

Published in cooperation with
The Wilderness Society

FALCON®

*A*FALCONGUIDE®

Falcon® Publishing is continually expanding its list of recreational guidebooks. All books include detailed descriptions, accurate maps, and all information necessary for enjoyable trips. You can order extra copies of this book and get information and prices for other Falcon® books by writing The Globe Pequot Press, P.O. Box 480, Guilford, CT 06437, or by calling toll-free 1-800-582-2665. Also, please ask for a copy of our current catalog. Visit our website at www.Falcon.com or contact us by e-mail at falcon@falcon.com.

Printed in the United States of America.

1 2 3 4 5 6 7 8 9 10 MG 06 05 04 03 02 01

All black-and-white photos by the author unless otherwise noted.
Elevation profile data provided by TOPO!/Wildflower Productions
375 Alabama Street, Suite 230/San Francisco, CA 94110
415-558-8700/www.topo.com

Cataloging-in-Publication Data is on file at the Library of Congress.

CAUTION

Outdoor recreational activities are by their very nature potentially hazardous. All participants in such activities must assume responsibility for their own actions and safety. The information contained in this guidebook cannot replace sound judgment and good decision-making skills, which help reduce exposure, nor does the scope of this book allow for the disclosure of all the potential hazards and risks involved in such activities.

Learn as much as possible about the outdoor recreational activities in which you participate, prepare for the unexpected, and be cautious. The reward will be a safer and more enjoyable experience.

♻ Text pages printed on recycled paper.

Contents

Acknowledgments

A funny thing happened when I set out to thank the people who made this project possible. I started thinking about all the hiking I'd done in the Trinity Alps over the last two years, which in turn led me to recall even more hiking I'd done there in previous years, and soon I was trying to remember the first time I ever went backpacking in the area. I couldn't. As far back as I can remember, I've *always* been hiking in the Trinity Alps. Thank you to my parents, Bob and Elaine, for putting me on the right path when I was just learning to walk.

Then I started hiking hundreds of miles of trails for this book and discovered my childhood trips barely scratched the surface of this vast wilderness. I got to rediscover the Trinity Alps all over again. Thanks to all the friends and strangers who made the last two seasons of hiking possible. Without friends and family who joined me on the trail from time to time I might still be talking to myself. And thanks especially to my wife, Jen, who joined me even when there was no trail.

Finally, I'd like to thank all the helpful people at the Weaverville Ranger Station, who never complained about the dirty, unshaved hiker who kept showing up with a list of questions (at least they never complained to me). A special thanks to Larry McLean of the Weaverville Ranger District, who reviewed the manuscript for this guide and answered an endless barrage of questions. And of course a big thank you to the folks at Falcon Press, without whom none of this would be possible.

Legend

Interstate	⬟(00)	Campground	⛺
US Highway	(00)	Cabins/Buildings	▪
State or Other Principal Road	(00) (000)	Peak	🏔 9,782 ft.
Interstate Highway	═══➤	Butte	🏔
Paved Road	▬▬▬➤	Elevation	9,782 ft. ✕
Gravel Road	═══➤	Gate	•—•
Unimproved Road	========➤	Mine Site	⚒
Trailhead	◯	Overlook/Point of Interest	▣
Main Trail/Route	•••—•••—•••		
Alternate/Secondary Trail/Route	---•---•---	National Forest/Park Boundary	⌐_¬_⌐
Cross-country Route	·············	Map Orientation	↑N
Parking Area	Ⓟ	Scale	0 0.5 1 Miles
River/Creek	～		
Spring	⟃	Waterfall	⫽
Forest Road	4165	Pass	)(
City	◯	Bridge	⏝⏝
Meadow	⊥		

Overview Map

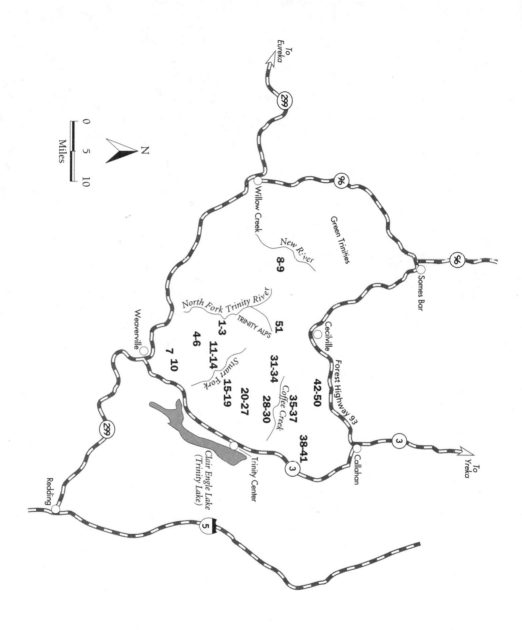

To Eureka

299

96

Willow Creek

Green Trinities

New River

8-9

96

Somes Bar

North Fork Trinity River

TRINITY ALPS

51

Ceciville

Weaverville

1-3

4-6

7 10

11-14

Stuart Fork

15-19

20-27

28-30

31-34

35-37

Coffee Creek

42-50

Forest Highway 93

38-41

3

Callahan

To Yreka

299

Redding

Clair Engle Lake
(Trinity Lake)

Trinity Center

3

5

0 5 10
Miles

N

Introduction

A sublime little alpine tarn is perched high on the flank of Red Rock Mountain in the Trinity Alps. No trail leads to the nameless pond, but an afternoon spent on its emerald green shores is well worth the steep cross-country hike. I once told a Trinity old-timer, a man in his 80s who still heads into the wilderness every summer, about coming across the peaceful pond.

"You know about that place, eh?" he responded, half-surprised I'd stumbled upon it, and half-glad to share the memory of such a beautiful place.

I understood the sentiment. It perfectly describes the way I feel about the entire Trinity Alps. Compared to California's more well-known wilderness areas, the Trinity Alps wilderness is much like that nameless little pond: a delightful place that any wilderness lover would be happy to stumble upon. Like the tiny tarn, what the Alps lacks in size and notoriety, it more than makes up for in true backcountry beauty. Granite peaks, glacier-carved canyons, lush meadows, sparkling lakes and streams, and a chance for real wilderness solitude await hikers, backpackers, and equestrians who find their way to the Trinity Alps.

Located in an isolated region at the southern end of the Klamath Mountains, along the headwaters of the Trinity and Salmon Rivers, the Trinity Alps Wilderness encompasses more than half a million acres—nearly 800 square miles—of rugged backcountry. The protected area constitutes one of the largest parcels of federally designated wilderness in California.

Elevations in the wilderness range from 2,000 to 9,000 feet. Within this zone you'll find a diverse environment that includes a multitude of jagged peaks, deep forested canyons, and gentle river valleys. Hundreds of miles of trails crisscross the wilderness, making it easy to reach the heart of the backcountry in just a day or two of hiking. There are also numerous drainages where no paths—and few humans—have yet to intrude. Whether you want an easy day hike or a challenging weeklong trek, you'll find exactly what you're looking for within the boundaries of the Trinity Alps.

WHAT TO EXPECT

Trails in the Trinity Alps are generally well-maintained and easy to follow. Most trails are signed, but don't expect to rely on signs alone: they disappear from time-to-time and may not be replaced for years. Except for early-season stream crossings, there are few trail hazards to worry about in the Trinity Alps. Elevations are relatively low, so altitude sickness and summer snowstorms are not much of a concern.

With more than 700 miles of trails and upwards of 100 lakes in the Trinity Alps, there's more than enough room for a large number of hikers to explore the backcountry and still enjoy the peace and solitude of the wilderness. Though the Alps have become more well known in recent years, the area is still relatively uncrowded compared to high-use regions like the Sierra Nevada. You can still show up without reservations, and land managers have yet to impose restrictions on where you can camp (except for those implied by standard Zero Impact practices; see below). The vast wilderness of canyons and forests and basins can absorb a lot of people without feeling crowded.

That said, you should avoid certain destinations or only go "out-of-season" if solitude is what you're after. Renowned lakes like Canyon Creek, Sapphire, Caribou, and Grizzly host a constant stream of human traffic all summer long, while less-publicized places like Bullards Basin may go weeks without a single visitor. Going midweek and after summer can also maximize solitude. I've been to each of the lakes mentioned above without another soul in sight—in October. For experienced backcountry travelers there are a limitless number of off-trail destinations with guaranteed solitude. A small number of off-trail routes are included in this guidebook, but they only constitute the tip of the iceberg.

Backpackers far outnumber equestrians in the Trinity Alps, but each trail user is apt to encounter the other at some point. Consideration and good trail etiquette can go a long way toward helping everyone get along. Hikers should step off the trail and let horses or other stock animals have the right of way (llamas have also become popular pack animals). It's much easier for hikers to make the accommodation. Likewise, stock users should observe good Zero Impact principles (see below). Everyone should keep in mind that the wilderness is public land—ours to share.

GETTING THERE

The Trinity Alps Wilderness is located in northwest California in a remote slice of backcountry between Redding and Eureka. The wilderness is within the boundaries of the Shasta–Trinity, Klamath, and Six Rivers National Forests. The main access routes from points north and south are off of Interstate 5 and US Highway 101. Depending on your destination, take either California Highway 299 or 3 to reach the wilderness area and trailhead roads. Weaverville, on CA 299 about 46 miles west of Redding, is the largest town on the outskirts of the Trinity Alps. Other settlements on the fringes of the forest include Trinity Center, Coffee Creek, Callahan, Cecilville, Willow Creek, and Junction City. The closest commercial airport (with rental cars available) is in Redding. Most trailheads are accessed via unpaved Forest Service roads. All roads included in this guidebook are passable to passenger cars.

SEASONS

The best hiking season in the Trinity Alps is the middle of June through the end of October. Keep in mind that snowfall changes dramatically year to year, so the early-season hiking sometimes varies by as much as a month (from late May to late June). Even when streams are high and lakes are frozen, however, there are often good alternative destinations in the lower elevations. Check with rangers for specific snowpack information if you plan a trip before late June.

Summer days tend to be warm and clear (80–95 degrees F) and nights cool (25–45 degrees F). Summer rain is rare and sporadic, arriving chiefly in the form of brief and intense thundershowers. In the fall the weather is generally dry and slightly cooler, with nights getting downright chilly in October. Autumn is a great time to hike if you want to avoid crowds (some of my favorite trips have been in early November, after most people leave and before the snow falls). Fall is also hunting season in the Trinity Alps. The USDA Forest Service locks gates across some access roads from October 31 to May 15.

For most people, winter means the wilderness is out-of-season. And with more than a dozen feet of snow in many years, the Trinity Alps is no exception. But for those with appropriate experience the area offers excellent opportunities for winter recreation and mountaineering. Just remember that you are truly on your own.

WATER

Water is readily available in streams and lakes throughout the Trinity Alps Wilderness. Unless otherwise noted, you can expect to encounter water sources frequently as you hike through the region. All water, however, should be treated before drinking. Many cases of giardiasis have been reported from drinking untreated water in the Trinity Alps. Boiling, filtering, and chemical purification tablets are all adequate treatments for preventing giardiasis and other water-borne illnesses.

BUGS

In general, mosquitoes and other biting bugs are not a major nuisance in the Trinity Alps, which is not to say the wilderness is bug free. Some of the lower elevation lakes and meadows host swarms of mosquitoes in early summer. But mosquito swarms, like everything else in Trinity, tend to the smaller end of the spectrum. If you're used to Sierra- or Alaska-size mosquito swarms, you may be pleasantly surprised by Trinity's gentler, kinder version, though you should still throw a tube of insect repellent into your pack.

Ticks may pose a threat if they carry Lyme disease, but they are extremely rare above the lower elevations (at least I have yet to encounter any). The best prevention is a daily body check and prompt removal of any ticks you find. Ticks must be embedded more than 24 hours to transmit Lyme disease. Using tweezers, grasp the tick's head right next to the skin and pull gently. Tugging on its body will make it act like a syringe, injecting tainted blood.

FISHING

Some hikers can't tell a fly rod from a fly on the wall, while others spend every moment in the backcountry either fishing or thinking about fishing. If you're one of the latter, you'll find plenty to occupy your time in the Trinity Alps. Stocking programs have filled many backcountry lakes and streams with eastern brook, rainbow, and brown trout. Salmon and steelhead also persist (in decreasing numbers) in the Trinity River and some of its tributaries. A valid California fishing license is required for all angling in the Trinity

Alps Wilderness. Because parts of the Trinity Alps watershed serve as spawning habitat for endangered salmon, it's vital that you check current California Fish and Game regulations before casting a line. Some streams (New River and North Fork Trinity River, for example) have been entirely closed to angling in recent years.

CATTLE

What's a cow doing in my camp? The Wilderness Act of 1964 allows livestock grazing to continue in Forest Service wilderness areas where it existed prior to the designation. In the Trinity Alps, that means you might run into cattle in some drainages between July and October. Fortunately (if you oppose cows in camp), grazing in the wilderness is now the exception rather than the rule. Most grazing permits have been phased out of a large portion of the Trinity Alps. If you want to avoid cows, stay away from the drainages on the north side of the Scott Mountains and a few areas north of Coffee Creek. Grazing is mentioned in hike descriptions where applicable.

WILDERNESS PERMITS

All overnight visitors to the Trinity Alps Wilderness must obtain wilderness permits before entering the backcountry. Permits are free and are available without reservation. Simply call ahead or stop by one of the ranger stations on the way to the trailhead (see Appendix A) and pick one up. If you arrive after hours you can fill out a permit form at a self-registration box located outside the stations. The Weaverville Ranger Station unveiled a slick computerized registration system in 1999. The system allows you to get your permit and current information on the route (including the number of people who are already there) in an instant. Campfire permits are also required, and you should always check to see if any special fire hazards or restrictions are in effect. See contact information in Appendix A.

EMERGENCY MEDICAL SERVICES

In case of emergency, 911 works in the Trinity Alps area. Cell phone coverage of the area is sparse, at best, so don't plan on calling for help when in the backcountry. The nearest major hospitals are in Redding, with limited medical services available in Weaverville.

Using this Guidebook

TYPE OF TRAIL

Suggested hikes have been split into the following categories:

Day hike: Best for a short excursion only, due to lack of water or suitable camping sites.

Backpack: Best for backpacking with at least one or more nights in the backcountry. Many of the overnight hikes can be done as day hikes if you have the time and/or stamina.

Loop: Starts and finishes at the same trailhead with no (or very little) retracing of your steps. Sometimes the definition of a "loop" includes creative shapes (like a figure eight or lollipop) and sometimes requires a short walk on a dirt road to get back to the trailhead.

Out-and-back: Traveling the same route coming and going.

RATINGS

Difficulty ratings are inherently flawed: what's easy for you might be difficult for me. Still, such ratings serve as a general guide and give a useful approximation of a hike's challenge. Remember that ratings are not the final word, and that the most important factor is to be honest about your own fitness level when planning your trip. In this guidebook, difficulty ratings consider both how long and strenuous a hike is. Here are general guidelines for ratings:

Easy: Suitable for any hiker—young or old. Expect no serious elevation gain, hazards, or navigation problems.

Moderate: Suitable for hikers who have at least some experience and average fitness level. Likely includes some elevation change and may have places where the trail is faint.

Strenuous: Suitable only for experienced hikers with above-average fitness level. Possible hazardous trail sections, navigation difficulties, and serious elevation change.

DISTANCE

Measuring trail distances is an inexact science at best. In this guidebook most distances have been taken from map measurements and from in-the-field estimates. Most trail signs in the Trinity Alps do not include distances, and when they do you can bet they are just somebody else's best guess. Keep in mind that distance is often less important than difficulty. A steep 2-mile climb on rocky tread can take longer than a 4-mile stroll through a gentle river valley. It may be helpful to note that most hikers average about 2 miles per hour.

MAPS

The maps in this book serve as a general guide only. Don't hit the trail without buying a better, more detailed map. There are a few choices when it comes to maps for the Trinity Alps. The USDA Forest Service Trinity Alps Wilderness map (1998; 1:63,360) is a comprehensive topographic map that covers the entire wilderness. It will serve most visitors who don't plan on doing extensive off-trail hiking. For those who do—or for anyone who wants a scale with more detail—try the USGS quads. The USDAFS map is available from the ranger stations listed in Appendix A. USGS quads can be special ordered from your local sports store, or you can order them directly from the USGS.

ELEVATION CHARTS

All hike descriptions include elevation charts. Use these charts to get a general picture of how much elevation gain and loss a hike entails. The charts are not meant to be a detailed foot-by-foot account of the route, but serve as a quick glimpse of the overall elevation change.

BACKCOUNTRY REGULATIONS

The Trinity Alps is a federally designated wilderness area. As such, it's been given the highest level of protection public lands receive. The underlying principle behind all wilderness regulations was best summed up by President Theodore Roosevelt in 1903. He was talking about the Grand Canyon at the time, but he might as well have been talking about all wilderness. "Keep this great wonder of nature as it now is," proclaimed Roosevelt. "Leave it as it is. You cannot improve on it; not a bit. The ages have been at work on it, and man can only mar it."

To that end, the following backcountry regulations are intended to help Trinity Alps visitors leave well enough alone.

- Get a wilderness permit for all overnight use (see Appendix A).
- Camp only in appropriate places (see Zero Impact, below).
- Stay on trails (where possible) and don't create shortcuts.
- Dispose of human waste in a cat hole at least 200 feet from all water sources and campsites. Bathing and dishwater should also be disposed of well away from water sources.
- Use campstoves rather than cooking fires whenever possible.
- Carry out all trash. If you can pack it in, you can pack it out.
- Limit group size to ten or fewer.
- Suspend food out of reach of bears.
- Do not feed or in any way disturb the wildlife. Do not leave behind food scraps.
- Do not operate any mechanized vehicle in the wilderness.
- Do not destroy, deface, disturb, or remove from its natural setting any plant, rock, animal, or archaeological resource.
- Please read Zero Impact (below) for more details on minimizing impact on the wilderness.

Zero Impact

Going into a wild area is like visiting a famous museum. You obviously do not want to leave your mark on an art treasure in the museum. If everybody going through the museum left one little mark, the piece of art would be quickly destroyed—and of what value is a big building full of trashed art? The same goes for pristine wildlands. If we all left just one little mark on the landscape, the backcountry would soon be spoiled.

A wilderness can accommodate human use as long as everybody behaves. But a few thoughtless or uninformed visitors can ruin it for everybody who follows. All backcountry users have a responsibility to know and follow the rules of zero-impact camping.

Nowadays, most wilderness users want to walk softly, but some aren't aware they have poor manners. Often their actions are dictated by the outdated habits of a past generation of campers who cut green boughs for evening shelters, built campfires with fire rings, and dug trenches around tents. In the 1950s, these "camping rules" may have been acceptable. But they leave long-lasting scars, and today such behavior is absolutely unacceptable. Wild places are becoming rare, and the number of users is mushrooming. More and more camping areas show unsightly signs of heavy use.

Consequently, a new code of ethics is growing out of the necessity of coping with the unending waves of people who want a perfect backcountry experience. Today, we all must leave no clues that we were there. Enjoy the wild, but leave no trace of your visit.

Leopard lilies along Boulder Creek.

THREE FALCON PRINCIPLES OF ZERO IMPACT

- Leave with everything you brought in.
- Leave no sign of your visit.
- Leave the landscape as you found it.

Most of us know better than to litter—in or out of the backcountry. Be sure you leave nothing, regardless of how small it is, along the trail or at your campsite. You should pack out everything, including orange peels, flip tops, cigarette butts, and gum wrappers. Also, pick up any trash others leave behind.

Follow the main trail. Avoid cutting switchbacks and walking on trailside vegetation. Don't pick up "souvenirs," such as rocks, antlers, or wildflowers. The next person wants to see them too, and collecting such souvenirs violates many regulations.

Avoid making loud noises on the trail (unless you are in bear country) or in camp. Be courteous—remember, sound travels easily in the backcountry, especially across water.

Carry a lightweight trowel to bury human waste 6 to 8 inches deep at least 300 feet from any water source. Pack out used toilet paper.

Go without a campfire. Carry a stove for cooking and flashlight, candle lantern, or headlamp for light. For emergencies, learn how to build a no-trace fire.

Camp in obviously used sites when available. Otherwise, camp and cook on durable surfaces such as bedrock, sand, gravel bars, or bare ground.

Leave no trace and put your ear to the ground and listen carefully. Thousands of people coming behind you are thanking you for your courtesy and good sense.

Details on these guidelines and recommendations of Zero Impact principles for specific outdoor activities can be found in the Falcon guidebook *Leave No Trace*.

Make it a Safe Trip

As a leader of wilderness trips for youth, I always tell my students to be prepared. For starters, this means carrying survival and first-aid materials, proper clothing, compass, and topographic map—and knowing how to use them.

Perhaps the second-best piece of safety advice is to tell somebody where you're going and when you plan to return. Pilots must file flight plans before every trip, and anybody venturing into a blank spot on the map should do the same. File your "flight plan" with a friend or relative before taking off.

Close behind your flight plan and being prepared with proper equipment is physical conditioning. Being fit not only makes wilderness travel more fun, it makes it safer. Here are a few more tips:

- Check the weather forecast. Be careful not to get caught at high altitude by a bad storm or along a stream in a flash flood. Watch cloud formations closely, so you don't get stranded on a ridgeline during a lightning storm. Avoid traveling during prolonged periods of cold weather.

- Avoid traveling alone in the wilderness and keep your party together.

- Study basic survival and first aid before leaving home.

- Before you leave for the trailhead, find out as much as you can about the route, especially the potential hazards.

- Don't exhaust yourself or other members of your party by traveling too far or too fast. Let the slowest person set the pace.

- Don't wait until you're confused to look at your maps. Follow them as you go along, from the moment you start moving up the trail, so you have a continual fix on your location.

- If you get lost, don't panic. Sit down and relax for a few minutes while you carefully check your topo map and take a compass reading. Confidently plan your next move. It's often smart to retrace your steps until you find familiar ground, even if you think it might lengthen your trip. Lots of people get temporarily lost in the wilderness and survive—usually by calmly and rationally dealing with the situation.

- Stay clear of all wild animals.

- Take a first-aid kit that includes, at a minimum, the following items: sewing needle, snake-bite kit, aspirin, antibacterial ointment, antiseptic swabs, butterfly bandages, adhesive tape, adhesive strips, gauze pads, two triangular bandages, codeine tablets, two inflatable splints, Moleskin or Second Skin for blisters, 3-inch gauze, CPR shield, rubber gloves, and lightweight first-aid instructions.

- Take a survival kit that includes, at a minimum, the following items: compass, whistle, matches in a waterproof container, cigarette lighter, candle, signal mirror, flashlight, fire starter, aluminum foil, water purification tablets, space blanket, and flare.

Lastly, don't forget that the best defense against unexpected hazards is knowledge. Read up on the latest in wilderness safety information in the recently published *Wild Country Companion*. Check the back of this guidebook for ordering information.

LIGHTNING: YOU MIGHT NEVER KNOW WHAT HIT YOU

Mountains are prone to sudden thunderstorms. If you get caught in a lightning storm, take special precautions. Remember,

- Lightning can travel far ahead of the storm, so be sure to take cover before the storm hits.
- Don't try to make it back to your vehicle. Instead, seek shelter even if the trailhead is a short distance away. Lightning storms usually don't last long, and from a safe vantage point, you might enjoy the sights and sounds.
- Be especially careful not to get caught on a mountaintop or exposed ridge; under large, solitary trees; in the open; or near standing water.
- Seek shelter in a low-lying area, ideally in a dense stand of small, uniformly sized trees.
- Stay away from anything that might attract lightning, such as metal tent poles, graphite fishing rods, or pack frames.
- Crouch with both feet firmly on the ground.
- If you have a pack (without a metal frame) or a sleeping pad with you, put your feet on it for extra insulation against shock.
- Don't walk or huddle together. Instead, stay 50 feet apart, so if somebody gets hit by lightning, others in your party can give first aid.
- If you're in a tent, stay in your sleeping bag with your feet on your sleeping pad.

THE SILENT KILLER

Be aware of hypothermia—a condition in which the body's internal temperature drops below normal. It can lead to mental and physical collapse and death.

Hypothermia is caused by exposure to cold and is aggravated by wetness, wind, and exhaustion. The moment you begin to lose heat faster than your body produces it, you're suffering from exposure. Your body starts involuntary exercise, such as shivering, to stay warm; it makes involuntary adjustments to preserve normal temperature in vital organs, restricting bloodflow in the extremities. Both responses drain your energy reserves. The only way to stop the drain is to reduce the degree of exposure.

With full-blown hypothermia, as energy reserves are exhausted, cooled blood reaches the brain, depriving you of good judgment and reasoning power. You won't be aware that this is happening. You lose control of your hands. Your internal temperature slides downward. Without treatment, this slide leads to stupor, collapse, and death.

To defend against hypothermia, stay dry. When clothes get wet, they lose about 90 percent of their insulating value. Wool loses relatively less heat; cotton, down, and some synthetics lose more. Choose rainclothes that cover the head, neck, body, and legs and provide good protection against wind-driven rain. Most hypothermia cases develop in air temperatures between 30 and 50 degrees F, but hypothermia can develop in warmer temperatures.

If your party is exposed to wind, cold, and wet, think hypothermia. Watch yourself and others for uncontrollable fits of shivering; vague, slow, slurred speech; memory lapses; incoherence; immobile, fumbling hands; frequent stumbling or a lurching gait; drowsiness (to sleep is to die); apparent exhaustion; and inability to get up after a rest. When a member of your party has hypothermia, he or she may deny any problem. Believe the symptoms, not the victim. Even mild symptoms demand treatment, as follows:

- Get the victim out of the wind and rain.

- Strip off all wet clothes.

- If the victim is only mildly impaired, give him or her warm drinks. Then get the victim into warm clothes and a warm sleeping bag. Place well-wrapped water bottles filled with heated water close to the victim.

- If the victim is badly impaired, attempt to keep him or her awake. Put the victim in a sleeping bag with another person—both naked. If you have a double bag, put two warm people in with the victim.

FORDING RIVERS

Early summer hiking in the Trinity Alps may involve crossing streams swollen with runoff. When done correctly and carefully, crossing a big river can be safe, but you must know your limits.

The most important advice is be smart. There are cases where you simply should turn back. Even if only one member of your party (such as a child) might not be able to follow larger, stronger members, you might not want to try a risky ford. Never be embarrassed by being too cautious.

One key to safely fording rivers is confidence. If you aren't a strong swimmer, you should be. This not only allows you to safely get across a river that is a little deeper and stronger than you thought, but it gives you the confidence to avoid panic. Just like getting lost, panic can easily make the situation worse.

You can build confidence with practice. Find a warm-water river near your home and carefully practice crossing it both with a pack and without one. You can also start with a smaller stream and work up to a major river. After you've become a strong swimmer, get used to swimming in the current.

When you get to the ford, carefully assess the situation. Don't automatically cross at the point where the trail comes to the stream and head on a straight line for the marker on the other side. A mountain river can change every spring during high runoff, so a ford that was safe last year might be too deep this year. Study upstream and downstream and look for a place

California Pitcher Plants.

where the stream widens and the water is not over waist deep on the shortest member of your party. The tail end of an island is usually a good place, as is a long riffle. The inside of a meander sometimes makes a safe ford, but in other cases a long shallow section can be followed by a short, deep section next to the outside of the bend where the current picks up speed and carves out a deep channel.

Before starting any serious ford, make sure your matches, camera, billfold, clothes, sleeping bag, and other items you must keep dry are in watertight bags.

In the Trinity Alps, most streams are cold, so have dry clothes ready when you get to the other side to minimize the risk of hypothermia—especially on a cold, rainy day.

Minimize the amount of time you spend in the water, but don't rush across. Instead, go slowly and deliberately, taking one step at a time, being careful to get each foot securely planted before lifting the other foot. Take a 45-degree angle instead of going straight across, following a riffle line if possible.

Don't try to ford with bare feet. Wear hiking boots without the socks, sneakers, or tightly strapped sandals.

Stay sideways to the current; turning upstream or downstream increases the current's force.

In some cases, two or three people can cross together, locking forearms with the strongest person on the upstream side.

If you have a choice, ford in the early morning when the stream isn't as deep. In the mountains, the cool evening temperatures slow snowmelt and reduce the water flow into the rivers.

On small streams, a sturdy walking stick used on the upstream side for balance helps prevent a fall, but in a major river with a fast current, a walking stick offers little help.

Loosen the belt and straps on your pack. If you fall or get washed downstream, a waterlogged pack can anchor you to the bottom, so you must be able to easily release your pack.

If you're 6'4" and a strong swimmer, you might feel secure crossing a big river, but you might have children or smaller hikers in your party. In this case, the strongest person can cross first and string a line across the river to aid those who follow. This line (with the help of a carbiner) can also be used to float packs across instead of taking a chance of a waterlogged pack dragging you under. (If you know about the ford in advance, you can pack a lightweight rubber raft or inner tube for this purpose.) Depending on size and strength, you might also want to carry children.

Be prepared for the worst. Sometimes circumstances arise where you simply must cross instead of going back, even though the ford looks dangerous. Also, you can underestimate the depth of the channel or strength of the current, especially after a thunderstorm when a muddy river hides its true depth. In these cases, whether you like it or not, you might be swimming. If this happens, don't panic. Do not try to swim directly across; instead, pick a long angle and gradually cross to the other side, taking as much as 100 yards or more to finally get across. If your pack starts to drag you down, get out of it immediately, even if you have to abandon it. If you lose control and get washed downstream, go feet first, so you don't hit your head on rocks or logs.

Finally, be sure to report any dangerous ford to a ranger as soon as you finish your trip.

BE MOUNTAIN LION ALERT

You're sure to see plenty of deer in the Trinity Alps Wilderness, which means mountain lions probably aren't far away. Cougars feed on deer, and the remote backcountry of Northern California constitutes some of the best cougar habitat in the West. Though many people consider themselves lucky indeed to see a mountain lion in the wild, the big cats—nature's perfect predators—are potentially dangerous. Attacks on humans are extremely rare, but it's wise to educate yourself before heading into mountain lion habitat.

To stay as safe as possible when hiking in mountain lion country, follow this advice:

- Travel with a friend or group. There's safety in numbers.
- Don't let small children wander away by themselves.
- Don't let pets run unleashed.
- Avoid hiking at dawn and dusk when mountain lions are most active.
- Know how to behave if you encounter a mountain lion.

What to do if you encounter a mountain lion: In the majority of mountain lion encounters, these animals exhibit avoidance, indifference, or curiosity that never results in human injury, but it is natural to be alarmed if you have an encounter of any kind. Try to keep your cool and consider the following:

Recognize threatening mountain lion behavior. A few cues may help you gauge the risk of attack. If a mountain lion is more than 50 yards away, and directs its attention to you, it may be only curious. This situation represents only a slight risk for adults, but a more serious risk to unaccompanied children. At this point, you should move away, while keeping the animal in your peripheral vision. Also, look for rocks, sticks, or something to use as a weapon, just in case.

If a mountain lion is crouched and staring at you from less than 50 yards away, it may be gauging the chances of a successful attack. If this behavior continues, your risk may be high.

Do not approach a mountain lion. Instead, give the animal the opportunity to move on. Slowly back away, but maintain eye contact if close. Mountain lions are not known to attack humans to defend young or a kill, but they have been reported to "charge" in rare instances and may want to stay in the area. It's best to choose another route.

Do not run from a mountain lion. Running may stimulate a predatory response.

Make noise. If you encounter a mountain lion, be vocal and talk or yell loudly and regularly. Try not to panic. Shout also to make others in the area aware of the situation.

Maintain eye contact. Eye contact shows the lion you are aware of its presence. However, if the mountain lion's behavior is not threatening (for example, grooming or periodically looking away), maintain visual contact through your peripheral vision and move away.

Appear larger than you are. Raise your arms above your head and make steady waving motions. Raise your jacket or another object above your head. Do not bend over, as this will make you appear smaller and more "preylike."

If you are with small children, pick them up. Bring the children close to you without bending over, maintaining eye contact with the lion. If you are with other children or adults, band together.

Defend yourself. If attacked, fight back. Try to remain standing. Do not feign death. Pick up a branch or rock; pull out a knife, pepper spray, or other deterrent device. Everything is a potential weapon, and individuals have fended off mountain lions with rocks, tree limbs, and even cameras.

Defend others. In past attacks on children, adults have successfully stopped attacks. Defend your hiking partners, but don't physically defend your pet.

Respect any warning signs posted by agencies.

Spread the word. Before leaving on your hike, discuss lions and teach others in your group how to behave in case of a mountain lion encounter.

Report encounters. If you have an encounter with a mountain lion, record your location and the details of the encounter, and notify the nearest land owner or land-managing agency. The land management agency (federal, state, or county) may want to visit the site and, if appropriate, post education/warning signs. Fish and wildlife agencies should also be notified because they record and track such encounters.

If physical injury occurs, it is important to leave the area and not disturb the site of the attack. Mountain lions that have attacked people must be killed, and an undisturbed site is critical for effectively locating a dangerous mountain lion.

See Falcon Publishing's *Mountain Lion Alert* for more details and tips for safe outdoor recreation in mountain lion country.

BE BEAR AWARE

The first step of any hike in bear country is an attitude adjustment. Being prepared for bears means having the right information as well as the right equipment. The black bears in the Trinity Alps rarely approach humans, but they may pose a danger if you handle your food improperly. At the very least, letting a bear get human food is like contributing—directly—to the eventual destruction of that bear. Think of proper bear etiquette as protecting the bears as much as yourself.

CAMPING IN BEAR COUNTRY

Staying overnight in bear country is not dangerous, but it adds an additional risk to your trip. The main difference is the presence of food, cooking, and garbage. Following a few basic rules greatly minimizes the risk to you and the bears.

Storing food and garbage: Be sure to finalize your food storage plans before it gets dark. It's not only difficult to store food in the dark, but it's easier to forget some juicy morsel on the ground. Also, be sure to store food in airtight, waterproof bags to prevent food odors from circulating throughout the forest.

The following illustrations depict three popular methods (Trinity Alps bears have yet to learn the tricks of their more sophisticated Sierra cousins, so bear canisters are not necessary). In any case, try to get food and garbage at least 10 feet off the ground.

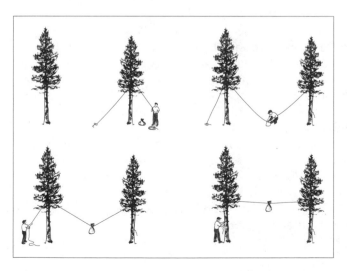

Hanging food and garbage between two trees.

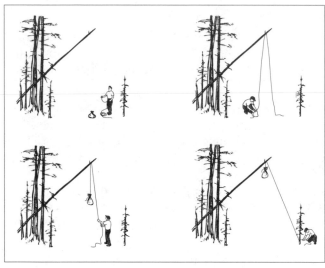

Take a special bag for storing food: The bag must be sturdy and water-proof. You can get dry bags at most outdoor specialty stores, but you can get by with a trash compactor bag. Regular garbage bags can break and leave your food spread on the ground.

You also need 100 feet of nylon cord. Parachute cord will usually suffice.

The classic method of hanging food and gear smelling of food is to tie a rock or piece of wood to the end of your rope and toss it over the branch. Attach it to the bag and hoist it up 10 feet or more. If the load gets too heavy, wrap it around a small tree or branch for leverage.

If you can't tie the rope to the rock, put the rock in a small bag and toss it over a high branch. Use gloves so you don't get rope burns. And of course, don't let the rock or wood come down on your head (it happens!). Also, don't let anybody stand under the bag until you're sure it's secured.

What to hang: To be as safe as possible, store everything that has any food smell. If you spilled something on your clothes, change into other clothes for sleeping and hang clothes with food smells with the food and garbage.

What to keep in your tent: You can't be too careful in keeping food smells out of the tent. Just in case a bear has become accustomed to coming into that camp-site looking for food, it's vital to keep all food smells out of the tent. This often includes your pack, which is hard to keep odor-free. Usually only take valuables (like cameras and binoculars), clothing, and sleeping gear into the tent.

Types of food: What food you have along is much less critical than how you handle it, cook it, and store it. Consider, however, the less dishes and/or packaging the better.

Hanging food at night is not the only storage issue: Also, make sure you place food correctly in your pack. Use airtight packages as much as possible. Store food in the containers it came in or, when opened, in zip-locked bags. This keeps food smells out of your pack and off your other camping gear and clothes.

Don't cook too much food, so you don't have to deal with leftovers. If you do end up with extra food, however, you only have two choices. Carry it out or burn it. Don't bury it or throw it in a lake or leave it anywhere in bear country. A bear will most likely find and dig up any food or garbage buried in the backcountry.

If you end up with lots of food scraps in the dishwater, drain out the scraps and store them in zip-locked bags with other garbage or burn them. You can bring a lightweight screen to filter out food scraps from dishwater, but be sure to store the screen with the food and garbage. If you have a campfire, pour the dish water around the edge of the fire. If you don't have a fire, take the dishwater at least 100 yards downwind and downhill from camp and pour it on the ground or in a small hole. Don't put dishwater or food scraps in a lake or stream. Do dishes immediately after eating, so a minimum of food smell lingers in the area.

REMEMBER RATTLESNAKES

Rattlesnakes strike humans only out of self-defense, when they're startled or otherwise afraid. The solution, of course, is to avoid scaring rattlesnakes. Look where you place your feet and hands when hiking in rattlesnake country (which means most of the trails in the Trinity Alps, but especially lower, warmer elevations).

If you encounter a rattlesnake, slowly back away and give it a chance to leave. Generally, it will seize the opportunity and slither away. If it doesn't, simply give the snake a wide berth and leave well enough alone. Do not throw rocks or sticks at it.

If bitten by a rattlesnake, don't panic. Rattlesnake bites are rarely fatal to healthy adults. Use a snakebite kit immediately to extract as much of the venom as possible. (It may actually be a "dry bite" in which no venom is delivered—intended only to frighten you.) Do not run or otherwise speed up your circulation, as that increases the spread of the venom in your blood stream. Keep the bite site below your heart to decrease the spread of venom. Seek medical attention immediately.

Natural and Cultural History

The story of human settlement in the Trinity Alps is a familiar one in the West: Native Americans were displaced by miners, who gave way to loggers and ranchers, who in turn have been largely replaced by outdoor recreationists.

In this case it was the Wintu who were here first. The relatively small Native American tribe met a fate similar to many other California tribes: they were nearly wiped out by the influx of European settlers. Starting in the early 1800s, disease, violence, and loss of their native lands decimated the Wintu population. In the mad rush for gold and good land, the Wintu were never awarded a reservation. There's little archaeological record of their presence in the wilderness. Arrowheads and other small items turn up now and then, small reminders that this remote slice of mountain country has a human history we can barely surmise. Today the remaining Wintu in the Shasta–Trinity region number about 2,000 and still preserve many of their ancient traditions.

Recorded history in the Trinity Alps region began in the early 1830s, when explorers and fur trappers first made forays through the area. These early visitors followed Native American trails to the Trinity River valley and headwaters. Jedediah Smith passed through, as did Major Pierson Reading, who named the Trinity River because he assumed (wrongly) that the river ran all the way to Trinidad Bay on the Pacific coast. In fact the Trinity River flows into the Klamath River.

The discovery of gold near Douglas City in 1848 put the Trinity River region on the map. Miners with gold in their eyes arrived in hordes. Weaverville was established in 1850 and four years later the boomtown boasted 22 stores, two banks, two drugstores, six hotels, four restaurants, six saloons, three bakeries, three blacksmith and carpenter shops, seven lawyers, and a population well over 1,000. Mining claims by the hundreds sprang up overnight in the rugged country, and soon a number of satellite towns appeared in the mountains: places like Saloon City, Lake City, and Old Denny housed hundreds of miners deep in the wilderness. As you hike through the backcountry, don't be surprised to come across a few nineteenth-century relics from the heyday of gold fever. Miners built cabins, roads, stamp mills, and flumes in what today appears to be the most remote of backcountry backwaters. A large Chinese population—some 2,000-strong— lived and worked in Weaverville during this era. The Joss House, a Taoist Temple built in Weaverville in 1874, has been preserved and today is a state historic park worth a visit.

The tide of mining rose and fell over the next 75 years or so, as first the placer mines played out, and then the more efficient hydraulic and dredge mining had their turn. The many tailing piles scattered around the region indicate just how extensive these operations were. Gold prices and the high price of corporate mining made prospecting in the Trinity Alps unprofitable by the 1930s, but not for long. In recent years, miners have again returned to the Trinity Alps, this time with wetsuits and high-tech dredges to gather gold the old-timers missed (the modern-day miners are not present in great numbers, but you may spot them is such places as the North Fork Trinity River and the New River drainages). These claims predate the area's wilderness designation. No new claims may be filed in the wilderness.

During the heyday of mining and settlement, the Trinity Alps region became the main thoroughfare between the Sacramento Valley and Oregon. The California–Oregon Stage Road, opened in 1860, closely followed the route of present-day California Highway 3, with numerous stops along the upper Trinity River and even a hotel up on Scott Mountain.

Industrial logging in the Trinity Alps region didn't start until the late 1800s and the coming of the railroads. Though you'll see evidence of clearcuts surrounding the wilderness, the heart of the Alps escaped the ax and saw. As early as 1926 a portion of the Alps had been set aside for its outstanding scenic and recreation value (in 1932 the Forest Service officially designated the Salmon–Trinity Alps Primitive Area). Even where logging occurred within the modern-day wilderness, enough time has passed that most visitors will be hard-pressed to identify it. Logging still occurs on private and national forest land outside the wilderness boundary.

Recreation in the region started as early as the 1920s, when a local couple, the Webers, established the Trinity Alps Resort on Stuart Fork. Legend has it this enterprising couple coined the term "Trinity Alps" after returning from a trip to Europe and the Austrian Alps. The Trinity Alps Resort, as well as other historic lodges like Coffee Creek Ranch, is still in operation today. Lodges, horse packers, hiking guides, hunting and fishing guides, and rafting companies are now an important part of the local economy. Consult the Trinity County Chamber of Commerce for a list of local services (see Appendix A).

GEOLOGY

The Trinity Alps Wilderness stands alone—an island of alpine splendor cut adrift from California's more well-known ranges. Geologically speaking, the Alps is distinct from most of its neighbors. The mountains are unrelated to both the nearby Coast Range and the volcanic Cascades, which include Mount Shasta and Lassen Peak to the north and east. In fact the Trinity Alps form the southern end of the Klamath Mountains.

Some 2.5 million years ago the region was much gentler in nature than today. But a general uplift caused valleys to deepen, and granitic magmas welled up at various times and pushed through the overlying rock (made up of various metamorphic and sedimentary rocks) to create many of the areas most spectacular peaks. A high iron content in some of the Alps' igneous rocks accounts for the rust-colored appearance of peaks like Red Rock Mountain and Seven Up Peak.

Glaciers delivered the finishing touches on the awesome scenery. In four separate glaciation periods over the last 1.5 million years, deep ice accumulated in the high mountains and slowly slid down the valleys, carving and slicing the terrain into the spectacular alps you see today. The glaciers left behind dramatic cirques with exquisite lakes and classic U-shaped valleys with polished sides and knife-edged ridges. Terminal moraines dammed low-lying valleys and created large lakes that eventually became the lush, sprawling meadows you see today. The most recent glaciers receded some 10,000 years ago. Two remnant "glacierets" from this last mini-Ice Age still persist on the high north-facing slopes of Thompson Peak.

PLANTS

The Trinity Alps is home to an incredible variety of trees, flowers, and shrubs. From giant ponderosa and sugar pines towering overhead to tiny and fleeting wildflowers like blue gentians, the plant communities in the Trinity Alps represent one of the most diverse ecosystems in the United States. What follows is a brief description of a few of the more common or noteworthy plants you can expect to see in the Trinity Alps. For a complete guide, several reference books are available. *Flowers and Trees of the Trinity Alps*, by Alice Goen Jones, is easy to use and illustrated with hundreds of color photos.

The lower elevations (below 4,000 feet) are dominated by mixed forests of Douglas-fir, ponderosa, and digger pines, as well as a healthy smattering of oaks (several varieties), madrones, bigleaf maples, and dogwoods. Ferns, berries, alders, and poison oak thrive in streamside riparian zones at this level. (Poison oak is uncommon on most hikes described in this guidebook, but it is prevalent along creeks and trails in the western, or "Green," Trinities.) Chaparral, consisting mostly of ceanothus and manzanita bushes, covers the dry, exposed hillsides at this elevation.

Between 4,000 and 6,000 feet you find Trinity's forest giants: Douglas-fir, ponderosa and sugar pine, and incense-cedar. Smaller conifers, including white fir, Jeffrey pine, lodgepole pine, and western white pine, also thrive at these elevations. The understory is dominated by azaleas (beautiful and fragrant in early summer), mountain ash, several kinds of berries, and manzanita. Scrub and black oaks also appear on dry slopes. Lush mountain meadows of thick grasses, corn lilies, and wildflowers exist at this and at higher elevations. You can even see a few aspen stands, rare in the Trinity Alps.

Above 5,000 feet, red fir starts to replace white fir (though they often overlap) and western white and Jeffrey pines outnumber their larger cousins. Cottonwoods and mountain ash appear in a few scattered riparian environments at this elevation. Alders and willows grow shrublike along the creeks and on the fringes of wet meadows. Sunny slopes at this elevation may be covered with manzanita, ceanothus, and other hardy shrubs. Do not be tempted to take a shortcut across one of these slopes if you value your skin.

The subalpine environment above 6,500 feet is dominated by stunted versions of some of the lower-elevation trees, plus a number of new species like foxtail pines, mountain hemlocks, and weeping spruce. Trees that grow along the rocky ridgelines and inhospitable granite cirques, chiefly between 6,500 and 7,500 feet, tend to be small, scattered widely, and often bent in gnarled shapes by the wind and poor soil.

Few trees grow between 8,000 and 9,000 feet, the only true alpine zone in the Trinity Alps. Near the highest peaks' summits, where snow persists well into the summer and the soil is mostly rock, there are only a few stubborn shrubs, lichens and, for a brief but spectacular period in late summer, a few bright wildflowers.

The wildflowers of the Trinity Alps could occupy an entire book unto themselves. From late June through September the Alps is awash in white, yellow, orange, purple, and red blossoms. Many flowers are specific to certain locations (forest fringes, meadows, rocky slopes, etc.) and seasons (early, middle, and late summer), so what you see depends largely on where and when you go. The most dependable flower-viewing time is typically the middle of July to the middle of August. Some of the more common species include leopard lilies, columbines, angelica, Indian paintbrush, lupines (both yellow and blue), sunflowers, penstemons, asters, and monkshood. One of the most interesting flowering plants in the Alps is the California pitcher plant. This rare insectivorous plant grows in wet meadows at mid-elevations, and should be treated with utmost care (don't pick them or trample their habitat).

WILDLIFE

Encountering animals in the wild is one of the most thrilling experiences in the outdoors. Unlike the animals in some of the more heavily visited wilderness areas in the West, the wildlife in the Trinity Alps is still mostly wild. Consider yourself lucky to see a black bear. The shy bruins, which can be any shade of brown or black or even cinnamon, are quite a sight when they lumber across a high meadow, trying to get out of view.

A more common sight, however, is the Columbian black-tailed deer; these animals are sometimes hard to avoid as they wander into camps in search of handouts and sweaty clothes to chew (they crave the salts). A friend of mine once fell asleep wearing a sweat-soaked cap. She jumped awfully high when she awoke with a deer nibbling her head. The deer jumped even higher.

Other mammals in the region include mountain lions, coyotes, martens, weasels, bobcats, foxes, porcupines, and ringtails. Consider yourself lucky indeed to spot one of these stealthy species. Mammals such as chipmunks, mice, squirrels, skunks, jackrabbits, and raccoons are much more common, especially in the mid-elevation forests. Bats often can be seen at dusk, swooping low through the twilight as they feed on insects.

Members of the cold-blooded animal kingdom are also well represented in the Trinity Alps. Rattlesnakes, gopher snakes, rubber boas, garter snakes, and lizards (on some trails there seems to be a lizard on every rock) are the most common reptiles. Rattlesnakes tend to remain out of sight in the warm lower elevations, and are easily avoided if you keep an eye peeled and give them time to get away. As for amphibians, you can find a variety of frogs, salamanders, and newts in the wet meadows, ponds, and lakes throughout the wilderness.

The most eye-catching birds in the Alps are raptors: hawks, golden eagles, ospreys, and even bald eagles nest and hunt here. Of the ear-catching variety, you might hear the songs of robins, finches, warblers, bluebirds, and jays. Hummingbirds also show up for the summer wildflowers, and the echo of a woodpecker hard at work can often be heard reverberating through the forest. The number and variety of avian species are far too numerous to list here. Dedicated birders should consult a field guide before heading out (see Appendix B, Further Reading, at the back of this book).

A NOTE ON THE GREEN TRINITIES

The western half of the Trinity Alps Wilderness is often called the "Green Trinities" because it is lower in elevation and more densely forested than the granite heart of the eastern half of the wilderness. Because the Green Trinities lack the alpine lakes and glacier-gouged canyons found in the east, the trails here have retained one of the most important natural wonders in the backcountry: solitude.

It wasn't always that way. During the mid- and late 1800s, the New River drainage was a bustling center of mining activity. Today, 21 miles of the stream are included in the National Wild and Scenic Rivers System. Two hikes described in this book (New River Loop and East Fork New River Loop, Hikes 8 and 9) sample some of the scenery and history to be found in the Green Trinities.

In addition to those routes, there are miles of trails that form a maze of possible hikes in the Green Trinities. Extended hikes of a week or more could easily be made along the Salmon Summit, Green Mountain, or Virgin Creek Trails. Keep in mind, however, that trails and trail signs are sometimes not well maintained due to low use. And because of the low elevation (except for a few ridgeline trails, most paths are below 5,000 feet) there are three things you should be aware of: hot weather in the summer, poison oak, and rattlesnakes. The first can be avoided by planning an early- or late-season trip; the second and third are best avoided by knowing what they look like and staying alert. Also note: In the 1970s and early 1980s, the area became a popular place to grow illegal marijuana crops. Marijuana cultivation has largely been eradicated since then, but visitors should report any suspicious activity to the local law enforcement and the Forest Service.

The Big Bar Ranger District (see contact information in Appendix A) is an excellent source of information on the trails in the Green Trinities. If you want to be alone and don't mind forgoing the lakes and peaks of the Trinity Alps proper, get out a map and plan a trip here.

Trail Finder Table

	EASY	MODERATE	STRENUOUS
Best Backcountry Lakes	25 Boulder Lakes 41 Tangle Blue Lake 35 Adams Lake 48 Hidden Lake	11 Stuart Fork (Emerald and Sapphire Lakes) 34 Caribou Lakes 4 Canyon Creek Lakes	1 Grizzly Lake 2 Papoose Lake 19 Lake Anna 27 Foster Lake
Best Hikes for Wildflowers	30 Union Creek	46 Pacific Crest Trail 20 Swift Creek 17 Long Canyon 21 Bear Basin–Granite Lake Loop	19 Lake Anna 1 Grizzly Lake
Best Hikes for Views	43 East Boulder	46 Pacific Crest Trail 21 Bear Basin–Granite Lake Loop 34 Caribou Lakes 40 Bear Lakes	33 Tri-Forest Peak 16 Granite Peak 38 Billys Peak 27 Foster Lake Loop
Best Hikes for Solitude	30 Union Creek 50 Fish Lake	36 South Fork Coffee Creek 31 Bullards Basin–Sunrise Creek Loop 23 Poison Canyon 9 East Fork New River Loop	2 Papoose Lake 33 Tri-Forest Peak–Deer Creek Loop 15 Stoney Ridge Trail

Author's Favorites

For Alpine Scenery	11 Stuart Fork 34 Caribou Lakes 46 Pacific Crest Trail 14 Smith Lake
For Swimming	18 Four Lakes Loop 20 Swift Creek 19 Lake Anna Loop 34 Caribou Lakes
For a Long Day Hike	4 Canyon Creek Lakes 17 Long Canyon 40 Bear Lakes 49 Trail Gulch and Long Gulch Loop
For Kids	25 Boulder Lakes 24 Lake Eleanor and Shimmy Lake 35 Adams Lake 41 Tangle Blue Lake 48 Hidden Lake
For Sunsets	15 Stoney Ridge/Echo Lake 27 Foster Lake Loop 18 Four Lakes Loop
For a Good Basecamp	30 Union Creek 20 Swift Creek 11 Stuart Fork 33 Tri-Forest Peak-Deer Creek Loop 46 Pacific Crest Trail

Lake Finder Table

Hike	Lake	Elevation	Acres	Depth	Why Go
35	Adams	6,300'	1.00	16'	Good for small children; nice day hike if you're short on time.
13	Alpine	6,150'	14.00	26'	Pretty detour off of busy Stuart Fork; good off-trail exploring.
19	Anna	7,550'	4.00	56'	Great swimming in unique setting; good wildflowers on the hike in.
40	Big Bear	6,500'	28.00	73'	Beautiful views from classic granite cirque; visit two companion lakes.
15,19	Billy-Be-Damned	7,400'	0.75	9'	Good solitude on a rocky terrace high above Bowerman Meadow.
5	Boulder Creek	5,750'	5.00	17'	Camp on granite slabs with great view of Sawtooth Mountain.
25	Boulder Lake (Big)	6,100'	8.00	27'	Good basecamp or day hike for families and novice hikers.
25	Boulder Lake (Little)	6,350'	4.50	19'	Easy hike to a pretty lake with good swimming.
43	Boulder Lake (East)	6,700'	32.00	60'	Unique setting in an open, grassy basin overlooking Scott Valley.
44	Boulder Lake (Middle)	6,500'	6.50	12'	Good basecamp for hikers on the Pacific Crest Trail.
44	Boulder Lake (West)	7,000'	7.00	29'	Excellent solitude near Scott Mountain crest.
4	Canyon Crk. Lake (Upper)	5,690'	25.00	86'	Spectacular granite setting with great views, several waterfalls on hike in.
34	Caribou	6,850'	72.00	72'	Jaw-dropping scenery with excellent swimming and camping.
27,28	Conway	6,850'	8.00	9'	Good solitude at lilypad-fringed pond off the beaten track.
17,18	Deer	7,150'	4.50	19'	Make snow cones in summer at this north-facing basin.
18	Diamond	7,250'	2.50	13'	Great wildflowers and beautiful sunsets at this little gem.
6	East Fork	5,900'	2.00		Isolated lake in a rugged basin; good chance for solitude.

Hike	Lake	Elevation	Acres	Depth	Why Go
7	East Weaver	6,350'	1.00	12'	Good for families with small children; good day hike destination.
15	Echo	7,250'	2.50	17'	Good chance for solitude and incredible sunsets.
24	Eleanor	4,950'	3.00	10'	Great for anglers who don't want to waste any time hiking.
11	Emerald	5,500'	21.00	68'	A premier lake in the Trinity Alps; interesting mining relics.
50	Fish Lake	6,000'	3.00		More of a pond than a lake, but makes a nice day hike.
5	Forbidden	6,250'	1.50	18'	Rugged cirque off the beaten track. Worth it just to say you've been to Forbidden Lake.
27	Foster	7,250'	5.50	20'	Plenty of exploring in the area; best sunset seat in the Trinity Alps.
26	Found	6,600'	2.50	9'	Rugged, isolated setting just stone's throw from Big Boulder Lake.
45	Fox Creek	6,600'	9.50	38'	Pleasant camping near the Scott Mountain crest.
21	Granite	6,000'	18.00	64'	Beautiful granite cirque marred only by steady stream of traffic.
1,51	Grizzly	7,100	42.00	173'	Tucked between the Trinity Alps highest peak and biggest waterfall. Worth every step.
48	Hidden Lake	6,700'	3.00	15'	Great destination for a short day hike or family with small children.
20	Horseshoe	6,850'	6.00	22'	Swimming and rock scrambling at the head of Swift Creek.
4	Kalmia	7,500'	1.00	13'	Small lake with a big view. Difficult to reach.
4	"L" or El	6,350'	2.00	29'	Good chance for solitude above perpetually crowded Canyon Creek Lakes.
22	Landers	7,100'	6.00	17'	Unique setting with good swimming and peak bagging potential.
23	Lilypad	6,300'	2.00	8'	Excellent solitude at this shallow lake; good basecamp.
27,28	Lion	7,000'	3.00	37'	Great view of Mount Shasta; rugged setting enclosed by cliffs.

Hike	Lake	Elevation	Acres	Depth	Why Go
49	Long Gulch	6,450'	14.00	21'	Makes a nice stop on a loop that crosses crest of the Salmon Mountains.
18	Luella	6,950'	2.50	13'	Beautiful little lake of cold, clear water perched above Deer Creek.
43	Marshy Lake (Big)	6,400	5.50	15'	Good place to find solitude a short ways from Pacific Crest Trail.
45	Mavis	6,700'	3.50	16'	A pretty place to basecamp on north side of Scott Mountains.
39	McDonald	6,100'	4.00	15'	Nice place to explore while at Stoddard Lake.
42	Mill Creek	6,600'	3.00	16'	A short hike to a small lake with a good chance for solitude.
11	Mirror	6,600'	14.00	25'	Spectacular setting in the granite heart of Trinity Alps. Tough hike.
14	Morris	7,350'	3.50	31'	Idyllic lake tucked just below the summit of Sawtooth Mountain. Challenging hike.
2	Papoose	6,600'	28.00	70'	Great swimming and rock scrambling at granite-enclosed lake.
7	Rush Creek Lake (Upper)	6,950'	2.00	44'	Tough hike to a sheer-walled basin; guaranteed cold water in August.
20	Salmon	7,150'	1.50	13'	Good chance for solitude; great view of Caribou Mountain.
11	Sapphire	6,100'	43.00	200'	Classic alpine setting in heart of Trinity Alps. Great swimming.
45	Section Line	7,100'	2.50		Scenic off-trail exploring on north side of Scott Mountains.
24	Shimmy	6,400'	1.50	10'	Good day hike with views of Trinity Lake.
14	Smith	6,950'	24.00	167'	Spectacular alpine setting near summit of Sawtooth Mountain. Rough off-trail hike.
34	Snowslide	6,700'	10.00	42'	Pretty lake in the popular Caribou Basin; popular basecamp area.
47	South Fork Lake (Upper)	6,720'	6.40	34'	Larger of two companion lakes perched on Scott Mountain crest.
39	Stoddard	5,900'	25.00	84'	Big, forest-fringed lake popular with equestrians and large groups.

Hike	Lake	Elevation	Acres	Depth	Why Go
29	Sugar Pine	6,600'	9.00	43'	Isolated lake in a beautiful setting high above Coffee Creek.
18	Summit	7,350'	13.00	34'	Stunning blue water; highest lake accessible by trail.
41	Tangle Blue	5,800'	12.00	17'	Easy hike to a pleasant lake; good for families with small children.
26	Tapie	6,500'	1.75	15'	Nice place to explore while in the Boulder Lakes basin.
44	Telephone	6,900'	3.50		Scenic stopover on loop across the Scott Mountain crest.
49	Trail Gulch	6,400'	10.00	17'	Makes a nice stop on a loop that crosses crest of the Salmon Mts.
30	Union	6,050'	3.50	14'	Good for equestrians; makes a nice early-season hike.
45	Virginia	6,900'	3.00	16'	Scenic off-trail exploring on north side of Scott Mountains.
20,32	Ward	7,100'	5.50	23'	Secluded lake at head of Swift Creek; good sunrises nearby.
42	Washbasin	7,000'	11.00	85'	Short hike with good chance of solitude in a pretty, rocky basin.

Hikes From California Highway 299

---

1 North Fork Trinity River to Grizzly Lake

Highlights: An outstanding ramble along the idyllic North Fork Trinity River to heavenly Grizzly Lake.
Type of hike: Backpack; out-and-back.
Total distance: 37 miles.
Difficulty: Moderate (last half-mile is strenuous).
Elevation gain: 4,123 feet.
Maps: USGS Thurston Peaks, Cecil Lake, and Thompson Peak quads; USDAFS Trinity Alps Wilderness map.

Finding the trailhead: From Weaverville drive 15 miles west on California Highway 299 to the turnoff for Old Helena (an old mining town, largely abandoned) and turn right (north) on County Road 421 (East Fork Road). Follow signs to Hobo Gulch Campground and Trailhead, 16 miles away on steep, unpaved Forest Road 34N07Y.

Parking and trailhead facilities: Campground, outhouse, and ample parking at the trailhead. The only water available is in the North Fork of the Trinity River. Be sure to purify it.

Key points:
- 0.0   Hobo Gulch Trailhead.
- 0.9   Backbone Creek and North Fork Low Water–Whites Creek Trails junctions.
- 2.8   North Fork Low Water Trail junction.
- 5.0   Rattlesnake Camp; Rattlesnake Creek (Hike 2) Trail junction.
- 7.1   Morrison Gulch Trail junction.
- 9.0   Jorstad Cabin.
- 12.8   Bobs Farm and Moliter–Cold Spring Trail junctions.
- 14.3   China Spring Trail junction.
- 17.7   Grizzly Meadows.
- 18.5   Grizzly Lake.

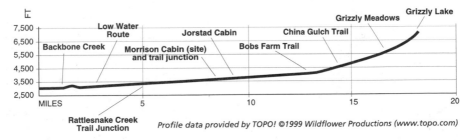

Profile data provided by TOPO! ©1999 Wildflower Productions (www.topo.com)

North Fork Trinity River to Grizzly Lake
Rattlesnake Creek to Papoose Lake • Bobs Farm Trail

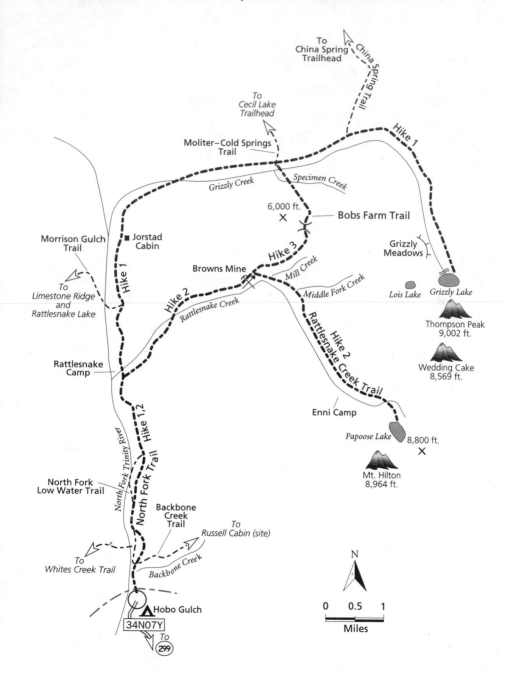

To
China Spring
Trailhead

China Spring Trail

Hike 1

To
Cecil Lake
Trailhead

Moliter–Cold Springs
Trail

Grizzly Creek

Specimen Creek

6,000 ft.
X

Bobs Farm Trail

Grizzly
Meadows

Morrison Gulch
Trail

Jorstad
Cabin

Hike 1

Hike 3

Mill Creek

Browns Mine

Middle Fork Creek

Lois Lake

Grizzly Lake

To
Limestone Ridge
and
Rattlesnake Lake

Hike 2

Rattlesnake Creek

Thompson Peak
9,002 ft.

Wedding Cake
8,569 ft.

Rattlesnake
Camp

Hike 2

Rattlesnake Creek Trail

Enni Camp

Hike 1,2

North Fork Trinity River

North Fork Trail

Papoose Lake

8,800 ft.
X

Mt. Hilton
8,964 ft.

North Fork
Low Water Trail

Backbone
Creek
Trail

To
Russell Cabin (site)

To
Whites Creek Trail

Backbone Creek

N

Hobo Gulch

34N07Y

To
299

0   0.5   1

Miles

30

The hike: If I were handed the raw materials—blocks of granite, sweet clear water, permanent snowfields, idyllic meadows, majestic waterfall—and allowed to assemble them however I pleased, I would no doubt come up with something that looks very much like Grizzly Lake. Perched on a glacier-gouged shelf below 9,002-foot Thompson Peak, with a 100-foot waterfall cascading from its sheer outlet and jaw-dropping vistas everywhere you look, Grizzly Lake is like a Hollywood set designer's vision of what a quintessential mountain lake should look like—but Grizzly is real.

Of course if this were a Hollywood version of an alpine lake, there'd also be an easy way to get here. Fortunately, there's not. A lot of hikers find their way to Grizzly, but you can rest assured that no one gets here without breaking a sweat. The shortest way to Grizzly is a sneak route via China Spring Trail. This steep, 6.7-mile trail (described in Hike 51) starts near Cecilville and enables hikers to reach Grizzly in one day.

Before the China Spring Trail was built, however, the only route to Grizzly Lake was this 18.5-mile trek from Hobo Gulch along the North Fork Trinity River. It still may be the best way. The route is mostly level and incredibly picturesque for the first 12 miles, offering hikers a leisurely stroll through magnificent wilderness, past historic cabins, and along the lush North Fork banks, accompanied by some of the best stream fishing in the Trinity Alps—all without the crowds that typically march over the China Spring Trail every summer weekend. (Note to anglers: Check with the California Fish and Game Department before casting a line. The North Fork is subject to fishing restrictions to protect endangered species.)

From the Hobo Gulch Trailhead, hike north on the North Fork Trail (12W01) along the North Fork of the Trinity River. The path meanders along the idyllic creek through shady woods of Douglas-fir, ponderosa and sugar pine, oaks, madrone, and dogwood. Just 0.9 mile from the trailhead, arrive at a three-way trail junction. The Backbone Creek Trail heads uphill to the right (east) and eventually ends at an old cabin site. To the left (west) is the North Fork Low Water Trail, which also leads to the Whites Creek Trail. The Low Water Trail crosses the river, so stay on the main path if you want to keep your feet dry.

Continuing on the North Fork Trail, the path climbs a little but mostly just hugs the east bank of the North Fork. The parklike walking is pleasant and easy-going. You may spot modern-day miners plying the river in wetsuits and operating high-tech dredges.

At 5 miles, you arrive at Rattlesnake Camp, a large forested flat at the confluence of Rattlesnake Creek and the North Fork Trinity River. A sign here indicates that Grizzly Lake lies to the left (north) and the Rattlesnake Creek Trail is to the right (northeast). See Hike 2 for a description of the trail along Rattlesnake Creek to Papoose Lake.

Take the left fork and immediately cross Rattlesnake Creek, a wide stream that could pose problems at high water. Just after the ford, the trail climbs a set of dusty switchbacks to gain a line high above the North Fork. Once around the nose of the ridge, an easy contour leads north across a wooded hillside, with good views of the river below and a gentle grade that makes it easy to enjoy the scenery.

At 7.1 miles, the trail dips down to river level again and arrives at the Morrison Gulch Trail junction, on a shady bench next to the water. A sign at the fork indicates Rattlesnake Lake to the left (up Morrison Gulch to the northwest) and Grizzly Lake to the right (north). Rattlesnake Lake, which is not much more than a glorified puddle up on Limestone Ridge, probably gets as many visitors in one summer as Grizzly Lake gets on a holiday weekend. Hikers who cherish solitude over scenery would do well to hang a left here.

Continuing on the North Fork Trail, ascend above the river again, then stroll upstream to a wide, level bench called Pfeiffer Flat. In the center of the grassy glade, shaded by mature ponderosa pines, Douglas-fir and incense-cedar, stands Jorstad Cabin. The ancient structure is a testament to the tough folks who carved a living out of the wilderness long before Gore-Tex and freeze-dried food were invented. Willard Jorstad and his wife Adzie built the cabin in 1937 and Willard lived here until he reached his 80s (Jorstad recorded an entertaining account of their first year here in his book *Behind the Wild River*). A few outbuildings and fencing still remain, and the trail passes through an old wooden gate on the way through the meadow. Jorstad wrote of discovering this spot, "Imagine a broad flat along the river, fairly open, set about with giant firs and pines, parklike in appearance, covered with grass growing out of a bed of fertile soil. What a find!"

After paying your respects to the Jorstads, continue north on the level, streamside trail. Soon the path reaches the confluence of the North Fork and Grizzly Creek, and veers right (east) to follow Grizzly Creek to its namesake lake. The path starts climbing a little more earnestly along Grizzly Creek, but the elevation is still relatively low (just 3,600 feet). Oak and maple are mixed liberally with the pine and fir. You can also see a number of tailing piles from mining done along Grizzly Creek.

The trail now climbs moderately but steadily to a junction with the Moliter–Cold Springs Trail and Bobs Farm Trail at 12.8 miles. On the west side of Mill Gulch, the Moliter–Cold Springs Trail climbs north over Salmon River Divide. On the east side of the gulch Bobs Farm Trail (signed Papoose Lake and Specimen Creek) heads south. Some hikers like to use this route to make a loop back to Hobo Gulch by way of Papoose Lake; others swear they'll never set foot on the trail again. I fall into the former camp, but freely admit that you have to be very open-minded to appreciate the redeeming qualities of Bobs Farm Trail. For a complete description see Hike 3.

The next 1.5 miles of the North Fork Trail contour steadily along the north bank of Grizzly Creek, in mixed forest cover high above the water. At 14.3 miles from Hobo Gulch the path meets the junction with the China Spring Trail (11W08). It's just under 3 miles from here to the trailhead at China Gulch, but bear in mind that nearly every yard of that is steep, steep, steep (up and down).

The last 4 miles of trail to Grizzly Meadows may seem like twice that distance if you're doing it at the end of a long day. The path parallels the ever steepening Grizzly Creek drainage on its final journey southeast to its source at the head of the canyon. Several small waterfalls, lush gardens of ferns and berries, and welcome vistas up and down the drainage soon appear. At the top of a rocky outcropping you're treated to your first glimpse of the cirque above Grizzly Lake, with Thompson Peak and its permanent snowfields towering over the basin.

Grizzly Lake.

After several more tantalizing glimpses, the path crosses a series of lush emerald meadows and deposits you in the heart of Grizzly Meadows, amid stands of red and white fir, summer wildflowers galore, granite-lined glades, and the crash of Grizzly Falls. The lake, of course, is hidden above the sheer cliff ahead, up where the falls pour from the sky. There's a way up there, but even the Forest Service hesitates to call it a trail.

It's called the Grizzly Scramble (its Forest Service title), which means a route exists but you'll need your hands free and good scrambling skills to follow it. From the meadow, cairns lead up the left (east) side of the boulder field. Before the base of the falls the route veers left (east) and climbs a loose talus slope up the side of the canyon. Pick your way up through the rock band (that's the scramble part), then traverse upwards and back to the southwest to reach lake level, 0.5 mile and 800 feet above the canyon floor. You should arrive at the shore near the lip of the waterfall.

Icy water fed by the glacieret on Thompson Peak (a fast-melting remnant from the last period of glaciation, about 10,000 years ago) fills the 42-acre lake. Swimming is excellent if you can bear the temperature, and sun-baked granite slabs are in abundance if you can't. A sparse scattering of stunted fir and mountain hemlock grows in the rocky basin, but mostly it's just rock and snow and water. Gray and massive Thompson Peak, at 9,002 feet the highest summit in the Trinity Alps, looms over all. Experienced peak baggers will have no problem finding a line to its top.

The fragile ecosystem around Grizzly Lake should not be camped in (take a look around the rocky basin and it's pretty obvious where all the human waste ends up), so do your back a favor and don't lug your pack up the steep scramble. There are plenty of great places to camp along Grizzly Creek.

Options: On the way back from Grizzly Lake you can make a loop using Bobs Farm Trail (Hike 3) and Rattlesnake Creek Trail (Hike 2). Experienced navigators can also make several off-trail hikes from Grizzly Lake. Besides Thompson Peak, other destinations in the area include Lois Lake, Little South Fork Lake, and Mirror Lake. Use the map and good judgement: the terrain around these places is steep, wild, and lonely.

2 Rattlesnake Creek to Papoose Lake

See Map on Page 30

Highlights: Historic mining relics along beautiful Rattlesnake Creek and a granite wonderland in the Papoose Lake basin.

Type of hike: Backpack; out and back.

Total distance: 25.6 miles.

Difficulty: Strenuous.

Elevation gain: 3,646 feet.

Maps: USGS Thurston, Mt. Hilton, and Thompson quads; USDAFS Trinity Alps Wilderness map.

Finding the trailhead: From Weaverville, drive 15 miles west on California Highway 299 to the turn-off for Old Helena (an old mining town, largely abandoned) and turn right (north) on County Road 421 (East Fork Road). Follow signs to Hobo Gulch Campground and Trailhead, another 16 miles away on steep, unpaved Forest Road 34N07Y.

Parking and trailhead facilities: Campground, outhouse, and ample parking at the trailhead. The only water available is in the North Fork of the Trinity River. Be sure to purify it.

Key points:

0.0	Hobo Gulch Trailhead.
0.9	Backbone Creek and North Fork Low Water–Whites Creek Trail Junction.
2.8	North Fork Low Water Trail junction.
5.0	Rattlesnake Creek Trail junction.
6.8	Rattlesnake Creek crossing.
8.6	Browns Mine.
8.7	Bobs Farm Trail junction.
11.5	Enni Camp.
12.0	Rattlesnake Creek ford.
12.8	Papoose Lake.

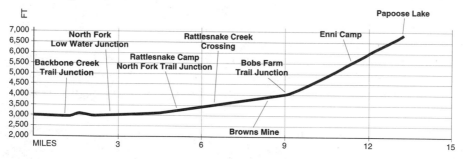

Profile data provided by TOPO! ©1999 Wildflower Productions (www.topo.com)

The hike: For years Papoose Lake has managed to fly just under the radar screen when it comes to renowned Trinity Alps destinations. Overshadowed by more prominent neighbors like Grizzly, Canyon Creek, and Emerald Lakes, Papoose is rarely crowded, but not for lack of charm. The jagged granite cirque overlooking Papoose is drop-dead gorgeous, and the clear, icy water is well worth the final steep scramble up to the lake (calling this last rough segment a trail is a stretch). Along the way you hike by many fascinating mining relics left along Rattlesnake Creek, a one-time booming center of gold prospecting. Rattlesnake Creek itself tumbles through a deep, lush drainage with mostly pleasant walking.

From the Hobo Gulch Trailhead, hike north on the North Fork Trail (12W01) along the North Fork of the Trinity River. The path meanders along the idyllic creek through shady woods of Douglas-fir, ponderosa and sugar pine, oaks, madrone, and dogwood, arriving at the Rattlesnake Creek Trail junction after 5 pleasant miles (see Hike 1 for a description of this section of the route). Rattlesnake Camp is a large forested flat at the confluence of Rattlesnake Creek and the North Fork Trinity River. A sign here indicates that Grizzly Lake is to the left (north) and Papoose Lake is to the right (northeast).

Turn right and continue up the south bank of Rattlesnake Creek on the Rattlesnake Creek Trail (11W05). The going is nearly level and mostly shady as you skirt the edge of the creek. After crossing a couple of small tributaries, the trail fords Rattlesnake Creek 1.8 miles from the junction. Use caution if the water is high. This is most likely a wet crossing, and the current may be swift in early season. Maples and oaks line the banks here, and numerous tailing piles (stacks of river boulders) are a testament to the enormous amount of mining work that occurred here a century ago.

Now on the north side of the creek, the trail ascends at a very moderate grade through more mixed oak, madrone, fir, and pine woodland. At times, the path widens considerably and you can easily imagine wagonloads of equipment and miners plying the route along Rattlesnake Creek. After 1.8 miles of gentle climbing arrive at Browns Mine, where scattered pieces of such equipment have been left to rust in their wilderness grave. History buffs may want to schedule a little extra time to linger here and try to identify the various machinery, gears, and odd items the miners left behind.

Just beyond Browns Mine, 8.7 miles from the trailhead, arrive at the junction with Bobs Farm Trail. A left (north) turn here leads steeply uphill to surmount a 6,000-foot ridge separating the Rattlesnake and Grizzly Creek drainages. Mile for mile, it is without doubt one of the most difficult trails in all of the Trinity Alps. On the plus side, it enables you to make a nifty loop between Papoose and Grizzly lakes. See Hike 3 for a complete description of Bobs Farm Trail.

Stay right (east) to continue on Rattlesnake Creek Trail. The path soon crosses Mill Creek (which you could follow to its source at little Lois Lake, should you be in the mood for a serious bushwhack), then Middle Fork Creek, which rises high on the ridge between Thompson Peak and Wedding Cake. Top off water bottles before moving on, as the next few miles tend to be hot and dry in the summer.

Papoose Lake.

The trail climbs along the course of Rattlesnake Creek but stays high above the water, offering only enticing views of the inviting swimming holes in the gorge down below. The ascent steepens at times as you climb through alternating stands of forest cover, berry bushes, and brushy fields of ceanothus and manzanita. You also pass through eerie, skeletal forests of charred trees left by a 1987 wildfire that swept through the drainage. Wildflowers now bloom where the fire burned.

A final push up the narrowing canyon brings you level with Rattlesnake Creek and to the site of Enni Camp (Enos on the USGS quad), an overused campsite that marks the end of the Papoose Lake Trail proper. From here it's a rock-hopping bushwhack up the Papoose Scramble, which is the Forest Service's official way of saying a trail is not a trail. (Another faint path leads left from Enni Camp to Bear Valley Meadows, 0.7 mile up the side of the drainage to the north and east.)

The path to Papoose continues southeast up the drainage along the north side of the creek, veering away from the water and following the course of a dry gully that runs along the edge of the canyon floor. The route is marked by cairns, but it's easy to lose the path among the downed trees, bushes, and boulders. Don't worry, just head east along the dwindling strip of land between the creek and canyon wall. After 0.5 mile the route crosses to the south side of the creek at a ford marked by several cairns.

Once across the creek, follow the faint path up a brushy, exposed slope to the base of a steep headwall guarding the final approach to Papoose Lake. Look for cairns leading the way past a snowmelt pond on a level bench just before what appears to be a sheer cliff. A zigzagging route winds up through the dark band of rock. The climbing is not technical, but it's a good idea to keep your hands free and use caution on the steep scramble. Above this section, the route heads generally left to right as you ascend, veering toward a field of light-colored granite boulders on the southwest side of the canyon. The lake is hidden from view, still high above and to the right (southeast), at the head of the drainage.

To your left (northeast) the outlet from Papoose Lake carves a deep, narrow gorge through naked gray rock. Cairns lead southeast along the lip of the gorge. Even without the cairns the route is obvious: just follow the path of least resistance until you top out on a granite apron at the mouth of the Papoose Lake basin, 12.8 miles from the trailhead.

The clear blue water, smooth granite shores, and spectacular cirque above the lake make for an ample reward. Stunted red firs and mountain hemlocks are scattered around the basin, but the shores consist mostly of sun-baked rock and bright-colored wildflowers. Indian paintbrush, scarlet gilia, angelica, and purple monkshood are just a few of the species that bloom here in the summer. Smooth slabs of granite slope down to the water's edge.

When you've recovered from the official scramble up to the lake, there's plenty of unofficial scrambling to be had on the ridge above Papoose. A stiff climb to the top of the sharp-edged ridgeline will earn you a spectacular view into the head of the Canyon Creek drainage and the heart of the Trinity Alps. Experienced climbers can also try their hand on 8,933-foot Mount Hilton, which is just beyond the ridge to the southeast.

Options: Make a loop over to Grizzly Lake using Bobs Farm Trail (Hikes 1 and 3). The detour adds about 25 miles to your route, but you won't be disappointed.

3 Bobs Farm Trail

See Map on Page 30

Highlights:	Guaranteed solitude; chance to link two of the Trinity Alps' most spectacular destinations.
Type of hike:	Backcountry connecting trail.
Total distance:	4.4 miles.
Difficulty:	Strenuous.
Elevation gain:	1,900 feet.
Maps:	USGS Thompson Peak quad; USDAFS Trinity Alps Wilderness map.

Finding the trailhead: Bobs Farm Trail runs between mile 12.8 on the North Fork Trail and mile 8.7 on the Rattlesnake Creek Trail.

Parking and trailhead facilities: See Hikes 1 or 2.

Key points:
- 0.0 North Fork Trail–Bobs Farm Trail junction.
- 0.1 Grizzly Creek crossing.
- 0.8 Specimen Creek crossing.
- 2.2 Horse camp/spring.
- 2.5 Bobs Farm.
- 4.4 Rattlesnake Creek Trail–Bobs Farm Trail junction.

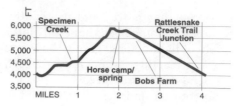

Profile data provided by TOPO!
©1999 Wildflower Productions(www.topo.com)

The hike: Any description of Bobs Farm Trail must start with a disclaimer: Do not attempt this route if you don't like steep trails. Mile for mile and switchback for switchback, this is one of the most difficult hikes in the Trinity Alps. The trail is steep, overgrown in places, and can be avoided by taking a longer, gentler route linking the North Fork and Rattlesnake Trails.

That said, Bobs Farm Trail is one of my favorite paths in Trinity Alps. What are its redeeming qualities? First, it allows you to make a spectacular loop between Grizzly and Papoose Lakes with a minimum of backtracking. Second, it's the only way to see—and marvel at—Bobs Farm, a lonely hill-side outpost, where long ago an entrepreneurial farmer named Bob grew produce to sell to local miners (or maybe not—it's possible that the legend of Bobs Farm was planted by a miner joking about the hillside's poor agri-cultural prospects). Finally, and perhaps most importantly, are bragging rights: you *hiked* Bobs Farm Trail. If the condition of the path is anything to go on, not many hikers can make that claim.

Starting at the North Fork end of the trail (11W03), the junction is just a few yards east of Mill Gulch. A couple of well-worn signs indicate the way to Papoose Lake and Specimen Creek (no mention of Bobs Farm at this end of the trail). Hike south, immediately crossing Grizzly Creek near a little-used campsite, then skirt the edge of Specimen Creek. Instead of crossing the creek here, however, the trail veers left (southeast) and climbs steeply up a dusty, oak-shaded ridge that separates Grizzly and Specimen Creeks. The ascent is short but attention getting: in places the trail climbs straight up the hillside. By the time you descend the other side of the ridge and cross Specimen Creek, you have a good taste of what's to come. (Be sure to fill water bottles before going further.)

After crossing Specimen Creek, the trail climbs steeply out of the drain-age and bends farther southeast, contouring along the base of the mountain across brushy slopes. In places the trail seems to disappear in dense cover of ceanothus bushes, but it's never so faint that you can't pick it up again on the other side. If it doesn't get you lost, however, this brush-choked section will do a number on bare legs. Take appropriate precautions.

Less than 0.5 mile after the creek crossing, the trail turns south and starts climbing in earnest. At times the path ascends what appears to be a primitive form of switchbacks: the idea is there, but they haven't been perfected. The steepness is somewhat abated by the old-growth fir forest that dominates the hillside, providing shade and a beautiful, open understory to walk through.

Eventually the trail tops out on the ridgeline separating Grizzly Creek and Rattlesnake Creek drainages, almost 2,000 feet above your starting point.

Mining relics at Bobs Farm.

Catch your breath and enjoy great views of the granite skyline to the east, then descend through manzanita and open slopes to an old hunters' camp in a stand of woods near a spring (two faint paths cross the short distance between the ridgetop and the camp). A few rusty old artifacts indicate the remote camp has a long history.

From the camp the trail descends almost due south, winding downhill through a ferny meadow and dropping into thicker forest cover. Don't worry if the spring doesn't look too inviting (it's at the edge of the meadow just east of the trail); there's plenty of water a few minutes away in the creek at Bobs Farm.

A set of more highly evolved switchbacks leads 0.3 mile down to Bobs Farm. The collection of old machinery pieces and the ruins of a shack are perched on a cramped-looking hillside above a clear-flowing little creek. A profusion of leopard lilies grows on the lush banks. Take a moment to look around the abandoned site and appreciate Bob's life—and how many times he must have walked his namesake trail.

From here the trail crosses the creek and descends southwest on rocky, dusty switchbacks. The terrain becomes more open and exposed as the path crosses hillsides covered in low-growing manzanita (sweltering on a hot day, but allowing for great views). Just over 4 miles from Grizzly Creek, Bobs Farm Trail descends to 4,000 feet (the same elevation you started at) and the junction with the Rattlesnake Creek Trail. Turn left (east) to reach Papoose Lake and right (west) to reach Rattlesnake Camp (see Hike 2). And yes, now you can start bragging.

4 Canyon Creek Lakes

Highlights:	Simply one of the most beautiful hikes in the Trinity Alps: lush meadows, spectacular waterfalls, gorgeous lakes, and awesome views. Expect lots of company.
Type of hike:	Backpack; out-and-back.
Total distance:	16 miles.
Difficulty:	Moderate.
Elevation gain:	2,602 feet.
Maps:	USGS Mt. Hilton quad; USDAFS Trinity Alps Wilderness map.

Finding the trailhead: From Weaverville, drive 8 miles west on California Highway 299 to Junction City. Turn right (north) on paved Canyon Creek Road (County Road 401) just before (east of) the bridge over Canyon Creek. Don't count on a sign, but the road is obvious (directly across from the general store). It's 13.5 miles from here to the trailhead at the end of the road (all paved but the last mile). Stay right at 10.5 miles and pass the East Fork Lake trailhead at 11 miles. Next comes a sign commemorating the old mining town

Canyon Creek Lakes • Boulder Creek Lakes and Forbidden Lakes

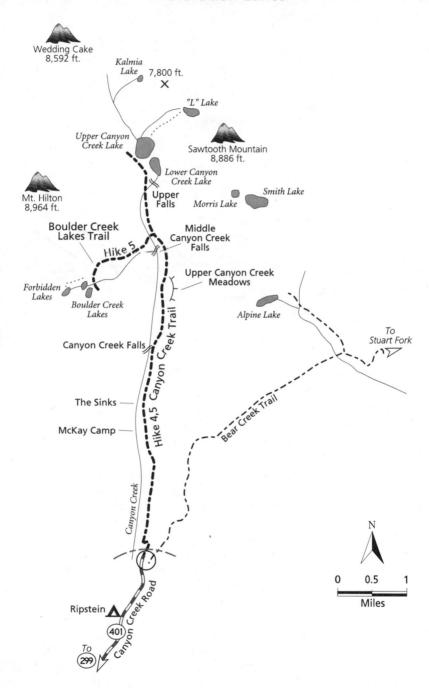

Wedding Cake
8,592 ft.

Kalmia
Lake   7,800 ft.
X

"L" Lake

Upper Canyon
Creek Lake

Sawtooth Mountain
8,886 ft.

Lower Canyon
Creek Lake

Upper
Falls

Morris Lake

Smith Lake

Mt. Hilton
8,964 ft.

Boulder Creek
Lakes Trail

Hike 5

Middle
Canyon Creek
Falls

Upper Canyon Creek
Meadows

Forbidden
Lakes

Boulder Creek
Lakes

Alpine Lake

To
Stuart Fork

Canyon Creek Falls

Canyon Creek Trail

Hike 4,5

Bear Creek Trail

The Sinks

McKay Camp

Canyon Creek

N

0   0.5   1

Miles

Ripstein

401

To
299

Canyon Creek Road

of Dedrick, now lost to history, which once did a bustling bit of business on the banks of Canyon Creek. The trailhead is at the end of the road.

Parking and trailhead facilities: Outhouse and ample parking; camping at nearby Ripstein Campground.

Key points:
- 0.0 Trailhead.
- 2.5 McKay Camp.
- 3.0 The Sinks.
- 3.9 Canyon Creek Falls.
- 4.5 Upper Canyon Creek Meadows.
- 5.5 Middle Canyon Creek Falls.
- 6.0 Boulder Creek Lakes Trail junction.
- 7.1 Lower Canyon Creek Lake.
- 8.0 Upper Canyon Creek Lake.
- 9.1 L Lake (optional, off-trail).

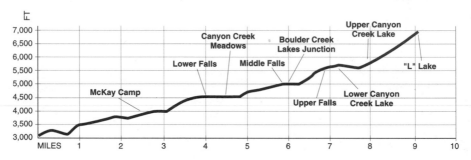

Profile data provided by TOPO! ©1999 Wildflower Productions (www.topo.com)

The hike: All of Canyon Creek's attractions—waterfalls, sweeping granite cliffs, sparkling lakes, spectacular views, swimming holes of near-perfect proportions—can be found elsewhere in the Trinity Alps. But you'd be hard-pressed to find anywhere else where they're all packaged into one pleasant hike. Such an abundance of beauty has not gone unnoticed.

Canyon Creek is without a doubt the most popular destination in the Trinity Alps. From the overflowing parking lot at the trailhead to the numerous tents dotting the meadows and creek along the way, you'll have no illusions about wilderness solitude here on a busy summer weekend. That said, Canyon Creek is still one of the most beautiful slices of mountain country you'll ever walk through. Hopefully, new restrictions on group size (maximum of 10 people) in the Trinity Alps should cut down on the gaggles of visitors that have been known to swarm up Canyon Creek in frighteningly high numbers. And if you plan your trip accordingly (out of season, midweek), you can still see Canyon Creek in all its glory with none of its crowds. I once spent a few peaceful days here in October without encountering one other person. If and when you come to Canyon Creek, camp well below the lakes. There are much better campsites along the creek leading

Lower Canyon Creek Falls near Canyon Creek Trail.

up the drainage. The lakes themselves are in granite-lined basins too vulnerable to human impact.

Two paths start at the trailhead: Canyon Creek Trail and Bear Creek Trail. For the Canyon Creek Trail, head north on the well-marked path. The trail ascends gradually through shady, low-elevation vegetation of dogwood, maple, Douglas-fir, and oak (with a smattering of pine and cedar thrown in). The path dips down to cross Bear Creek, then climbs moderately to a low ridge, continuing north parallel to and high above Canyon Creek's east bank.

It's pleasant going for the next 2.5 miles to McKay Camp. A spur trail to the left (west) leads down to Canyon Creek and McKay Camp, a little island nestled between two clear arms of the creek. In particularly dry years, the water may disappear under The Sinks (a pile of debris from a massive rock fall) just upstream, then reappear at the downstream end of the island. Normally, however, you can expect to see impossibly clear, aquamarine water flowing by the island.

After McKay Camp, the trail climbs more steeply on a short series of switchbacks to reach a ledge high above Canyon Creek. A dependable little creek crosses the trail three times as you switchback up its course, so consider waiting for the highest crossing to get water if you need it (purify all water in this heavily traveled drainage).

Ascending moderately along the granite-lined ledge, you first hear, then glimpse, the fabled Canyon Creek Falls. The crashing waterfall is commonly called the Lower Canyon Creek Falls to distinguish it from the Middle and Upper Falls, but when most people refer to *the* Canyon Creek Falls, this is the one they're talking about. Years ago, the trail climbed right up Canyon Creek and passed within spitting distance of the falls. Now, however, the path rejoins the creek above the falls, 3.9 miles from the trailhead.

Trail and creek meet at a pleasant site with a minifalls, a refreshing little swimming hole, and a rather poor trailside campsite marked by weeping spruce. Much better campsites can be found half a mile ahead and for the next 3 miles, in Upper Canyon Creek Meadows and beyond.

Continuing upstream from the falls, the trail meanders alongside the east bank of the now peaceful creek. The creek winds tranquilly through a lush, parklike forest of incense-cedars, ferns, willows, and inviting meadows of corn lilies and mullein. The trail runs mostly level to the base of Middle Canyon Creek Falls, about 5.5 miles from the trailhead. A use trail branches left (west) to the base of the falls, easily accessible through the open understory. To the right (east) is the beginning of a difficult off-trail route to Smith and Morris Lakes (Hike 14).

From the base of the Middle Falls, the Canyon Creek Trail climbs a series of switchbacks to reach the junction with the Boulder Creek Lakes Trail on a level, forested flat 6 miles from the trailhead. A left turn leads 2 miles up to Boulder Creek Lakes and Forbidden Lakes (Hike 5).

Past the junction, the Canyon Creek Trail continues north, climbing gently through weeping spruce, ponderosa pine, manzanita, incense-cedar, and more meadows. Near the end of a forested flat, after another set of falls and just before the last hill at the base of Lower Canyon Creek Lake, the trail crosses to the west side of the creek. A trail sign should indicate the crossing, and a couple of downed trees may be present to help keep your feet dry. The old route (which some people still use) goes up the east side of the creek along the falls. The problem with going up the east side is you have to cross the outlet at the top of the falls—a very bad idea in high water. Hikers have died trying it. The newer trail on the west side ascends a series of granite ledges (follow the cairns) and abruptly arrives at Lower Canyon Creek Lake, 7.1 miles from the trailhead.

If all the waterfalls, meadows, and swimming holes weren't enough, the sight from here should make you understand why there may be 50 cars at the trailhead on summer weekends. The deep blue 14-acre lake sits at an elevation of 5,600 feet in a trough gouged out of smooth slabs of granite. The east side of the lake ranges from steep to very steep, with 8,886-foot Sawtooth Mountain towering directly overhead. The west side is littered with sloping granite benches that are perfect for warming yourself after a dip in the cold, clear water. Framed in a notch at the north end of the lake are Thompson Peak and Wedding Cake.

To reach Upper Canyon Creek Lake, simply follow the orange blazes painted on rocks on the west side of the basin (yes, painted, but at least the shade isn't too bright). Stay high as you follow them northwest through a steep gully to the southwest corner of Upper Canyon Creek Lake.

The upper lake is 400 feet higher, 10 acres bigger, and maybe just a tad more spectacular than its lower companion. A sloping granite dike holds the water back on the south side, sheer slabs of gray rock plunge into the lake's northwest shore, and a lush green meadow surrounds the inlet on the northeast. Above all looms the secluded headwaters of Canyon Creek, topped by 9,002-foot Thompson Peak and its slightly lower neighbor, 8,592-foot Wedding Cake. If it's solitude you're after, set your sights on one of those granite summits.

Options: In the upper reaches of the Canyon Creek drainage lie two little lakes rarely seen by the crowds down below. Only experienced hikers should attempt these routes. All travel above Upper Canyon Creek Lake is off-trail.

Side trip to L (or Ell) Lake: Cross the outlet at Upper Canyon Creek Lake (carefully) and make your way to the northeast side of the lake. L lies in the basin that bends around to the northeast, directly below the northwest face of Sawtooth Mountain. Follow cairns up the gully and ascend the south side of the creek tumbling down from L. There's only one place little 2-acre L Lake can be up there, and that's where you find it. A mile of fairly easy scrambling and a few steep bands of granite lie between you and the lake. Finally, pick your way through the trees on the basin's west side and discover that L Lake is, indeed, shaped like an L. The lake sits at 6,350 feet.

From a granite seat near the lake's outlet you look directly across the Canyon Creek drainage at the sheer western wall and steep slopes leading up to 8,964-foot Mount Hilton. The peak was named in honor of James Hilton, who himself honored Weaverville by comparing the town to the mythical Shangri-La in his book *Lost Horizon*.

Side trip to Kalmia Lake: This tough scramble is recommended only for strong hikers with good route-finding ability. To reach tiny, 1-acre Kalmia, perched high on the shoulder of an unnamed peak at the head of Canyon Creek drainage, you've got to tackle the steep gully northwest of L Lake and ascend to the ridge between Canyon Creek and Stuart Fork headwaters. Follow the ridgeline northwest, up and over the shoulder south of the unnamed peak. Drop down to Kalmia after climbing about 1,500 feet and 1 mile from L. The tiny, shallow lake, gouged into the side of the mountain at 7,500 feet, is so close to Wedding Cake it feels like you can reach out and grab a slice.

Two extremely steep gullies lead from Kalmia down to the headwaters of Canyon Creek. The gullies are not a good way to get down, much less up. Still, I must admit I was rather pleased with the loop formed by traveling counterclockwise from Upper Canyon Creek Lake to L to Kalmia and back along Canyon Creek. The headwaters along upper Canyon Creek comprise some of the best alpine scenery in the Alps, with flower-filled meadows, sparkling waterfalls, and amazing vistas in every direction. No maintained trail leads between the upper drainage and Upper Canyon Creek Lake, but you'll pick up cairns and traces of use trails as you get closer to the lake.

5   Boulder Creek Lakes and Forbidden Lakes

See Map on Page 41

Highlights:	A steep and scenic detour out of the Canyon Creek drainage. Though it's a short distance from the most crowded trail in the Trinity Alps, this pretty little granite basin doesn't get as much traffic as you might expect.
Type of hike:	Backpack (2–3 nights); out-and-back.
Total distance:	17 miles.
Difficulty:	Moderate (off-trail hike to Forbidden Lakes is strenuous).
Elevation gain:	3,040 feet.
Maps:	USGS Mt. Hilton quad; USDAFS Trinity Alps Wilderness map.

Finding the trailhead: From Weaverville, drive 8 miles west on California Highway 299 to Junction City. Turn right (north) on paved Canyon Creek Road (County Road 401) located just before (east of) the bridge over Canyon Creek. Don't count on a sign, but the road is obvious (directly across from the general store). It's 13.5 miles from here to the trailhead at the end of the road (all paved but the last mile). Stay right at 10.5 miles and pass the East Fork Lake trailhead at 11 miles. Next comes a sign commemorating the old mining town of Dedrick, now lost to history, which once did a bustling bit of business on the banks of Canyon Creek. The trailhead is at end of the road.

Parking and trailhead facilities: The parking lot can accommodate as many as 50 cars; outhouse available. Developed camping at Ripstein Campground.

Key points:

0.0 Trailhead.
2.5 McKay Camp.
3.0 The Sinks.
3.9 Canyon Creek Falls.
4.5 Upper Canyon Creek Meadows.
6.0 Boulder Creek Lakes Trailhead.
8.0 Boulder Creek Lakes.
8.5 Forbidden Lakes.

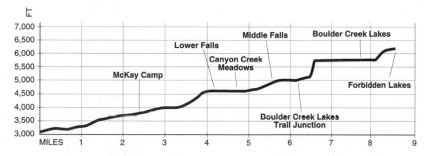

Profile data provided by TOPO! ©1999 Wildflower Productions (www.topo.com)

The hike: Boulder Creek Lakes is a collection of shallow pools and mini-lakes spread over a wide granite bench that hangs above the west side of the Canyon Creek drainage, just 2 miles off the crowded thoroughfare. The hanging cirque is protected by a sheer headwall the trail skirts on the north. It's an impressive sight and makes for a strenuous climb up sunny, exposed switchbacks. Once there, you find a delightfully different setting than exists at Canyon Creek Lakes. While Boulder Creek Lakes may not be as stunning as its glamorous neighbors, neither will it stun the sensibilities with crowds. The basin gets a lot of sunshine, so the shallow water warms up earlier than most lakes, and smooth granite slabs offer abundant places to lie down in peace and quiet. If that's not enough, the Forbidden Lakes hang hidden and mysterious in a concealed cirque above the basin. Who can resist a name like Forbidden Lakes?

Start at Canyon Creek Trailhead and hike 6 miles to the trail junction just above Middle Canyon Creek Falls (see Hike 4 for details on this part of the route). At the signed junction, turn left (west) and proceed over a little rise before reaching Canyon Creek just upstream from the falls. Cross to the west side of the creek. You can keep your feet dry with some creative boulder hopping, but use caution when the water's high—the falls isn't far away. Go farther upstream to cross if needed. (And refill water bottles here; there's none on the steep hillside ahead. Purify all water.)

Once across the creek, the trail heads south and then west through mixed conifers and alongside a secluded little meadow. (The trail heading north .

Forbidden Lake above Boulder Creek Lakes.

from the crossing leads to campsites along Canyon Creek.) Climb moderately parallel to and above Boulder Creek, which remains a good distance to the south.

After leaving the last of the meadows behind, the trail climbs more steeply up the north side of the drainage. There are great views of the headwall below the lake, but there's a price to pay: open vistas mean hot, sunny hiking. The trail is rough and rocky. All in all, it's a far cry from the cool fern grottoes you left behind along Canyon Creek. But the switchbacks soon deposit you on a granite slope leading over the lip of the basin, and from there it's just a matter of following cairns around the north side. Though you can see the lake from here, you can't go directly to it because of a wide and deep chasm that lies in the way. The cairns lead to the western, narrow edge of the ravine, where you can cross the little stream it contains. Continue from there to Boulder Creek Lakes, 2 miles from the junction (8 miles from the trailhead).

The wide, spacious basin has only a few Jeffrey pines and weeping spruce. Mostly it's just granite, water, and views. According to a few Sawtooth aficionados, the Trinity Alps' best view of Sawtooth Mountain is from here. It's also a good place to eye one of several off-trail routes up to Smith Lake, on the opposite side of the Canyon Creek drainage (see Hike 14).

To reach the Forbidden Lakes, aim for the notch in the canyon above and to the west, where the stream emerges. If the route looks forbidding, maybe that's how the lake got its name (not everyone thinks it's so bad; some people—and maps—identify Lower Forbidden Lake as Upper Boulder Creek Lake). In any case, the way up isn't too difficult. Cairns lead up the north side of the outlet (look for a path that starts where you crossed the ravine on the way in). On the south side, boulder hop and scramble your way up to the notch, then push through the bushes to the lower lake. Either way you go, the last hundred yards is going to be a bushwhack (maybe that's the forbidding part).

Lower Forbidden Lake is a picturesque little slip of a thing, tucked between high, steep walls that barely let much sunshine in even in midsummer. You can count on a permanent snowbank on the far west side of the basin that holds Upper Forbidden Lake and a little meadow that remains emerald green well into September. The two little lakes lie side by side at 6,250 feet, with not much more than rocks and cold water and a view of Sawtooth Mountain framed in the outlet notch—a truly wonderful place.

If you like to scramble over the granite high country, explore the largely untraveled terrain above Boulder Creek Lakes. It's possible to climb nearby Mount Hilton (8,964 feet) from here.

Options: Canyon Creek Lakes (2 miles from the trail junction on Canyon Creek, Hike 4). You can also make a difficult, off-trail journey to Smith Lake by scaling the drainage directly across from the Boulder Creek drainage (Hike 14).

6 East Fork Lakes

Highlights:	A secluded granite cirque with a shallow little lake at its base; no crowds.
Type of hike:	Day hike or backpack (1–2 nights); out-and-back.
Total distance:	10.4 miles.
Difficulty:	Moderate.
Elevation gain:	2,758 feet.
Maps:	USGS Rush Creek Lakes and Dedrick quads; USDAFS Trinity Alps Wilderness map.

Finding the trailhead: From Weaverville, drive 8 miles west on California Highway 299 to Junction City. Turn right (north) on paved Canyon Creek Road (County Road 401) just before (east of) the bridge over Canyon Creek. Don't count on a sign, but the road is obvious (directly across from the general store). Drive north 11 miles to the signed turn for the East Fork Lakes trailhead on Forest Road 35N47Y. Turn right (east) and continue up the unpaved road (road closed October 30 to May 1). Stay left at the fork at 1.2 miles. Arrive at the signed trailhead at 2 miles.

Parking and trailhead facilities: Parking but no facilities. The nearest developed campgrounds are just a few miles away: Ripstein Campground is located 2 miles farther north on Canyon Creek Road; Junction City Campground is on CA 299 west of Junction City.

Key points:

0.0	Trailhead.
0.2	Maple Mine.
2.1	Bucks Ranch.
5.2	East Fork Lake.

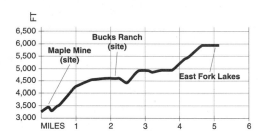

Profile data provided by TOPO!
©1999 Wildflower Productions (www.topo.com)

The hike: East Fork Lakes is one of those lost-and-forgotten corners of the Trinity Alps. The small lake is not much more than a little pond, really, tucked up in a pretty but isolated basin on the north side of Monument Peak. This obscurity, ironically, is highlighted by the multitude of people who drive by the trailhead each summer. The East Fork Lake Trail is on the way to Canyon Creek, which means 99.9 percent of the people who pass the trailhead just keep on going. Of course, that's not too surprising, considering Canyon Creek (Hike 4) is arguably the most spectacular destination in the Trinity Alps. It's also one of the most crowded, so if you've already seen it—or you're after solitude—just hang a right at the sign for East Fork Lake and rest assured no one else is likely to follow.

The East Fork Lake Trail (9W22) zigzags steeply uphill through a low-elevation mixture of oak, madrone, and brush. The path soon settles into a more moderate grade, climbing past old mining relics as it switchbacks up

East Fork Lakes

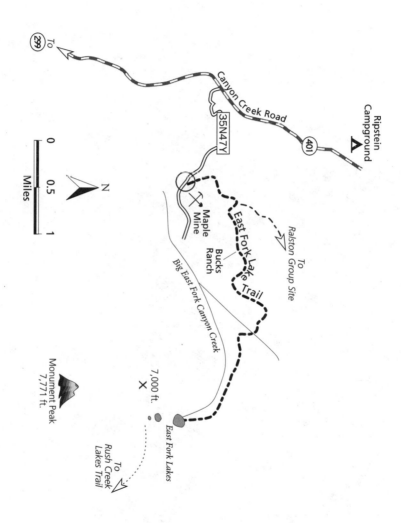

To 299

Canyon Creek Road

35N47Y

401

Ripstein Campground

Maple Mine

Bucks Ranch

East Fork Lake Trail

To Ralston Group Site

Big East Fork Canyon Creek

N

0   0.5   1
Miles

Monument Peak
7,771 ft.

7,000 ft.

East Fork Lakes

To Rush Creek Lakes Trail

East Fork Lake.

the slope. Watch for an obscure, unmarked fork a half-mile in. The main trail, well defined, goes right (north). At 0.8 mile gain the ridgeline and turn right (east) along the spine of the ridge (another unmarked path goes west).

The sparse forest becomes more dense as you ascend, with more pines appearing with the elevation gain. At another fork located just over a mile in, the main trail is signed (right, or east) where it follows a gentle contour with good views across the drainage (the left fork leads north 1 mile to Ralston Group site). Just over 2 miles from the trailhead, arrive at the old Bucks Ranch site, where traces of an ancient flume lead to a perennial creek (first dependable water source; it should be purified).

Break into an open and sunny section after the creek crossing. This part of the trail, though not long, is hot and dry in the summer. The tread is steep and rocky, lined by manzanita, and exposed to the sun. Fortunately, the path soon re-enters the canyon bottom, where a cool forest of cedar, fern, and alder line Big East Fork Canyon Creek.

The last mile of trail may be overgrown in places—a sign of just how few hikers make it up here. Finally, climb steeply to the south and reach the top of a granite shelf, where East Fork Lake is cupped in a grass- and boulder-lined bed gouged into the narrow canyon. Take a seat on the lip of granite and enjoy the views down the drainage, or relax and enjoy the picturesque cascade of the lake's inlet stream.

The cirque above the lake is a gradual slope of sweeping gray granite blessed with an inviting level bench. No trail leads to the bench, but with some creative rock hopping it's not difficult to pick your way up the boulder fields and brushy slopes to get there (though you do have to fight your way through a few dense thickets to get beyond East Fork Lake). Stick to the slope on the east side of the inlet creek.

It's worth the effort. The bench is a hanging garden of wildflowers, emerald meadows, fir and hemlock trees, a waterfall, and several delightful ponds of crystal clear water. It's because of these ponds that some maps call the basin East Fork Lakes (plural). Hike up to the ridgeline on either side for spectacular views. Return the way you came.

Options: A difficult, off-trail route to Rush Creek Lakes (Hike 10) is possible for ambitious hikers: go over the ridge southeast of the lake and descend to the Rush Creek Lakes Trail.

7 East Weaver Lake; Rush Creek Lakes

Highlights:	A steep hike (partly off-trail) to a sparkling little chain of lakes set deep in the jaws of a rocky cirque.
Type of hike:	Day hike or backpack (1–2 nights); out-and-back.
Total distance:	8 miles.
Difficulty:	Strenuous.
Elevation gain:	2,198 feet.
Maps:	USGS Rush Creek Lakes quad; USDAFS Trinity Alps Wilderness map.

Finding the trailhead: The journey to the trailhead is a trip in itself. In fact, some people drive the 9 miles up to the fire lookout on top of Weaver Bally Mountain just to watch the sunset. From Weaverville, drive west on California Highway 299 (but not too fast; the turn is on the edge of town). Turn right (north) on Memorial Drive, just past the Trinity County Office of Education, and proceed a few blocks to the beginning of unpaved Weaver Bally Road (Forest Road 33N38). Go straight (north) and gain 5,000 feet over the next 9 miles. The road is rough but passable for passenger cars (the main road is obvious, but go uphill if there's any confusion). The trailhead is on the right, just before the fire lookout at the end of the road.

Parking and trailhead facilities: Ample parking and a picnic area. You could throw a sleeping bag on the ground here (sunsets are extraordinary), but no available facilities or water.

Key points:
- 0.0   Trailhead.
- 1.0   East Weaver Lake.
- 1.5   Bear Gulch Trail junction.
- 2.5   Start of off-trail route.
- 4.0   Upper Rush Creek Lake.

Profile data provided by TOPO!
©1999 Wildflower Productions (www.topo.com)

The hike: The Rush Creek Lakes (there are four, plus assorted ponds) are close to Weaverville as the bird flies, but birds are about all you'll find here on most days. People just don't seem to believe the kind of spectacular scenery found in Rush Creek Lakes' craggy cirque could be so close to town. It can and is. (Please note: This off-trail route is the recommended way to the lakes, but not the only way. Hikers who don't like steep, off-trail scrambles should use the Rush Creek Lakes Trail to walk a path the whole way. See Hike 10).

That the trailhead elevation and the elevation at Upper Rush Creek Lake are nearly the same (just under and just over 6,900 feet, respectively) might lead you to believe this is an easy hike. Don't be misled. In between you descend 600 feet, ascend 1,200 feet, then drop another 600 to end up where

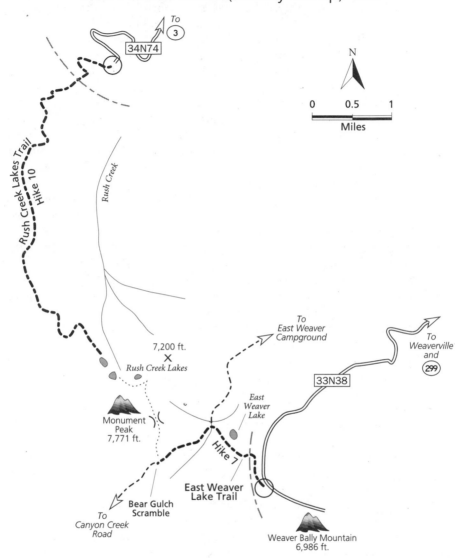

you started (in terms of altitude). In terms of scenery, you enter another world. The trail starts on a brushy, exposed ridge on the side of Weaver Bally Mountain, and finishes with a steep scramble down a rock-strewn chute to the rugged interior of the Rush Creek basin. The descent doesn't require any technical skills or special ability, just caution. Still, if negotiating a steep gully doesn't sound appealing, take the maintained Rush Creek Lakes Trail.

There are three reasons to take the Weaver Bally (off-trail) route to Rush Creek Lakes instead of using the trail. First, it's simply shorter and more elegant. It shaves 3 miles off the maintained route and lets you drop into the basin from above—always a nice way to finish a hike. Second, the route passes within a few hundred feet of Monument Peak's craggy summit. If you came the other way you might never make the climb all the way up to the peak from the lake, and that would be a shame. Finally, the Rush Creek Lakes Trail itself is a waterless, much maligned path in its own right (actually, it's been called worse, but there's no reason to be mean).

From East Weaver Lake Trailhead, walk east on the signed East Weaver Lake Trail (10W11). Almost immediately, the path leads past the remains of a ridgetop track cut during efforts to stop the 1987 East Fire. A Forest Service sign explains that fire crews prepared to set a backfire here as the wildfire approached from Bear Gulch. Fortunately, the fire was controlled before it crossed the ridge so they didn't have to. Still, there is evidence of vegetation cutting, especially on the slope below Monument Peak, where a number of mature red firs had to be felled.

After passing the East Fire sign (stay right), the trail heads east across slopes of ceanothus and manzanita. You soon reach a prominent shoulder above East Weaver Lake, where the trail turns sharply left to contour around the basin above the north side of the lake and drop down on steep, rocky switchbacks. The ridge is a good place to pause and survey the route ahead.

Below is East Weaver Lake, a mile from the trailhead. The little 1-acre lake is more of a stop along the route than a destination itself, though there are a couple of campsites nearby and people often come here for the day. No matter what your length of stay at East Weaver on the way in, you're sure to appreciate its cool water on the way out.

To the south is the road you came up on and a view of Weaverville. To the northeast is 7,771-foot Monument Peak and the high ridge between you and Rush Creek Lakes. Once you're standing on the low spot on that ridge, the lake will be at your feet.

First you must descend into (and out of) the drainage below East Weaver Lake. Follow the trail downhill to its junction with the Bear Gulch Scramble, a half mile past the lake (the junction is signed; turn left, or west). After eyeing that ridge next to Monument Peak, don't be discouraged by the descent. This is where people get into trouble. It appears you can save yourself some climbing if you leave the trail early and cut across the brush-covered slope. After all, what's a little manzanita when you can save all that elevation? Don't be tempted. Unless you're the type who likes to impress your friends with backpacking battle wounds, stay on the trail. If you are that type, you're guaranteed to impress. I know because I once tried to impress a girlfriend by showing her this "shortcut." She forgave me, eventually.

After turning onto the Bear Gulch Scramble, head uphill through shady forest cover and small meadows. The path wanders up a dry creekbed for a short way (usually marked by a cairn) then continues up steep, rocky switchbacks for the final push to the ridge between Bear Gulch and East Weaver Creek drainages. Take a breather and look at the near-impenetrable wall of brush you just avoided by staying on the trail. Good decision.

From here it's an easy mile along the ridgeline and up to the base of Monument Peak. The Bear Gulch Scramble drops down the hill to the west, while you head cross-country to the north. The off-trail route passes right along the burn line from the 1987 fire, past charred logs and giant firs felled by the fire fighters, and up to the ridge just east of Monument Peak. It's easy to pick your way through the open terrain. A fairly obvious use trail ascends through mature firs to the ridgeline, though the "trail" is steep and has very little zig or zag (and is badly eroded because of it; this is a good place to spread out and make your own, better, trail).

Once atop the ridge, it's a matter of controlling your descent to Upper Rush Creek Lake. Two steep chutes lead down to the lake, and the routes are fairly obvious with rock cairns and signs of use. Take it slow. A granite "island" midway down forces you right or left; the right side is steeper. At the bottom, you'll be at water's edge and at nearly the same elevation you started.

The lake itself has icy blue water and a pleasing mixture of evergreens and rock terraces. The 2-acre lake sits at 6,950 feet and its craggy, high-walled basin keeps the sun out and the water chilly all summer. In fact, the basin often holds snow until late summer.

Head down canyon through the basin to explore the other Rush Creek lakes. The ponds and 1-acre lakes are spread out in a curving basin that bends north and then east. No maintained trail leads between them.

On the way in or out, don't pass up the chance to scramble up Monument Peak. The 7,771-foot summit commands a 360-degree view of northwest California: the Alps, Mount Shasta, Lassen Peak; and a bird's eye view of Rush Creek Lakes. A use trail marked by cairns leads up the ridge to the base of the peak. The final push to the summit is on huge blocks of rock, one of which supports a small white cross. It reads: "Soaring with the Eagles."

8 New River Loop

Highlights:	Hike through wild canyon country to the fascinating historic mining district.
Type of hike:	Backpack; semi-loop.
Total distance:	23.4 miles.
Difficulty:	Moderate.
Elevation gain:	3,000 feet.
Maps:	USGS Jim Jam Ridge and Dees Peak quad; USDAFS Trinity Alps Wilderness map.

Finding the trailhead: From Hawkins Bar (on California Highway 299, 10 miles east of Willow Creek) drive north on Denny Road (County Road 402). Continue for 20 miles, past a Forest Service campground (at 18 miles) and the tiny settlement of Denny. It's slow going on the twisting, winding road. At 21.5 miles from the highway, turn left (west) at the sign for New River

New River Loop

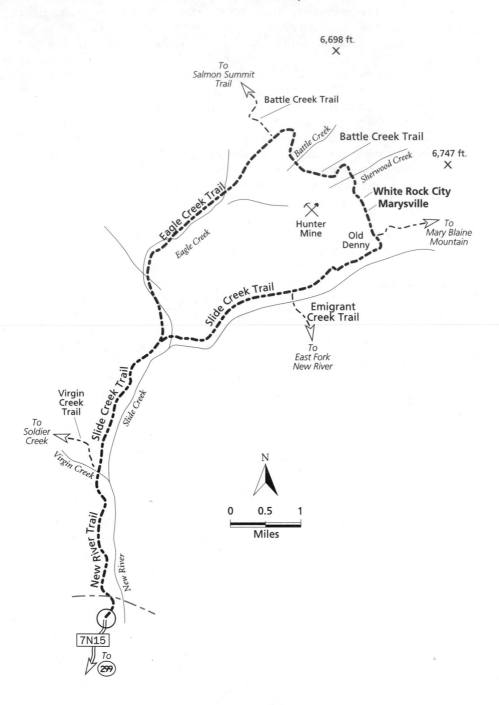

6,698 ft.
✕

To
Salmon Summit
Trail

Battle Creek Trail

Battle Creek

Battle Creek Trail

Sherwood Creek

6,747 ft.
✕

**White Rock City
Marysville**

Eagle Creek Trail

Eagle Creek

Hunter
Mine

Old
Denny

To
Mary Blaine
Mountain

Slide Creek Trail

Emigrant
Creek Trail

To
East Fork
New River

Virgin
Creek
Trail

Slide Creek Trail

Slide Creek

To
Soldier
Creek

Virgin Creek

New River Trail

New River

N

0   0.5   1
Miles

7N15

To
(299)

trailhead (Forest Road 7N15). Continue 6 miles to the end of the unpaved road (the way is marked by trailhead signs). The trailhead is at the end of the road, 27.5 miles from CA 299.

Parking and trailhead facilities: Parking and a toilet. Nearest developed campground at Denny.

Key points:
0.0	Trailhead.
2.8	Slide Creek Trail and Virgin Creek Trail junctions.
5.4	Eagle Creek Trail junction.
7.9	Emigrant Creek Trail.
10.5	Old Denny.
10.8	Mary Blaine–Cinnabar Trail and Battle Creek Trail junctions.
11.0	Marysville.
11.2	White Rock City.
14.0	Eagle Creek Trail.
18.2	Slide Creek Trail.
20.6	New River Trail.
23.4	Trailhead.

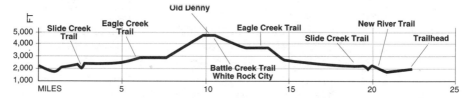

Profile data provided by TOPO! ©1999 Wildflower Productions (www.topo.com)

The hike: This journey into the heart of the "Green Trinities" is dramatically different from the classic hikes in the better-known eastern part of the wilderness. Rather than the high alpine lakes, granite peaks, and glacier-gouged valleys that draw numerous visitors to the east side, the west side of the wilderness is a land of thick-forested mountains and wild river canyons where few people venture. In the Green Trinities, elevations tend to be a little lower (and temperatures a little warmer), wildlife is more wild, and trails a lot less traveled. Solitude reigns supreme. Note: this area was nearly all burned in the 1999 Megram Fire.

But it wasn't always that way. In the late 1800s, the New River drainage was home to a number of mining settlements. Old Denny boasted 500 residents in its heyday. Due to the rugged, remote nature of the drainage, it was the last major river in the region that prospectors explored (hence the name "New River"). Once discovered, however, New River became a center of mining activity, with bustling communities at New River City (now called Old Denny), White Rock City, and Marysville. After a half-century of quiet, the Green Trinities again attracted cash-hungry entrepreneurs in the 1970s and 1980s. The area became a popular place to grow illegal marijuana crops. Marijuana cultivation has largely been eradicated since then, but visitors should report any suspicious activity to local law enforcement or Forest Service personnel.

Today, the area has been all but abandoned (though a few modern-day miners might be seen plying the rivers in wet suits), and the most common visitors are hikers who appreciate history and truly wild terrain. The trails are in good condition most of the way, but route-finding skills are required in a few places where the path is not obvious. Except for a few miles of trail, the hike is chiefly below 4,000 feet. The low elevation means there are three things you should be aware of: hot weather in midsummer, poison oak, and rattlesnakes. The first can be avoided by planning an early- or late-season trip; the second and third are best avoided by knowing what they look like and staying alert. Despite the lack of lakes, water is plentiful along the route. Creeks and streams are sparkling clear, with refreshing swimming holes and year-round flows. In fact, an abundance of water poses the only problem with hiking this route too early in the year. The ford at Virgin Creek, 2.8 miles in, may be uncrossable in high water. Check with the ranger station before heading out.

The hike starts on the New River Trail (7E05), meandering along the canyon high above the river and heading north up the drainage. The vegetation at this low elevation is a mix of oaks, madrone, maple, and dogwoods, with a fir thrown in here and there for good measure. The initial hike is an easy stroll downhill and along the river.

At 2.8 miles, arrive at the junction of Virgin Creek and Slide Creek (which forms New River). Already, you'll see evidence of an old flume and historic mining camps. The trail jogs to the left (west) to cross Virgin Creek slightly upstream from the confluence. If you can cross here you should have no problem at the route's other crossings. On the opposite bank, ascend immediately to a trail junction marked "Soldier Creek" to the left (west) and "Old Denny" to the right (east). Turn right toward Old Denny on the Slide Creek Trail (12W03).

Climb the point of a spur ridge separating Virgin and Slide Creeks, then amble up and down along Slide Creek for 2.6 miles. The forest is still a mix of oak, maple, and fir through here, with plenty of good swimming holes along the way. At the confluence of Slide and Eagle Creeks, 5.4 miles from the trailhead, arrive at another junction. To the right (east) is the Slide Creek Trail; to the left (north) is the Eagle Creek Trail (8E11), signed "Battle Creek–Salmon Summit." The Eagle Creek Trail is the path you'll return on to this point.

To continue the loop in the recommended direction, turn right and stay on the Slide Creek Trail. You descend and cross Eagle Creek a few hundred yards upstream from the confluence of the two creeks. From the crossing, it's a steep haul up and over the ridge separating the drainages, then another pleasant hike along and above the course of Slide Creek (with a few more uphill sections thrown in here and there, but nothing difficult). Top off water bottles at the crossing, as the next few miles are apt to be dry.

Just under 3 miles from the last junction, drop down to a grassy flat along Slide Creek. More well-preserved mining relics litter the clearing (look for an intact wood-and-metal hand-truck). Past the mining camp, the trail climbs moderately and crosses a couple of small tributaries, one of which boasts an ancient wooden bridge that's suitable only for looking at—not walking on. After crossing a fern-filled meadow about 0.2 mile beyond the camp, arrive at a somewhat confusing trail junction. To the right (south) is Emigrant Creek Trail (8E05), signed "Milk Camp–Pony Creek." The left (east) fork that goes straight is the trail that leads to Old Denny. Apparently unsigned at first, you'll eventually spot a sign for "Mary Blaine Meadows" soon after you start uphill.

Climb moderately but steadily for about 2 miles, reaching an elevation where pine, fir, and incense-cedar start dominating the forest, then arrive at Old Denny in a wooded flat high above Slide Creek. A weathered sign tells you the short version of the town's history: founded by Clive Clements in 1882; originally called New River City; abandoned in 1920. Looking around the wild setting, it's hard to imagine 500 people lived here at the turn of the century. Water is available from a spring 50 yards east of the Old Denny sign.

The trail heads north from Old Denny, climbing switchbacks to a ridge-top junction. Another ancient sign points right (east) to Mary Blaine–Cinnabar and left (north) to Marysville. The Cinnabar Mine, just a mile away toward the crest of the Salmon Mountains, is a great place to explore if you have time. This route continues north through Marysville (not much to see) and White Rock City (lots of artifacts and nice views). The White Rock City site is perched high on the ridgeline, a more aesthetically pleasing location than Old Denny's cramped forest quarters, and water is available from nearby Sherwood Creek. If you want to explore another old mine site, look for an unmarked trail (no longer on current Forest Service maps) heading west just after you pass Marysville. The path leads a mile to the Hunter Mine. There are enough relics and mines in the immediate vicinity to keep history buffs busy for a couple days. Use caution around old mine sites, which may be unstable and dangerous.

Old Denny historic town site along New River Loop.

To continue the loop, head north and west from White Rock City on what is now the Battle Creek Trail (8E19). The trail crosses Sherwood Creek and descends on moderate switchbacks to cross Battle Creek, less than 2 miles from White Rock City. Partway down, an indistinct and overgrown path veers right (north) from a sharp bend in the wide track and cuts across the hillside to reach the Battle Creek crossing. The section of trail between here and Eagle Creek, just over the ridge to the southwest, is likely to be overgrown and sometimes difficult to follow.

After the creek crossing, climb a rocky slope 0.5 mile to reach the crest of the ridge between Battle and Eagle Creeks. Arrive at a poorly marked junction on the forested crest. To the right (north), Battle Creek Trail leads north along the ridge to the spine of the Salmon Mountains. To the left (south), the Eagle Creek Trail (8E11) heads downhill to the southwest and an eventual meeting with Eagle Creek. A broken sign indicates that Slide Creek lies in that direction. The Eagle Creek Trail plunges straight over the side of the ridge, then immediately turns south to begin a sloping descent into the drainage. The trail steepens on a rocky, open hillside before finally leveling off in the wild, forested terrain at the bottom of the canyon. The path may be indistinct here (look for cairns), but the drainage naturally funnels you down to Eagle Creek (stay right, or west, and you'll run into it). The trail crosses to the west side of Eagle Creek just upstream from the confluence with Battle Creek, less than 2 miles from the ridgetop trail junction. From here the path is once again easy to follow.

The next 3.3 miles is another up-and-down affair as the creekside trail parallels the course of Eagle Creek. Plenty of water, inviting swimming holes, and a return to oak and maple woodland highlight the delightful little stream. The path crosses Eagle Creek two more times on the way down the drainage. Look for an ancient wooden ladder in a flat near one of the crossings. Arrive at the Slide Creek trail junction, 18.2 miles from the beginning, and retrace your steps to the trailhead.

Options: From Old Denny, follow signs to Mary Blaine Meadows–Cinnabar Mine to reach the Salmon Summit Trail (12W02), which runs along the spine of the Salmon Mountains, and can be used to make a longer loop connecting with the Battle Creek Trail. Likewise, a 40-plus mile loop can be created by linking the Salmon Summit Trail with the Virgin Creek Trail. Yet another loop can be made by heading east on the Salmon Summit Trail and linking the Mullane Corral, Pony Creek, and Emigrant Creek–Milk Camp Trails. The possibilities are endless in this corner of Alps. Just study the map, and rest assured that no matter where you go, you're not likely to have company.

9 East Fork New River Loop

Highlights:	A rugged hike through deep canyons in the remote "Green Trinities"; solitude.
Type of hike:	Backpack; loop.
Total distance:	19.8 miles.
Difficulty:	Moderate.
Elevation gain:	3,900 feet.
Maps:	USGS Cecil Lake and Dees Peak quad; USDAFS Trinity Alps Wilderness map.

Finding the trailhead: From Hawkins Bar (on California Highway 299, 10 miles east of Willow Creek) drive north on Denny Road (County Road 402). Continue for 20 miles, past a Forest Service campground and the settlement of Denny (population 20). It's slow going on the twisting, winding road. Four miles past Denny, cross New River and proceed on unpaved Forest Road 7N01 (stay left at a signed fork). The trailhead is at the end of the road, 7.5 miles from the Denny campground.

Parking and trailhead facilities: Ample parking, a horse corral, and an outhouse. Nearest developed campground is at Denny.

Key points:

0.0	Trailhead.
0.4	Footbridge across East Fork New River.
2.5	Pony Creek Trail junction.
3.2	Semore Gulch Trail junction.
7.7	Mullane Corral Trail junction.
10.2	Pony Creek Trail junction.
13.2	Pony Creek.
15.0	Lake City.
15.1	Milk Camp Trail junction.
17.3	East Fork Trail junction.
19.8	Trailhead.

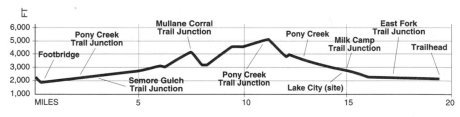

Profile data provided by TOPO! ©1999 Wildflower Productions (www.topo.com)

The hike: The East Fork New River is a smaller version of the New River drainage: a deep and shady canyon, dotted with oak and maple and madrone at the lower elevations, that leads up to a rugged, untraveled pine- and fir-forested wilderness at the higher end. It's a fine sampling of the "Green

East Fork New River Loop

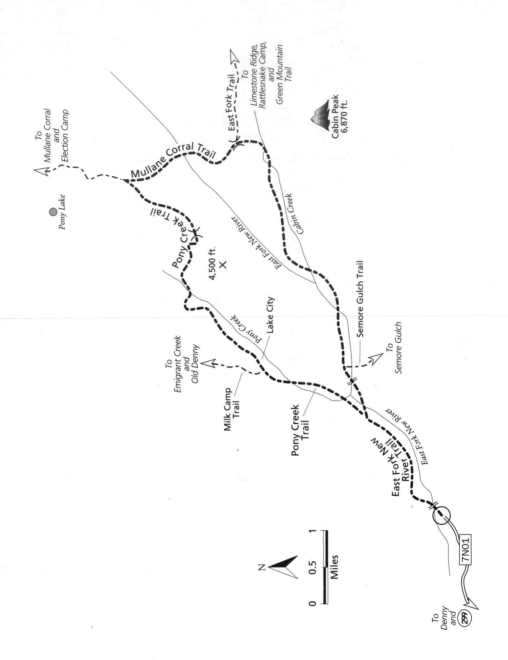

Trinities," the western part of the Alps known for thick-forested mountains, wild river canyons, and solitude. As at New River, you come across a few old mining relics along the East Fork (though not nearly as many). There are numerous connections to a maze of little-used trails that make it easy to disappear for a couple of weeks if that's your desire. You won't find the spectacular lakes and peaks of the eastern Trinity Alps here. What you do find is wilderness with a capital W, where you're more likely to come across a bear than another backpacker. Most two-legged guests are hunters who come here in the fall, and there are still active mining claims in the drainage that draw modern-day prospectors.

In the 1970s and early 1980s, the area became a popular place to grow illegal marijuana crops. Marijuana cultivation has largely been eradicated since then, but visitors should report any suspicious activity to the local law enforcement or Forest Service personnel. Today the most common visitors are hikers who appreciate truly wild terrain. The trails are in good condition most of the way, but route-finding skills may be required in a few places where the path is not obvious. Much of the hike is below 4,000 feet. The low elevation means there are three things you should be aware of: hot weather in midsummer, poison oak, and rattlesnakes. The first can be avoided by planning an early- or late-season trip, the second and third are best avoided by knowing what they look like and staying alert. Despite the lack of lakes, water is plentiful along the route. Creeks and streams are sparkling clear, with refreshing swimming holes and year-round flows.

From the trailhead, the East Fork Trail (12W08) descends to a solid wood-and-steel bridge, where you cross the East Fork New River and switchback up the canyon wall before heading northeast along the river. The gentle ascent meanders along the north bank for 2 miles, winding under shady stands of deciduous trees and alternating between meandering right beside the water and climbing the canyon wall above it. Swimming holes appear regularly along the course of the hike and you're never far from water (though be sure to purify everything you drink). In the early summer, the first section of this hike can be like walking through a green leafy tunnel, while in the fall you walk on a carpet of red and gold. Here and in numerous other places along this hike you see mine tailings and other remnants of mining activity.

At 2.5 miles from the trailhead, arrive at a trail junction on a level bench near the confluence of East Fork New River and Pony Creek (the sign may be on the ground). The Pony Creek Trail (12W07) veers left (north) and the East Fork Trail continues straight (east) along the canyon bottom. It's 2.3 miles up Pony Creek to Lake City if that's where you're headed. To do this route in the recommended direction, stay right and follow the East Fork Trail. You return to this point via the Pony Creek Trail and Lake City (it's a city in name only; there's not much there).

Just after the junction, cross the East Fork on a wood-and-steel bridge, then continue up the drainage on the south bank. Ignore the unmarked paths that meander along the river bank; they're left over from old mining activity. In 0.5 mile pass the signed junction with the Semore Gulch Trail (8E08, to the right). Stay left and descend to the East Fork, where for the

East Fork New River bridge, beginning of East Fork New River Loop.

first time you need to cross it without benefit of a bridge. The crossing should pose no problem at normal water levels, but beware when runoff is high in the early season.

Back on the north bank, climb an open, brushy slope and continue upstream. The canyon becomes more rocky and narrow through here, with a deep swimming hole tucked into a bend in the river. The trail climbs moderately through the forested canyon, crossing the East Fork twice more in quick succession near the confluence with the South Fork of East Fork New River, then crossing it one last time just below the confluence with Cabin Creek. The trail leaves the East Fork and follows Cabin Creek for about a mile. Just before starting the climb out of the Cabin Creek drainage, cross and re-cross the creek, then head uphill to the north.

On the short but steep ascent—the first real climb of the hike—you break out of the forest and pass through a rocky, open clearing with the first good view of your surroundings. To the south is the imposing hulk of 6,870-foot Cabin Peak. Once on top of Blue Ridge, 7.7 miles from the trailhead, you command an unobstructed vista of the East Fork drainage, as well as the sea of forested ridgelines that make up the Green Trinities.

On the crest of Blue Ridge is the Mullane Corral Trail junction (12W04). The East Fork Trail goes right (east) here, running along the ridgetop to Green Mountain Trail (12W09) on the crest of Limestone Ridge (the route is also known as the New River Divide Trail, because this ridge separates the New River drainage from that of the North Fork Trinity River). Rattlesnake Lake is 2 miles away from the junction on Limestone Ridge. The "lake" is really not much more than a mud puddle, so only hang a right here for two reasons: 1) you want to camp at Rattlesnake Camp (where a spring offers the only water in the vicinity) and watch the sunset over the New River drainage; or 2) you want to extend this hike by following the Green Mountain Trail north to the Salmon Summit Trail, then picking up the Mullane Corral Trail for the return (adds about 12 miles). You also may want to allow time to scramble up the easy summit of nearby Cabin Peak (with a view so good it used to host a fire lookout).

Staying left (north) at the junction, follow the Mullane Corral Trail down the north side of Blue Ridge, which the trail descends as abruptly as it climbed the south side. The trail up and over the ridge is not always obvious, but the route is generally marked with rock ducks and blazes. Keep your map handy and you shouldn't have any problem.

A 1,200-foot descent brings you quickly to the East Fork again, where you cross the stream and climb the ridge between East Fork and Pony Creek. After 2 miles of moderate climbing with plenty of great views, arrive at the signed junction with the Pony Creek Trail. This junction affords another opportunity for side trips to Pony Lake (a little pond, difficult to reach because there's no trail) or the historic sites of Mullane Corral and Election Camp.

Election Camp, just a couple of miles north of the junction, has an interesting story behind it. When miners fled nearby Lake City after a band of Native Americans burned the town to the ground, they had nowhere to vote in the upcoming 1864 presidential election. According to local lore, miners wanted to cast their votes for President Lincoln, so they arranged to have the election in the forest at a major trail junction. A hollow cedar tree was used for a ballot box, and upwards of 300 miners participated in the election.

To complete the East Fork loop, turn left (southwest) on Pony Creek Trail and contour through mixed forest dominated by mature fir and incense-cedar. The trail follows a mostly level contour around the point of the ridge, serving up more great views along the open, rocky crest, before finally plunging over the side and dropping down to Pony Creek. The path is easy to follow as you return to the land of oaks and maples.

At Pony Creek, hop across the water and follow the trail downhill along the stream. An easy 1.8-mile descent leads downstream, past more swimming holes and mining relics (plus a cabin of more recent vintage used by owners of a current claim). Lake City, a mining settlement founded in the 1850s, is in a clearing high above Pony Creek, just before the Milk Camp Trail junction. There's not much left here, but you can still see an old sign on a tree that identifies the site. As many as 1,500 miners lived here in the early 1860s. The town was never rebuilt after its destruction in 1863.

On the west side of the clearing, the Milk Camp Trail (8E16) turns north and heads uphill (eventually connecting with Slide Creek in the New River drainage). Go left (south) at the signed junction to stay on the Pony Creek Trail. It's an easy 2.2 miles downhill (with one climb over a spur ridge), crossing the creek two times, to the junction with the East Fork Trail. Retrace the first 2.5 miles back to the trailhead.

Options: Numerous connecting trails along this route offer extended trips into the rugged drainages of the Green Trinities. For a scenic loop that runs along the spine of Limestone Ridge, follow Green Mountain Trail to Salmon Summit Trail, then return via Mullane Corral Trail.

Hikes From California Highway 3

10 Rush Creek Lakes (Kinney Camp) Trail

See Map on Page 55

> **Highlights:** A tough ridgeline hike to scenic Rush Creek Lakes.
> **Type of hike:** Backpack; out-and-back.
> **Total distance:** 14.4 miles.
> **Difficulty:** Strenuous.
> **Elevation gain:** 3,500 feet.
> **Maps:** USGS Rush Creek Lakes quad; USDAFS Trinity Alps Wilderness map.

Finding the trailhead: From Weaverville drive 10 miles north on California Highway 3 to the signed turn for the Rush Creek Lakes Trail. Turn left (west) on Forest Road 34N74 and proceed 2 miles to the trailhead.

Parking and trailhead facilities: Limited parking for up to six cars. The closest developed campground is Rush Creek, just 2.5 miles south on CA 3.

Key points:
- 0.0 Trailhead.
- 6.5 Lowermost Rush Creek Lake.
- 7.2 Uppermost Rush Creek Lake.

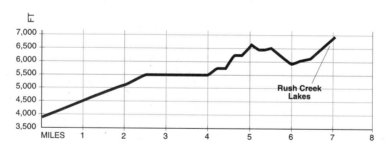

Profile data provided by TOPO! ©1999 Wildflower Productions (www.topo.com)

The hike: This is the alternative route to Rush Creek Lakes. The recommended route (described in Hike 7) is 3 miles shorter, but requires a steep off-trail scramble that some hikers may prefer to avoid. If you want to visit this beautiful chain of lakes (see Hike 7 for description) but would like to hike on a trail the whole way, use the Rush Creek Lakes Trail (10W10, sometimes called the Kinney Camp Trail). The 7.2-mile route (one way) has its own drawbacks, but falling rocks is not one of them.

The Rush Creek Lakes Trail has a poor reputation because it follows a ridgeline instead of a drainage bottom. It's hot in the summer, waterless, shadeless, and generally held in low regard by rangers and hikers alike (though there are some good views). There is also abundant poison oak along the first 2 miles of the trail. On the plus side, the trail deposits you safely in the Rush Creek Lakes basin without the elevatorlike descent of the off-trail route. And you'll probably have the path all to yourself. Just carry plenty of water.

From the trailhead, the path winds uphill through mixed forest that at least provides some welcome shade. Ascending higher, the trail heads northwest, climbing the spine of a ridge and eventually bending around to the west. It's a straightforward ascent most of the way, though because of low use it's not high on the Forest Service's list of maintenance priorities (downed trees could sit for awhile). The trail dips down several hundred feet and climbs back up again just before arriving at the basin. It's a very demoralizing end to an already tough hike. Arrive at the first of the Rush Creek Lakes at 6.5 miles. If you still have the energy, make your way another 0.7 mile to the uppermost lake in the chain, where you'll find the best swimming and coldest water. The maintained trail ends at the first lake, but the terrain beyond the lake is not difficult to negotiate.

Options: Monument Peak is within reach, but you'll have to ascend the steep gully used in the off-trail route (see Hike 7).

11 Stuart Fork

Highlights:	Together with Canyon Creek and Caribou Lakes, Stuart Fork forms the Holy Trinity of the Trinity Alps. Emerald and Sapphire Lakes, at the head of the canyon, are the crown jewels of the wilderness.
Type of hike:	Backpack (3–5 nights); out-and-back.
Total distance:	29 miles.
Difficulty:	Moderate (last optional off-trail mile to Mirror Lake is strenuous).
Elevation gain:	3,300 feet.
Maps:	USGS Siligo Peak, Mt. Hilton, Caribou Lake, and Rush Creek Lakes quads; USDAFS Trinity Alps Wilderness map.

Finding the trailhead: From Weaverville, drive 13 miles north on California Highway 3 to Trinity Alps Road (Forest Road 35N33Y). Turn left (west) just beyond a highway bridge and proceed 3.5 miles to the trailhead (the last mile is unpaved, but easily passable to passenger cars). The road passes through Trinity Alps Resort, a private collection of cabins on the banks of Stuart Fork. Last-minute supplies are available at the general store. The road dead-ends at the trailhead, 100 yards after passing Bridge Camp Campground.

Stuart Fork

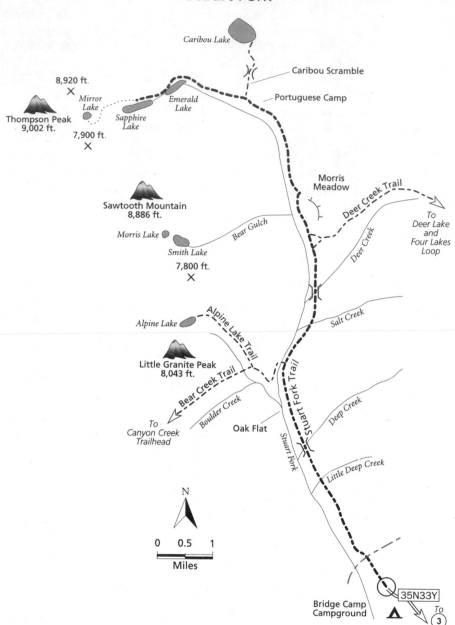

Caribou Lake

Caribou Scramble

Portuguese Camp

8,920 ft.
X
Mirror
Lake
Emerald
Lake
Sapphire
Lake

Thompson Peak
9,002 ft.

7,900 ft.
X

Morris
Meadow

Deer Creek Trail

Sawtooth Mountain
8,886 ft.

Bear Gulch

Deer Creek

To
Deer Lake
and
Four Lakes
Loop

Morris Lake

Smith Lake

7,800 ft.
X

Salt Creek

Alpine Lake

Alpine Lake Trail

Little Granite Peak
8,043 ft.

Stuart Fork Trail

Bear Creek Trail

Boulder Creek

Oak Flat

Deep Creek

To
Canyon Creek
Trailhead

Stuart Fork

Little Deep Creek

N

0   0.5   1
Miles

Bridge Camp
Campground

35N33Y

To
3

Parking and trailhead facilities: Parking only; camping, toilets, and potable water available at adjacent Bridge Camp Campground.

Key points:

0.0	Trailhead.
4.1	Deep Creek.
4.5	Oak Flat.
5.0	Bear Creek Trail.
8.0	Deer Creek Trail.
8.8	Morris Meadow.
10.0	Bear Gulch.
11.9	Portuguese Camp.
12.1	Caribou Scramble.
14.0	Emerald Lake.
14.5	Sapphire Lake.

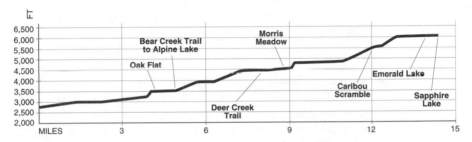

Profile data provided by TOPO! ©1999 Wildflower Productions (www.topo.com)

The hike: Stuart Fork Trail is like a highway into the heart of the Trinity Alps. Not so much because it's as crowded as a freeway during rush hour (though it can be), but because it leads so swiftly and smoothly into the inner sanctum of the Trinity Alps Wilderness. The trail seems to whisk you right up the drainage, through oaks and maples, into mixed conifers, past peaceful meadows, and finally to the treeless granite splendor of the Stuart Fork headwaters, tucked into a deep, glacier-carved slice in the wild terrain between Thompson Peak, Sawtooth Mountain, and Sawtooth Ridge. All the while you follow the spectacular course of Stuart Fork, one of the largest rivers in the Alps proper.

Expect plenty of company on summer weekends (and during fall hunting season; Stuart Fork is a popular basecamp among deer hunters). But don't let the crowds scare you. Like Canyon Creek and Caribou Lakes, there's a good reason people flock here. And with plenty of secluded, dispersed campsites between Morris Meadow and Portuguese Camp, the drainage can absorb a lot of visitors. (Don't even try camping at Emerald or Sapphire Lakes, which have only poor, fragile sites and very little room.) From a basecamp in Morris Meadow, you can make any number of day hikes into the surrounding wilderness.

The path starts out wide and level, following an old dirt road to the wilderness boundary at Cherry Flat. This first mile crosses private property (well marked, with white "trail" signs indicating the way at all junctions). The road ends after the wilderness boundary and you start climbing moderately on well-trodden trail, paralleling Stuart Fork as you head northwest. The river remains below as you travel up the east bank, but water is readily available in tributaries like Salt Creek, Little Deep Creek, Deep Creek, and so on, all the way up. Purify all water.

After ascending a moderate grade, return to river level and enjoy easy walking on a path shaded by fir, incense-cedar, maples, dogwoods, and both sugar and ponderosa pines. If you got a late start (coming or going), there are many fine riverside campsites on the east bank of Stuart Fork, between here and Oak Flat, an oak- and conifer-forested bench 4.5 miles from the trailhead. Just before Oak Flat, the trail dips down to cross Deep Creek on a footbridge. An inviting swimming hole awaits at the base of waterfall here, but swim at your own risk: the current is swift and the rocks downstream treacherous. Pause for a moment on the bridge and gaze up Deep Creek. If you tire of the human company in Stuart Fork and want to be truly alone for awhile, bushwhack your way up Deep Creek and you won't see another soul until you arrive at Siligo Meadows, several steep and trailless miles away. Good luck.

Arrive at the signed junction for Alpine Lake 5 miles from the trailhead. A left turn here leads to the beginning of the Bear Creek Trail, which connects the Stuart Fork drainage to the Canyon Creek Trailhead, and Alpine Lake via the Alpine Lake Trail (Hike 13). Alpine Lake is the most popular jumping off point for the off-trail route to Smith and Morris Lakes (Hike 14). The Bear Creek Trail is across the river, and fording Stuart Fork at high water should not be taken lightly. Use good judgment at all creek crossings.

To continue up Stuart Fork, stay right (north) at the junction. Walking up a gentle grade, look for signs of Buckeye Ditch and La Grange Ditch, which carried water from this drainage to mining operations miles away. The trail follows the historic ditch in some places, and you can see the last vestiges of the once lengthy flume. The Buckeye Ditch, which carried water to a mining operation some 40 miles away, was reputed to be one of the longest such flumes ever constructed. During the miners' heyday, a wagon road led all the way up Stuart Fork.

The path proceeds moderately for the next several miles, climbing a few switchbacks in and out of tributaries when necessary, but generally maintaining the gentle grade Stuart Fork is known for. Salt Creek is the next major tributary. Look for a few pieces of weathered, long-abandoned lumber on the forested hillside after Salt Creek. Next comes Deer Creek, just over 7 miles from the trailhead. Cross Deer Creek on a solid steel bridge (the Forest Service must have decided to build something dependable after the previous bridge washed away). There's also a refreshing swimming hole here if it's a hot day. Return to the ledge above Stuart Fork after climbing out of the Deer Creek drainage and bend farther east, out of sight of the river.

Arrive at the Deer Creek Trail junction 8 miles from the trailhead. Signed 9W17A, this trail climbs east up the Deer Creek drainage to a beautiful, secluded canyon with a good chance for solitude (Hike 12). You can also access the northern spur of the Deer Creek Trail (9W17) at another junction in Morris Meadow, a short distance ahead.

Soon after the Deer Creek junction, you start seeing the beginnings of Morris Meadow; then, just after the northern spur of the Deer Creek Trail, you enter the lower end of Morris Meadow proper (about 9 miles from the trailhead). The idyllic meadow fans out in green splendor from here, serving up one of the best late-summer wildflower displays in the Alps. Yarrow, Indian paintbrush, lupine, and lush grasses grow in profusion throughout the wide valley. Campsites are liberally sprinkled in the forested fringes in each direction. A little island of pine and cedar sits at the head of the meadow where you come in, and the historic Morris Meadow horse camp lies on the western edge of the clearing. Water may be available in meadow streams, or you may have to trek over to Stuart Fork, which is hidden in dense trees on the west side of the valley.

Be wary of rattlesnakes in the area, which are notoriously plentiful here (I seem to see one on every trip). It's likely that too many campers dropping crumbs have increased the local rodent population, which in turn has drawn the snakes. Ditto the local bears, which come to munch on unprotected food everywhere from Bridge Camp at the trailhead to Sapphire Lake. On one memorable afternoon trail run along Stuart Fork, I nearly ran headlong into a bear who himself (or herself) was lumbering along at a good clip. Our paths were about to intersect when we saw each other, put on the brakes, and narrowly avoided disaster. I don't know who was more surprised. Don't feed the bears—and don't run into them.

Dedicated bushwhackers who want to use Bear Gulch to reach Smith Lake should start their trek here (Hike 14). A number of use trails meander north through Morris Meadow to the upper end, where the main trail picks up again near an impressive double-trunked ponderosa pine. Enter the forest proper and pass another pile of historic lumber on the left, as well as more campsites and good access to the river. The trail winds up the drainage, passing through shady forest, brushy slopes, and lush glens of ferns and wildflowers.

As the canyon starts bending from north to west, bigger and bigger views of the granite peaks and ridges hanging over the headwaters start to open up. Alder, maple, and wildflowers of several persuasions turn some parts of the trail into a green jungle midsummer. Portuguese Camp, a historic Stuart Fork camp that offers the last good site to throw down your pack before the lakes, is located just before the junction with the Caribou Scramble.

At the signed junction with the Caribou Scramble, at a rocky intersection 12.1 miles from the trailhead, stop and contemplate the route up to Sawtooth Ridge. You better have a good idea of what lies above before you set out for the saddle between Stuart Fork and Caribou Lake. Some 100 switchbacks and 2,500 feet of elevation gain are packed into the shadeless, waterless route above. The view from up there is spectacular, but start early and carry plenty of water if you decide to do it.

After the Caribou junction, the Stuart Fork Trail continues to bend west and starts climbing more steeply toward the head of the canyon, now plainly visible through breaks in the trees. The last mile is steep and rocky and offers little shade on a sunny day. A crystal clear spring flows across the trail and helps take the bite out of the climb. On the way up this last haul, you can glimpse to your left (south) the deep gorge cut in the rocky canyon by the Stuart Fork headwaters emerging from the lip of Emerald Lake. Save time to explore the waterfalls and pools down there before leaving. The trail gains the top of Emerald's granite dike at the lake's northeast corner, passing through a sparse stand of firs and an overused campsite before winding over the last few boulders and arriving at water's edge (14 miles from the trailhead).

Twenty-one-acre Emerald Lake lives up to the promise of its name: cold, clear water, granite piled on granite, and the mass of Sawtooth Mountain's northern shoulder towering overhead. It's hard to believe the lake sits at a mere 5,500 feet. Remnants of the dam built by miners are still visible along Emerald's eastern shore.

To reach Sapphire Lake, make your way around Emerald's north shore on a rough trail marked by cairns. After passing through a stand of trees above the lake's northeast corner, cross the boulder piles littering the north shore, where a trail has been literally blasted into the rock. The granite-lined path switchbacks steeply up the north side of Sapphire's outlet (the lake is 600 feet higher than Emerald). On the way, look for rusty remains of the heavy equipment laboriously dragged in here a century ago, as well as still-solid remnants of the dam at Sapphire's eastern edge.

The 43-acre lake is sunk into a narrow, east-west trough in the canyon, with stunning views at both ends and jumbled piles of blindingly white granite around the shoreline. Thompson Peak looms over the western edge of the cirque, where Mirror Lake lies concealed in a hidden basin, and

Sapphire Lake, Stuart Fork Trail.

Sawtooth Ridge dominates the eastern vista, where Stuart Fork drainage falls away precipitously. The visible evidence left behind by the glacier that carved out this basin is impressive enough, but just as astounding is what you can't see—Sapphire's blue water is 200 feet deep, which makes it the deepest lake in the Alps.

Off-trail to Mirror Lake: No maintained trail leads to little Mirror Lake, in a secluded cirque at the upper end of the Stuart Fork canyon. Mirror Lake sits atop a steep formation of vertical cliffs and narrow gullies. The difficult, off-trail approach keeps at bay most of the visitors who come as far as Emerald–Sapphire Lakes. It's a mile farther and 500 feet higher than Sapphire Lake.

Start the route to Mirror by traversing the north shore of Sapphire. Walk first along the water's edge, then climb up to a shelf above the lake and continue west. A fairly well-established use trail leads to the west end of the lake, then fades away in the brush. There are two ways to go from here. Aim for the waterfall on the north side of the basin if you prefer the short and steep route. Pass just beneath the falls and continue around to the southwest, where you can scramble up the ledges to a chimney that allows passage (barely) to the top. This is by no means the best way, just the shortest.

The safer and slightly longer route simply follows the talus field up the south side of the basin to the lake. At the west end of Sapphire, stay low and pick your way across the drainage to the talus-filled gully, then boulder-hop the rest of the way up to Mirror's lonely cirque.

Mirror Lake is aptly named. Gaze at its smooth waters on a calm, still evening and you will find one of the most perfect reflections in the Alps. Thompson Peak soars overhead. Sawtooth Mountain looms to the southeast. And back the way you came, beyond Sapphire and Emerald lakes, is Sawtooth Ridge and Caribou Mountain. Mirror Lake manages to gather it all in. Mirror has a few stunted foxtail pines and hemlocks, but it's mostly bare rock and water, with several granite islands breaking the surface of the clear, shallow lake.

Options: Stuart Fork drains the heart of the Alps, and has arteries connecting with a number of the area's other drainages. Alpine Lake (Hike 13), Caribou Lakes (Hike 34), and Deer Creek (Hike 12) are all easily reached via trails. A long loop back to the Stuart Fork trailhead can be made by linking the Deer Creek, Stonewall Pass, and Weber Flat Trails (requires several miles of walking on roads at the end). Experienced hikers will find off-trail routes to Canyon Creek Lakes (Hike 4), Smith Lake (Hike 14), and Grizzly Lake (Hike 1).

12 Deer Creek Trail

Highlights:	A connecting trail between Stuart Fork and the Four Lakes Loop.
Type of hike:	Backcountry connecting trail.
Total distance:	5.5 miles.
Difficulty:	Moderate.
Elevation gain:	1,800 feet.
Maps:	USGS Siligo Peak quad; USDAFS Trinity Alps Wilderness map.

Finding the trailhead: The Deer Creek Trail runs between mile 8.0 on the Stuart Fork Trail and the Four Lakes Loop at the head of Deer Creek drainage. Start at either end. Description here is from Morris Meadow.

Parking and trailhead facilities: None.

Key points:

0.0   Morris Meadow–Stuart Fork Trail.

3.0   Willow Creek Trail junction.

4.5   Deer Creek Camp.

4.5   Black Basin Trail junction.

5.5   Granite Lake Trail–Four Lakes Loop Trail junction.

Profile data provided by TOPO!
©1999 Wildflower Productions(www.topo.com)

The hike: The Deer Creek Trail is a useful connecting trail that links Stuart Fork to the Four Lakes Loop. It can also be used to create a number of loops that start and end at Swift Creek and Big Flat Trailheads. This description starts in Morris Meadow on the Stuart Fork Trail.

Approaching from the south, you find the first of two trail junctions for the Deer Creek Trail (9W17) 8 miles from the Stuart Fork Trailhead. The next junction is just before the lower end of Morris Meadow. Turn right (east) here and begin a steep climb over the ridge that separates the Stuart Fork and Deer Creek drainages. A series of switchbacks leads up the slope, then you crest the ridgeline and start a much more moderate ascent along the course of Deer Creek. Forest cover is a shady mixture of mature ponderosa and sugar pine, Douglas-fir, and incense-cedar.

Three miles from Morris Meadow, arrive at Willow Creek and the junction with the Tri-Forest Trail (Hike 33). This little-used path leads up to a pass at the base of Tri-Forest Peak, then on to Big Flat Trailhead 8 miles away. The pass affords easy access to spectacular views along Sawtooth Ridge, and makes a good day hike if you basecamp along Deer Creek.

Continuing along the Deer Creek Trail, a very pleasant 1.5 miles of streamside hiking brings you to Deer Creek Camp. Look for beautiful gardens of leopard lilies and other wildflowers that grow in little riots of color along

Deer Creek Trail

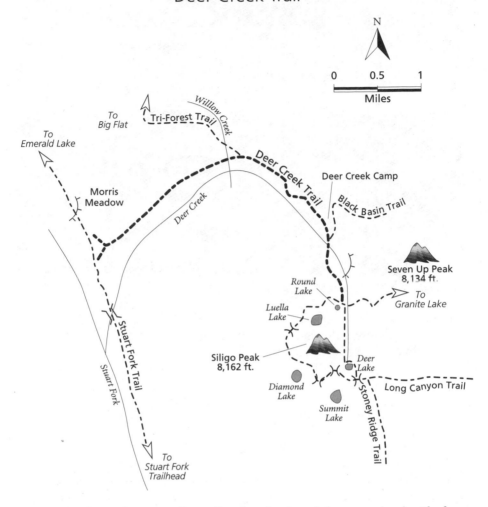

the creek. The path crosses Deer Creek twice in quick succession just before arriving at historic Deer Creek Camp, a series of old hunting and cow camps spread out along the north bank of the creek. The cows are long gone, but the area is still a popular basecamp for hunters and horsepackers.

The junction with the Black Basin Trail (9W12) is located on a rocky flat near the beginning of an open meadow at the southeastern end of Deer Creek Camp. The little-used Black Basin Trail leads uphill and connects with two paths that cross the divide between Deer Creek and Swift Creek drainages (see Hike 20). Anyone looking for solitude will find it up there on the lonely divide.

The Deer Creek Trail continues southeast from the junction, skirting the edge of the first of a series of beautiful meadows leading up to the head of the canyon. The open valley affords great views of Seven Up and Siligo peaks at the head of the drainage. A few hundred yards from the junction

View of the Deer Creek drainage from the Tri-forest Trail.

the trail crosses the creek for the last time and ascends a moderately rising slope past more wildflowers and great views up and down the valley.

The final mile brings you to a spectacular meadow sprawling across the entire breadth of the valley. Little Round Lake (not named on some maps) sits in the southwest corner of the meadow. From here you have three trail junctions from which to choose. Two junctions are for the Four Lakes Loop (Hike 18), which continues up to Deer Lake or Luella Lake and circles Siligo Peak. The first fork, 0.3 mile before arriving at the upper meadow, is an unmarked junction with a spur trail that forks right (southwest). This faint path is an old trail that connects with the Four Lakes Loop on the west side of the valley, on the way to Luella Lake. The second junction with the Four Lakes Loop is at the head of valley, where the steep ascent to Deer Lake starts. Just before the second meeting with the Four Lakes Loop you arrive at the Granite Lake Trail (Hike 21), which heads east over Seven Up Pass to Granite Lake and eventually Swift Creek.

Options: Use Deer Creek Trail to connect with the Four Lakes Loop and climb Siligo Peak (Hike 18). In the other direction, follow Deer Creek to Morris Meadow in the Stuart Fork drainage (Hike 11). From there you can access Emerald and Sapphire Lakes.

13 Alpine Lake

Highlights: A scenic detour off the popular Stuart Fork Trail. Brave an early-season crossing of Stuart Fork and you'll have Alpine to yourself.
Type of hike: Backpack; out-and-back.
Total distance: 16.6 miles.
Difficulty: Moderate.
Elevation gain: 3,400 feet.
Maps: USGS Siligo Peak quad; USDAFS Trinity Alps Wilderness map.

Finding the trailhead: From Weaverville, drive 13 miles north on California Highway 3 to Trinity Alps Road (Forest Road 35N33Y). Turn left (west) just after a highway bridge and proceed 3.5 miles to the trailhead (the last mile is unpaved, but easily passable to passenger cars). The road passes through Trinity Alps Resort, a private collection of cabins on the banks of Stuart Fork. Last-minute supplies are available at the general store. The road dead-ends at the trailhead, 100 yards after passing Bridge Camp Campground.

Parking and trailhead facilities: Ample parking; camping, toilets, and potable water at the adjacent campground.

Key points:
0.0   Trailhead.
4.5   Oak Flat.
5.0   Bear Creek Trail.
5.7   Alpine Lake Trail.
8.3   Alpine Lake.

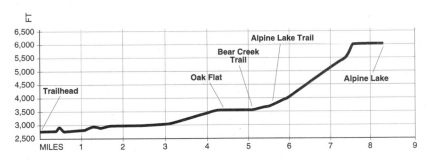

Profile data provided by TOPO! ©1999 Wildflower Productions (www.topo.com)

The hike: The trail to Alpine Lake has a split personality: first comes an easy, mostly level stroll along the shady banks of Stuart Fork, followed by a stiff climb up dry, brush-choked, rocky slopes. Fortunately the lake itself is not the least bit schizophrenic—just pure, tranquil mountain splendor. If you don't want to lug your pack up the final steep 3 miles, Alpine Lake

Alpine Lake

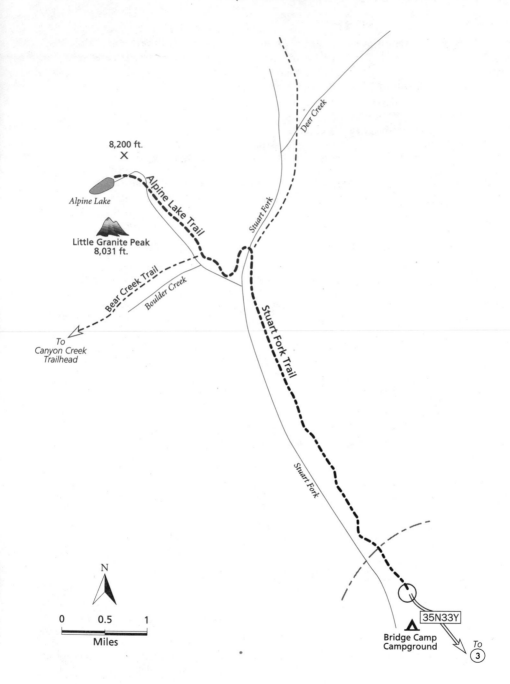

8,200 ft.
X

Alpine Lake

Little Granite Peak
8,031 ft.

Alpine Lake Trail

Deer Creek

Stuart Fork

Bear Creek Trail

Boulder Creek

To
Canyon Creek
Trailhead

Stuart Fork Trail

Stuart Fork

N

0   0.5   1
Miles

35N33Y

Bridge Camp
Campground

To
3

makes a great day hike from a number of streamside camps along Stuart Fork. (Besides, the few campsites at the lake are too close to the water and too close together.) Most of the traffic on the Stuart Fork Trail is heading for Emerald and Sapphire Lakes, so making a detour to Alpine is often a good way to leave the crowds behind.

The gentle half of the route's Jekyll and Hyde personality comes in the first 5 miles of nearly level, parklike walking on the Stuart Fork Trail. For a detailed description of this section, see Hike 11.

Once you reach the signed junction for Alpine Lake (5 miles from the trailhead), turn left and proceed downhill to a crossing of Stuart Fork. This ford is the crucial factor in reaching Alpine Lake in early summer (the current is typically too high and swift to cross before July). Use extreme caution crossing Stuart Fork if the river is high. If the water is too high but you are nonetheless determined to reach Alpine Lake, you can bypass the ford by starting at the Canyon Creek Trailhead and using the Bear Creek Trail to reach the Alpine Lake Trail. This route is only 2 miles longer than starting at the Stuart Fork trailhead, but it's much steeper (you have to cross the ridge between Canyon Creek and Stuart Fork drainages) and rarely maintained (expect to negotiate your way under, over, and around downed trees).

Once you're safely across Stuart Fork, the trail climbs away from the creek on an easy contour to the south, then turns northwest just before reaching Boulder Creek and ascends more steeply. Just under a mile from Stuart Fork, arrive at a fork in a small clearing next to a large snag. A couple of old signs indicate that Stuart Fork is back the way you came, Canyon Creek is straight (west) on the Bear Creek Trail, and Alpine Lake lies to the right (north).

Alpine Lake.

Turn right on the Alpine Lake Trail (the path is dubbed a "scramble" on the Forest Service wilderness map, though it's in much better condition than the term would lead you to expect). It's only 2.6 miles from here to Alpine Lake, but the hike may seem quite a bit longer on a hot, sunny afternoon. Now comes Mr. Hyde.

Climbing generally northwest through a mixed forest of oak and conifers, the trail follows the course of Alpine Lake's outlet creek to its source. The only problem is, the path stays well east of the creek, keeping the refreshing stream at arm's length for most of the way. You have one opportunity to fill water bottles when the trail nearly touches the creek in the first mile. Use it. (Like all other water sources in the wilderness, the water here should be purified.)

The final 1.5 miles climb steadily through manzanita and ceanothus. The rocky, brush-covered tread has a southern exposure, so you can expect the final push to be brutally hot on a sunny summer afternoon. A quarter-mile before reaching the lake, the trail crosses the outlet stream for the first time. The creek crossing is just upstream from a series of pretty cascades and tremendous views down the Stuart Fork drainage. Hikers looking for the off-trail route to Smith and Morris Lakes (see Hike 14) should turn right (north) at the rock cairns just before the creek crossing.

The last few hundred yards of the trail traverse a series of open, rocky benches and grass-fringed ponds. Just before reaching the lake, look for a rock cairn that marks the last crossing of the outlet creek (if you miss this last creek crossing you'll soon run into a wall of steep boulders and head-high brush). Once on the north side of the stream, follow an obvious path through a lush green meadow and arrive at the narrow, southeast end of the lake.

Alpine Lake sits in a narrow, steep-sided basin topped by a jumble of gray granite crags. Little Granite Peak (8,031 feet) is almost directly south of the lake. A sparse forest of stunted fir and weeping spruce grows on the southern side of the lake, while rocks, wildflowers, and shoreline meadows dominate the northern side. Except for a few spots near the outlet, the entire basin is too steep for camping. Rest assured, however, that the 14-acre lake is clear, cool, and perfect for swimming after trudging up the trail on a sunny day. Return the way you came.

Options: Experienced hikers can make their way off trail to Smith and Morris Lakes, as well as Sawtooth Mountain (see Hike 14).

14 Smith and Morris Lakes

Highlights: A tough off-trail hike that amply rewards the effort. Smith Lake is a gem.

Type of hike: Backpack; out-and-back or possible loop.

Total distance: 20.6 miles for Alpine Lake (recommended) route.

Difficulty: Strenuous.

Elevation gain: 5,100 feet.

Maps: USGS Siligo Peak quad; USDAFS Trinity Alps Wilderness map.

Finding the trailhead: From Weaverville, drive 13 miles north on California Highway 3 to Trinity Alps Road (Forest Road 35N33Y). Turn left (west) just beyond a highway bridge and proceed 3.5 miles to the trailhead (the last mile is unpaved). The road passes through Trinity Alps Resort, a private collection of cabins on the banks of Stuart Fork. Last-minute supplies are available at the general store. The road dead-ends at the trailhead, 100 yards after passing Bridge Camp Campground.

Parking and trailhead facilities: Ample parking; camping, toilets, and potable water at the adjacent campground.

Key points:

0.0	Trailhead.
4.5	Oak Flat.
5.0	Bear Creek Trail.
5.7	Alpine Lake Trail.
8.1	Off-trail route to Smith Lake.
10.3	Smith Lake.

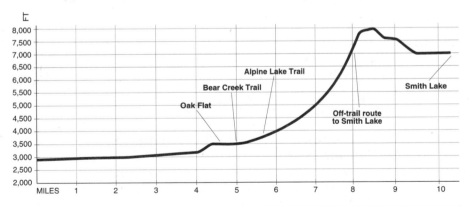

Profile data provided by TOPO! ©1999 Wildflower Productions (www.topo.com)

The hike: If there were a queen of the Trinity Alps, her throne would be somewhere in the vicinity of Smith Lake. Perched on a majestic bench below Sawtooth Mountain, in the granite heart of the Alps, the lake and its awesome cirque have natural wonders like a queen has jewels: a misty waterfall pours

Smith and Morris Lakes

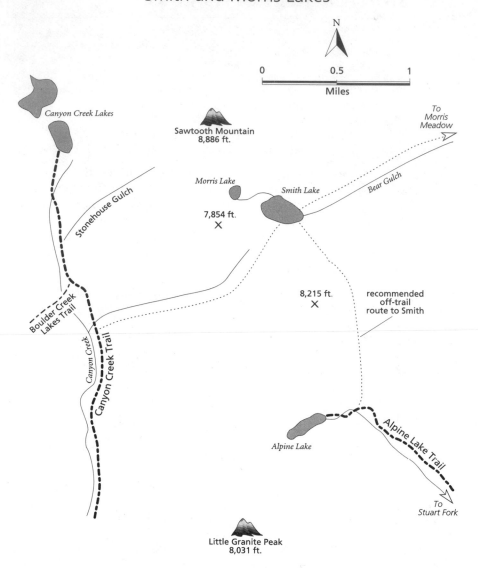

over a cliff at the inlet; the sun rises over the awesome drop of Stuart Fork; the jagged profile of Sawtooth towers overhead. Seat yourself on a slab of gray granite near the lake's outlet, and you'll feel like royalty indeed.

Of course, such alpine splendor doesn't come without effort. Dense brush and steep granite slopes surround Smith like a mountainous moat. No trail leads to the basin. Only hikers who are experienced with route-finding and comfortable with off-trail travel should attempt this hike. Though not technical, some of the hiking gets quite steep. Everyone's comfort level is different.

Alpine Lake route: This is by far the most popular way to reach Smith Lake. It's only 2.2 miles from the Alpine Lake Trail to Smith Lake, but most

Hiking along granite benches above Smith Lake.

hikers take several hours to complete the off-trail route. See Hike 13 for a description of the Alpine Lake Trail to this point. Leave the trail about a quarter mile before Alpine Lake (just before the trail crosses the outlet creek) and head north, up the drainage. Cairns lead the way. Thick brush here used to make this the most difficult part of the route, but the last time I was here a reasonably worn path had been cut through the bushes. Once through the brush, continue north up steep granite slabs, over the ridge, then make your way down and across an open cirque to the outlet of Smith Lake. This part is often snow-covered until August. Be prepared. With the brushy section of this route getting so much easier in recent years, the number of visitors at Smith Lake has increased dramatically. Expect to share.

Canyon Creek route: The approach hike to this route is shorter and easier than the Alpine Lake route, but the final 2 miles are grueling. For a description of the Canyon Creek Trail, see Hike 4. Leave the trail a half-mile before reaching the junction with the Boulder Creek Lakes Trail junction. Your route lies up the big drainage to the east. Good luck with the brush guarding the entrance. After the initial bushwhack (bring plenty of Band-Aids), it's a fairly straightforward scramble up the south side of the drainage and around the head of the canyon (the route never drops down to the gully at the bottom). As an alternative, gluttons for steep stuff can continue up Canyon Creek another mile to Stonehouse Gulch. This sheer gully leads to the ridge above Morris Lake, from where you descend into the basin (only for extremely experienced hikers).

Bear Gulch route: This route has the longest approach hike (12 miles), but in some ways it's the most elegant way to reach Smith: just hike up its outlet creek. From Morris Meadow in Stuart Fork (see Hike 11), battle your way through the brush to gain the granite slopes of Bear Gulch, then climb the north side of the creek. I've looked down on this route from above, and it looked slightly better than the Canyon Creek route. But looks can be deceiving. Others say it's just as bad—or worse.

Smith Lake: Whichever way you choose, allow plenty of time to enjoy this beautiful basin once you arrive. The steep-sided, 24-acre lake takes time to explore (just making your way around its shores requires some effort). On a hot day, try swimming to the base of the 50-foot waterfall cascading into the lake.

Above Smith Lake lies tiny Morris Lake, a little gem of a pond hanging on a bench that feeds Smith's inlet stream. Above Morris Lake the granite soon gives way to sky. The ridgeline above Morris leads to the steep, craggy slopes of 8,886-foot Sawtooth Mountain. Proceed at your own risk.

A few stunted firs and mountain hemlocks grow in the basin, but mostly it's a world of rock and water. In late summer, wildflowers thrive in colorful little minigardens where seeps and soil combine to create the right environment. One of my most cherished memories of the Alps is an evening I spent next to one of these little gardens. A friend and I sat on a slab of granite and watched a bald eagle hunt for trout as the evening light turned the gray rocks red and orange and the stars began twinkling above.

Options: Ambitious hikers can make a loop by combining two of the routes described above. I recommend starting with the Alpine Lake route, then exiting via one of the other two (the Bear Creek Trail will get you from the Canyon Creek Trailhead back to Stuart Fork, or you can drop a car shuttle).

15 Stoney Ridge Trail

Highlights:	A seldom-used trail (it's steep and dry) that leads to beautiful Siligo Meadows and the Four Lakes Loop; most direct route to Echo Lake.
Type of hike:	Backpack (2-4 nights); out-and-back.
Total distance:	17 miles.
Difficulty:	Strenuous.
Elevation gain:	4,000 feet.
Maps:	USGS Siligo Peak and Covington Mill quads; USDAFS Trinity Alps Wilderness map.

Finding the trailhead: From Weaverville, drive 15 miles north on California Highway 3 to the signed turnoff for the Stonewall Pass Trailhead. The dirt road is on the left (west), just past Trinity Alps Road and before Stoney Creek swim area. Proceed 6 miles up the road (Forest Road 35N72Y) to the trailhead. Stay right at 4.3 and 5.3 miles. The route is well marked. The road is closed from October 31 to May 1 each year.

Parking and trailhead facilities: Ample room for parking but no facilities. The closest developed campground is at Stoney Point on CA 3.

Key points:
- 0.0 Trailhead.
- 4.0 Granite Peak Trail junction.
- 4.2 Red Mountain Meadow.
- 6.0 Stonewall Pass.
- 6.7 Echo Lake.
- 7.1 Little Stonewall Pass.
- 8.0 Siligo Meadows.
- 8.5 Deer Creek Pass.

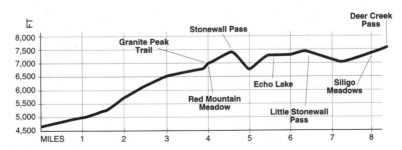

Profile data provided by TOPO! ©1999 Wildflower Productions (www.topo.com)

Stoney Ridge Trail

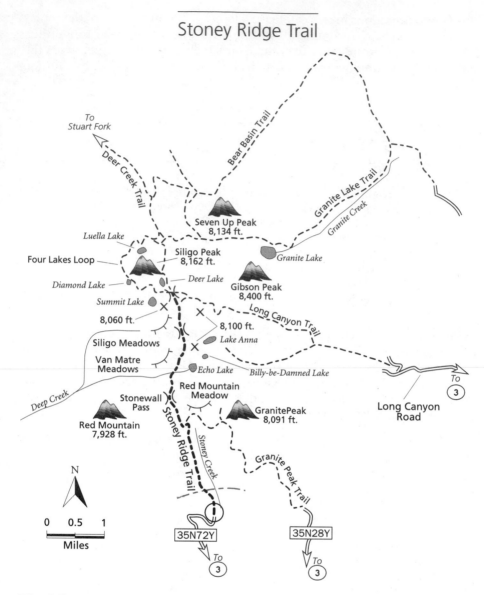

The hike: It's a long haul up the Stoney Ridge Trail, and one could make a strong argument for using a less daunting route to reach the same destination (Long Canyon is the alternate path). But it's precisely the unrelenting nature of this trail that makes it so appealing: the view from Stonewall Pass is all the more beautiful for every switchback you climb on the way up. At the end of the trail you find Echo Lake, one of the overlooked gems of the Trinity Alps, and ample reward for your effort.

Consider Stoney Ridge Trail the seldom-used backdoor route to the popular Four Lakes Loop (Hike 18). Long Canyon (Hike 17) is the front door, and wastes no time ushering you into magnificent alpine scenery. Stoney Ridge, however, makes you wait for the best stuff. If they were books, Long Canyon would be a fast-paced thriller and Stoney Ridge a more literary novel. Fortunately hikers, like readers, have varied tastes.

If you're the type who appreciates a good read, you'll like the way Stoney Ridge builds to a climax atop Stonewall Pass. The trail climbs a seemingly endless staircase of switchbacks (about 6 miles) through mixed forest, brushy slopes, and high meadow. The moderate switchbacks take the steepness out of the ascent, but expect a hot, tough hike on a midsummer day.

So why use the Stoney Ridge Trail? Solitude, first and foremost. The route gets much less traffic than its more flashy neighbor. And because Echo Lake and Van Matre Meadow are the first things you encounter at the end of the hike, as opposed to the last if you're coming from Long Canyon, fewer people visit the area. For peak baggers, there's also the added allure of three 8,000-foot summits within easy striking distance: Red Mountain (7,928 feet); Granite Peak (8,091 feet); and Middle Peak (8,095 feet).

The Stoney Ridge Trail (9W21) starts uphill and trends generally northwest up the flanks of Red Mountain. The mountain is named for the reddish peridotite rock of which it's composed. The mixed-conifer forest is similar to other areas of the Alps, but the red rock lends a remarkably different feel to Stoney Ridge.

Past logging has left a relatively young and open forest of fir, incense-cedar, and pine at the lower elevations. The trail is laid atop a soft cushion of duff. After a mile of gradual but steady ascent, the forest cover gets thicker and shadier, and the trail gets noticeably steeper. Look for a seasonal creek decorated with dogwood, incense-cedar, and fern near the wilderness boundary. The first dependable water source comes shortly after, at 2 miles, and should be purified. There isn't much water along the Stoney Ridge Trail, so fill up at one of these early streams if your bottle needs topping off.

A long contour east around the shoulder of the ridge reveals a fine view of Trinity Lake. Climbing steadily, the route gets sunnier and manzanita lines both sides of the trail. You soon get your first good view of Red Mountain, still high above. The junction with the Granite Peak Trail is at 4 miles. The junction is not well marked but you can see a fairly obvious path leading northeast away from the main trail. A right at the fork leads east across a gully (dry by late season) and up the side of Granite Peak. Stoney Ridge Trail continues to the left and northwest.

A quarter mile after the junction, the trail arrives at Red Mountain Meadow (elevation 6,900 feet). The fringes of the meadow offer the first place to camp on the route. Compared to the meadows on the other side of Stonewall Pass, Red Mountain Meadow can appear small, dry, and uninviting, but don't be deceived. The sunrise from here is spectacular.

From the meadow, the trail winds the rest of the way through open, rocky terrain to Stonewall Pass, elevation 7,400 feet. Allow time for a long break on the pass (your legs will probably need it anyway). The pass commands an incredible view directly into the heart of the Alps. Looking north, the vista includes Middle Peak, Gibson Peak, Siligo Peak, Sawtooth Mountain, and Little Granite Peak. At your feet lie the emerald green fields of Van Matre Meadows. Interspersed among the meadows are little subalpine ponds

Van Matre Meadows along the Stoney Ridge Trail.

that keep the grasses green all summer long. The ponds are filled with life, like the mountains' own tidepools, and great care should be taken in exploring this fragile environment.

Stonewall Pass does, indeed, have a stone wall running along it. The fence and a few remnants of barbed wire remain from the not too distant days when cattle were allowed to munch on the lush meadows. Fortunately, cows are no longer among the animals that drink from the alpine pools.

A steep descent on rocky tread leads down into the drainage below Echo Lake. The trail levels out after 0.5 mile and crosses a creek and then the outlet from Echo. These small streams, along with the tributary arising in Siligo Meadows, join to form Deep Creek, which drains the entire basin at your feet. Downhill from here lies one of the Alps' truly wild and half-forgotten corners. Deep Creek, with no formal trail and very little human traffic, remains off the map in all but the most literal way.

No maintained trail leads to Echo Lake, but if you're anxious to reach the lake you can pick your way 0.3 mile up the rocky, boulder-strewn outlet (which you cross before heading uphill again toward Little Stonewall Pass); or, for the more leisurely route, stay on the trail as it climbs up to Little Stonewall Pass on the way to Siligo Meadows and beyond. But don't go over the pass. Just before Little Stonewall, an obvious use trail heads southeast (right) across a level area that holds a snowmelt pond (that shrinks to a mudflat by late summer). Pick your way across the meadow and through the boulder field on the other side of the pond. Just over the rise lies Echo Lake.

Though Echo Lake is only a couple of miles from the Four Lakes Loop and Long Canyon, both of which host a stream of hikers all summer long, Echo doesn't get nearly as much attention as its neighbors. In this case, ignorance is not bliss.

The Forest Service's 1984 Trinity Alps Wilderness map (no longer in print) had a brief description of each lake in the Alps. The map pegs Echo at 2.5 acres and 7,250 feet, then notes simply: "Many daytime activities possible in the surrounding area. Sunsets breathtaking." Translation from Forest Service speak into plain English: no fewer than six lakes, five peaks, four meadows, and three of the most stunning canyons in the Alps are within striking distance of Echo Lake. The lake itself sits in a rocky cirque perched on the north side of Middle Peak. Only a few stunted firs and mountain hemlocks grow in the basin, but summer flower gardens around the east side of the lake are glorious. The inlet is a gurgling, crystal clear creek that tumbles through a slide of rocks and tiny pockets of meadow grass. The balcony of red rock on Echo's western edge offers a magnificent view of wild Deep Creek drainage and Sawtooth Mountain. Finally, topography has conspired to place the setting sun directly in the V-notch cut by Echo's outlet. Take a seat on the eastern side of the bowl and watch the sun slip into the perfectly cut notch and disappear in a blaze of glory. Breathtaking indeed.

To reach the Four Lakes Loop from Echo Lake, return to the Stoney Ridge Trail and continue north, over Little Stonewall Pass and down into Siligo Meadows. The trail descends on rocky switchbacks to the bottom of the drainage, then crosses a small stream in a stand of trees (this is the headwaters of Deep Creek). More alpine tidepools dot the meadows downstream from the crossing.

Across the creek, the sometimes-obscure trail is on the west side of the wide meadow. Old cattle paths and light human traffic on foot trails can make the going a little confusing in this area. Fortunately, the route is easy to see. Once you come down from Little Stonewall Pass and cross the creek, look up to the head of the drainage. The saddle on the left (northwest) is Deer Creek Pass and the saddle on the right (northeast) is Bee Tree Gap. Midway up the valley you reach a signed junction. The right fork leads to Bee Tree Gap and Long Canyon, while the left fork leads to Deer Creek Pass and the beginning of the Four Lakes Loop. Another spur trail at the top of the valley links the two passes. Both saddles are just under 2 miles from Echo Lake.

Options: Start at Deer Creek Pass (described in text) and descend 100 yards to the beginning of Four Lakes Loop, a beautiful trail that circles Siligo Peak (described in Hike 18).

Side trip to Lake Anna and Billy-be-Damned Lake: The best way to reach Lake Anna and Billy-be-Damned Lake is through the narrow gap directly east of Echo Lake. There's no trail on the rocky scramble across the ridge, but the route is fairly obvious (and very steep). From the east side of Echo, pick your way up the rocky slope to the narrow notch on the ridgeline, directly above the lake. After stopping for a moment to admire a perfect view of Mount Shasta, contour north across the open, rocky slope to little Billy-be-Damned Lake (7,400 feet, 1 acre).

Billy-be-Damned is set in a treeless basin on a dramatic ledge overlooking Bowerman Meadows. Colorful wildflowers dot the rocky cirque in midsummer, views are spectacular, and it's a fine place to wile away a day in the Alps. A rock dam forms the eastern edge of the lake and offers an incredible thronelike seat from which to watch the sunrise. Beneath your throne there's nothing but a thousand feet of pure mountain air between you and the meadow far below.

Lake Anna is one more ridge to the north. Follow the use trail north over the grassy ridge between the lakes, then pick your way down the rocky slope to Lake Anna. The lakes are about a half-mile apart. Anna, 4 acres of deep blue paradise, is one of the best swimming lakes in the Alps. Take a dip in the sparkling turquoise water, lay your body out on Anna's sun-warmed rocks, feel your goosebumps melt away, and just try to imagine a place you'd rather be.

16 Granite Peak Trail

Highlights: A steep hike to a spectacular vista atop 8,091-foot Granite Peak.
Type of hike: Day hike: out-and-back.
Total distance: 8.4 miles.
Difficulty: Strenuous.
Elevation gain: 4,400 feet.
Maps: USGS Covington Mill quad; USDAFS Trinity Alps Wilderness map.

Finding the trailhead: From Weaverville, drive 18 miles north on California Highway 3 to the signed turn for Granite Peak Trail (Forest Road 35N28Y). Turn left (west) and proceed 3 miles to the dead-end trailhead.

Parking and trailhead facilities: Ample parking at the trailhead (on an old logging landing) though no water or camping facilities; however, two Forest Service campgrounds are nearby on CA 3 (Bushytail and Minersville).

Key points:
0.0   Trailhead.
1.4   East Fork Stoney Creek.
1.5   Wilderness area boundary.
3.9   Stoney Ridge spur trail.
4.2   Granite Peak.

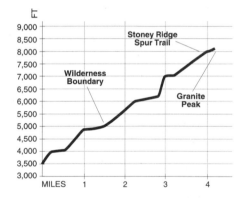

Profile data provided by TOPO!
©1999 Wildflower Productions (www.topo.com)

The hike: If you're a glutton for punishment and a pushover for great views, you'll love the hike to Granite Peak. Rising 4,400 feet in 4.2 miles, the route is like one long Stairmaster to the sky, but the view from the top of the 8,091-foot peak is worth every grueling step. All of the inner Trinity Alps, as well as Mount Shasta, Lassen Peak, and Trinity Lake are laid out before you like a relief map of rock and water. Most people tackle Granite Peak as a day hike, but you can definitely lay your sleeping bag out if you want to sleep with your head in the stars. If you do, you'll get a small taste of what it was like for those who spent their summers up here on the old (now gone) Granite Peak fire lookout. Water is readily available along the way (but not on top).

The Granite Peak Trail (9W18) starts wide and steep on an old jeep track, climbing steadily northwest through mixed forest of Douglas-fir, incense-cedar, and sugar pine. Oak, madrone, and dogwood also grow at this lower elevation.

Look back over your shoulder as you climb. There's a nice view of Mount Shasta every time the trees open up. After about a mile, the wide track gives way to real trail—a well-defined path that snakes upward in a series of seemingly endless switchbacks. Cross East Fork Stoney Creek just before the

Granite Peak Trail

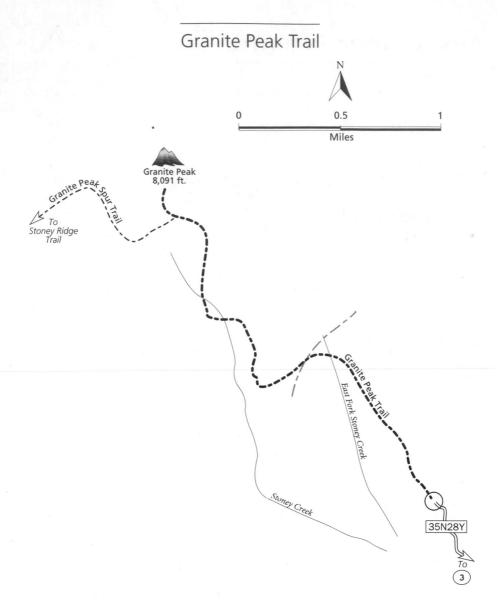

wilderness boundary, then continue the zigzagging ascent through open, mature forest dotted with large boulders.

At 2.5 miles from the trailhead, the path enters a steep, rocky gully. For the next 0.5 mile it's more steep switchbacks, but now the route hugs the gully, meandering back and forth through wildflowers, stands of brush and ferns, and green grassy glades. It's an idyllic setting, which helps somewhat to alleviate the disappointment you feel when you reach what looks like the summit straight above you. It's not.

After the false summit, climb 0.5 mile to the junction with the spur trail to Stoney Ridge. A left (west) turn here leads to Red Mountain Meadow and the Stoney Ridge Trail (just over a mile away). Stay straight (north) to reach the old lookout site at the trail's end, 4.2 miles from the trailhead. Allow plenty of time to enjoy the view. It's magnificent.

Options: The only option from Granite Peak is a side trip to Red Mountain Meadow by way of the spur trail to Stoney Ridge, which offers fine camping on the south side of Stonewall Pass. You can reach Van Matre and Siligo Meadow by going over Stonewall Pass, but it makes more sense to use the Stoney Ridge Trail if that's your destination (Hike 15).

17 Long Canyon

Highlights:	A steep hike up a canyon that boasts one of the best summer wildflower shows in the Alps; the most direct route to the Four Lakes Loop (Hike 18), a popular trail that circles Siligo Peak and its four scenic lakes.
Type of hike:	Backpack; out-and-back.
Total distance:	13.6 miles (plus optional 5.2-mile Four Lakes Loop).
Difficulty:	Moderate.
Elevation gain:	3,900 feet.
Maps:	USGS Siligo Peak and Covington Mill quads; USDAFS Trinity Alps Wilderness map.

Finding the trailhead: From Weaverville, drive 24 miles north on California Highway 3 to the signed Long Canyon turnoff. Turn left (west) on Long Canyon Road (County Road 115) and proceed 3 miles to the trailhead (bear right at the signed fork just before the trailhead). Long Canyon Road is unpaved after the first mile.

Parking and trailhead facilities: Ample parking but no facilities; numerous Forest Service campgrounds nearby on CA 3.

Key points:
- 0.0 Trailhead.
- 1.3 Bowerman Meadows Trail.
- 4.0 Off-trail route to Lake Anna.
- 5.3 Bee Tree Gap.
- 6.1 Deer Creek Pass.
- 6.8 Deer Lake.

The hike: Fortunately, Long Canyon is prettier than it is long—otherwise the hike up this steep-sided gorge might seem long indeed. As it is, a stunning array of summer wildflowers, lush meadows, and breathtaking views can make the uphill haul seem entirely too short. If it's wildflowers you're after, late July is your best bet for hitting Long Canyon at its peak.

Water is readily available at numerous stream crossings (purify all water) along the Long Canyon Trail (9W14). From the trailhead, begin walking

Long Canyon

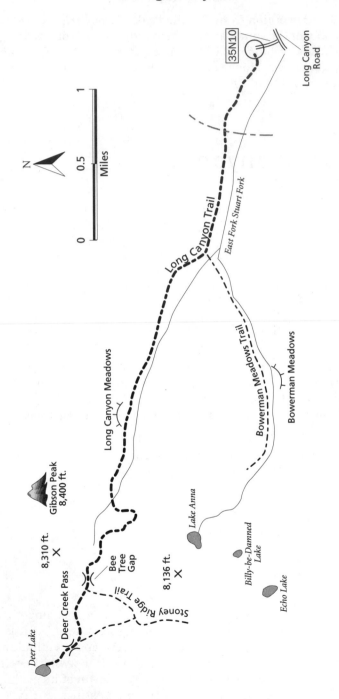

35N10

Long Canyon Road

East Fork Stuart Fork

Long Canyon Trail

N

0   0.5   1

Miles

Long Canyon Meadows

Bowerman Meadows Trail

Bowerman Meadows

Gibson Peak
8,400 ft.

8,310 ft.
X

Bee
Tree
Gap

8,136 ft.
X

Deer Creek Pass

Stoney Ridge Trail

Lake Anna

Billy-be-Damned
Lake

Echo Lake

Deer Lake

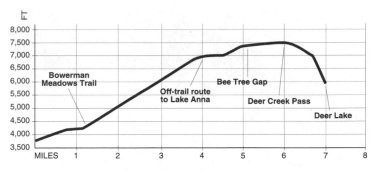

Profile data provided by TOPO! ©1999 Wildflower Productions (www.topo.com)

west with a short uphill push on wide, smooth track. This initial climb is only a few hundred yards, but it gives a good taste of what's to come.

After the brief ascent, the route levels out on a more narrow path. The trail is shaded by mixed forest of fir, pine, and incense-cedar. The route parallels (but remains high above) the East Fork of Stuart Fork for just under a mile, climbing very gradually and crossing two tributaries in short succession.

Shortly after crossing the second tributary, the trail turns uphill (northwest) and ascends to a junction with the Bowerman Meadows Trail 1.3 miles from the trailhead. To continue up Long Canyon from the junction, bear right at the fork and start climbing. The trail ascends steeply on a series of switchbacks, then climbs more moderately after reaching a meadow marked by a grandfather incense-cedar—one of the biggest I've ever seen in the Trinity Alps. Cross two small, flower-crowded creeks shortly after the meadow, then climb gradually to a pleasant clearing next to the canyon's main stream, just under 3 miles from the trailhead. Be sure to get water out of the stream here, if only to view the lovely little garden of leopard lilies and other wildflowers.

The trail then continues up the north bank of the creek, with Bee Tree Gap, the pass at the head of Long Canyon, coming into view for the first time. You're now in Long Canyon proper. Sheer walls rise on either side as the trail ascends the ravine. Lake Anna is behind the ridge on the left (south) and Granite Lake is behind the ridge on the right (north).

Bee Tree Gap may look close in the clear alpine air, but it's still a steep 2 miles away. As you continue up, look for colorful explosions of summer wildflowers along the trail where little streams nourish sprays of monkshood, leopard lilies, Indian paintbrush, and scarlet gilia. Just before reaching the top of the meadow, the trail descends briefly on rocky tread to cross the creek at the bottom of the canyon, passes a golden field of yellow lupine, then climbs the south wall on several switchbacks to a hanging meadow. An icy stream emerges from under a semipermanent snowbank here (after ascending most of Long Canyon, you might want to allow time for at least a short snowball fight).

A miniature forest of western pasque flowers (mountain anemones) makes this an idyllic spot to rest awhile—even if you pass on the snowballs. In late summer, the anemones turn into tiny imitations of Dr. Seuss's Truffula Trees

Siligo Meadows.

(there's no record of Dr. Seuss having been in Long Canyon, but the resemblance is uncanny). The steep gully up the south side of the canyon is the off-trail route to Lake Anna.

The Long Canyon Trail turns back to the north, contours up to the heart of the canyon, then bends west for the final push to Bee Tree Gap. The little stream in this uppermost meadow is the last chance for water. The trail climbs through rocks on the south side of the upper canyon, then ascends two steep switchbacks to the saddle. Enjoy your much deserved rest—and the awesome views—on Bee Tree Gap. You can see the striking difference between two different geological features that nearly come together here: red metamorphic rock to the south and gray granite to the north. Not so eye-pleasing are the remains of barbed wire fencing still hanging from a few trees near the pass, relics from the not-so-distant days when cattle grazed here (you won't see any cows today).

From the saddle, bear right on the signed trail to Deer Creek Pass. The left fork heads down into Siligo Meadows and then over Little Stonewall Pass, passing within a stone's throw of Echo Lake. On your way, note the enormous foxtail pine specimens; one has an average diameter of more than 8 feet.

The route to Deer Creek Pass follows an easy path that dips down and then up across the top of the basin, leading 0.8 mile to the saddle above Deer Lake. The view from the pass is even better than the one you just left behind, with Deer Lake literally at your feet, Siligo Peak to the west, and the pristine wilderness of Deer Creek drainage falling away to the north. (Siligo Peak is the gray summit between Deer and Diamond Lakes, not the unnamed red peak rising immediately above the pass you're standing on.)

Steep switchbacks lead 0.7 mile down to the shoreline of Deer Lake (passing the Four Lakes Loop junction on the way). The red talus slopes above the north-facing basin usually hold snow until late summer. Deer is a pretty little 4.5-acre lake, sitting at 7,150 feet, with emerald green grass around most of its shoreline and, in late summer, an eye-catching display of blue gentians on its western edge. The basin is nearly treeless, with just a few foxtail pines on its northeastern side. Walk up the granite shelf to the north for excellent views down the Deer Creek drainage and into the heart of the Alps.

Options: The four lakes at the end of the hike (Deer, Summit, Diamond, and Luella) are linked by the aptly named Four Lakes Loop (see Hike 18 for complete description). The 5.2-mile roller coaster of a path is a stunning trail by any standard. It boasts more views per mile than just about any other trail in the Alps, with many good swimming, fishing, and camping opportunities along the way. You can also make a sidetrip to Echo Lake (Stoney Ridge Trail, Hike 15) by veering south at Bee Tree Gap and going over Little Stonewall Pass. To make a loop back to the trailhead, you can hike cross-country to Lake Anna (Hike 19) and then follow the Bowerman Meadows Trail to its junction with the Long Canyon Trail.

18 Four Lakes Loop

Highlights:	A stunning hike around Siligo Peak, dipping in and out of four distinctive cirques, each with its own lake.
Type of hike:	Backcountry trail, accessible from several trailheads; loop.
Total distance:	5.2 miles.
Difficulty:	Moderate.
Elevation gain:	2,000 feet.
Maps:	USGS Siligo Peak quad; USDAFS Trinity Alps Wilderness map.

Finding the trailhead: Use Long Canyon (Hike 17), Stoney Ridge (Hike 15), Granite Lake (Hike 21) or Deer Creek (Hike 12) Trails to access the Four Lakes Loop.

Parking and trailhead facilities: None.

Key points:
- 0.0 Deer Lake.
- 1.0 Summit Lake.
- 1.9 Diamond Lake.
- 3.5 Luella Lake.
- 4.2 Deer Creek Trail junction.
- 5.2 Deer Lake.

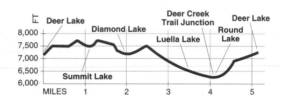

Profile data provided by TOPO!
©1999 Wildflower Productions(www.topo.com)

The hike: The Four Lakes Loop is one of those alpine delights that almost seems unnatural it's so well arranged. If Disneyland designed a trail, this would be it (though maybe not so steep). The Four Lakes Loop roller coasters around 8,162-foot Siligo Peak, dipping in and out of four different cirques, skirting four inviting lakes, and presenting more views per mile than any other hike in Trinity.

It's best done as a day hike while base camping nearby, in either the Deer Creek drainage or Siligo/Van Matre Meadows. End the day (or start it) with a walk up Siligo Peak, and you will definitely sleep well that night. Like all beautiful places, of course, this one attracts a fair amount of admirers. You won't find Disneyland-size crowds, but don't expect solitude on a summer weekend. Avoid camping at the lakes en route. There's very little space, and the fragile environments have suffered from the impact.

This description starts at the Four Lakes Loop junction above Deer Lake. The closest access is from the Long Canyon Trailhead (Hike 17).

On the south side of Deer Lake, midway up the slope to Deer Creek Pass, go west on the Four Lakes Loop Trail (9W13), toward Summit Lake. The loop can be hiked in either direction. There's no obvious advantage to either.

After turning onto the Four Lakes Loop, start the traverse across a broad talus slope above Deer Lake. Beautiful bouquets of rock fringe, veronica, and Indian paintbrush bloom among the reddish rocks in July and August.

Four Lakes Loop

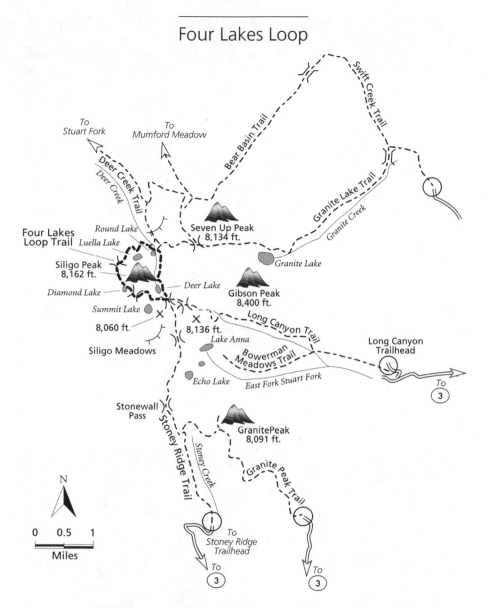

The north-facing cirque often holds snow well into the summer. The path is carved directly into the rocky hillside, but a moderate grade makes for easy walking until you get to the final, sandy switchbacks that lead up to the saddle. Near the start of the switchbacks you can still see remnants of the old trail that plunged almost straight down the hillside to the lake.

Once you gain the saddle, it's an easy half-mile descent to Summit Lake. The startlingly clear blue water of Summit (at 7,350 feet and 13 acres, it's the highest and biggest of the four lakes) is perched in a basin of red metamorphic rock. The lake appears to sit in a volcanic crater, but in fact it's in a glacier-carved bowl like other lakes in the Alps.

Before descending to the lake, take a look up the hill to the right (north). This is the way up Siligo Peak. Scattered use trails lead to a steep but non-technical walk-up of the 8,162-foot peak. On top of Siligo, you can see three of the four lakes on the loop (Luella remains hidden to the north). The 360-degree view encompasses Sawtooth Mountain to the west, Seven Up Peak to the east and, on the eastern horizon, Mount Shasta and Lassen Peak. As far as peak-bagging goes, Siligo offers more view for the effort than just about any other summit in the Alps.

Back down on the main path, descend a quarter mile west to a signed junction with a spur trail that leads down a series of switchbacks to Summit Lake. The forested north shore offers easy access to the clear blue water. Swimming is superb—and cold—all summer long. A steep, rocky slope and a nameless 8,061-foot red peak dominate the other side of the lake. The only water available is usually from the lake itself (no inlet, and the outlet runs only in early season, though you can find a dependable little stream in the meadow to the west below the lake).

Return to the main trail above Summit Lake and head left (west) on an easy quarter-mile leg to the saddle above Diamond Lake. From the pass, descend a staircase of switchbacks down a rocky, barren slope decorated with bright-colored summer flower gardens. Diamond Lake sits in a grassy bowl on a shelf overlooking Stuart Fork and the heart of the Alps. A castle-like rock on the western edge of the lake offers an incredible throne from which to watch the sun go down over Sawtooth Mountain.

To continue on the loop, follow the trail north through a lush meadow sloping away from the lake, then start climbing as the path contours north up the hill into mixed forest (stock up on water before leaving the lake, as

Camp along Deer Lake, Four Lakes Loop.

nothing dependable lies between here and Luella). After 0.5 mile, several moderate switchbacks lead northeast up to the third pass on the loop.

A grassy, tree-shaded saddle offers another spectacular place to rest and enjoy expansive views before dropping down to little Luella Lake. Looking east across Deer Creek drainage, you're looking directly at Seven Up Peak (named after a card game, not the soft drink). The reddish, rounded summit is distinctly different from nearby Gibson Peak (sharp gray granite), though Seven Up is often confused with its granite neighbor. You can also see the route to Granite Lake—a seemingly endless series of switchbacks carved into the eastern side of the drainage. The sight should give you a good idea of what lies between you and Deer Creek far below.

Descend on moderately steep switchbacks that zigzag down to little Luella, 1 mile below. Luella is tucked into a treeless, rocky shelf midway down the canyon wall (just under 7,000 feet elevation). The 2.5-acre lake rivals Summit Lake for the clearest water in the Alps, and a near-permanent snowbank on its western shore ensures that the water remains bracingly cool all summer long.

To reach Deer Creek and complete the loop, continue east on the trail as it descends another series of switchbacks. A gradual descent to the south finally brings you to the canyon floor at the head of a large and beautiful meadow. An unmarked trail to the northeast is just a spur trail that joins Deer Creek Trail down the canyon. Continue southeast, rounding the meadow near a clear-flowing creek that meanders through the deep grass. The source of the pretty little creek is Round Lake—a beautiful but tiny pond that stretches the definition of "lake."

Follow the path through the meadow to a signed junction at the edge of Deer Creek. Turn right (south) to return to Deer Lake and complete the loop. A left turn leads north down the Deer Creek Trail to Stuart Fork (Hike 11). Just 100 yards north is the junction with the Granite Lake Trail, which leads over the ridge to Swift Creek (Hike 21).

Heading south on the Four Lakes Loop, you begin the only really challenging section of the hike. It's only a mile from here to Deer Lake, but it's all uphill. Fill up water bottles before starting. The first part of the ascent is shaded by mixed forest, but the final push up to the lake can be sunny and hot. Cool off in Deer Lake and return to the starting point.

19 Lake Anna Loop

Highlights: An off-trail hike in one of the Alps' most unique settings to beautiful Lake Anna, a turquoise-colored gem in a red-rock basin.
Type of hike: Backpack (2–3 nights); out-and-back, or possible semi-loop.
Total distance: 9.3 miles, loop; 9 miles out-and-back.
Difficulty: Strenuous.
Elevation gain: 3,900 feet.
Maps: USGS Covington Mill and Siligo Peak quads; USDAFS Trinity Alps Wilderness map.

Finding the trailhead: From Weaverville, drive 24 miles north on California Highway 3 to the signed Long Canyon turnoff. Turn left (west) on Long Canyon Road (County Road 115) and proceed 3 miles to the trailhead (bear right at the signed fork just before the trailhead). Long Canyon Road is unpaved after the first mile.

Parking and trailhead facilities: Ample parking but no facilities; numerous Forest Service campgrounds nearby on CA 3.

Key points:

0.0	Trailhead.
1.3	Bowerman Trail junction.
4.0	Off-trail route to Lake Anna.
4.5	Lake Anna.
5.5	Bowerman Meadows.
8.0	Long Canyon Trail junction.
9.3	Trailhead.

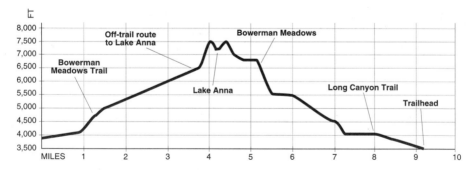

Profile data provided by TOPO! ©1999 Wildflower Productions (www.topo.com)

The hike: Lake Anna's appeal doesn't lie in overwhelming alpine scenery or granite splendor like some of Trinity's other lakes. Rather, Anna's charms are hidden modestly in a red-rock cirque below Mount Temple. A moonscape of red rock lies on the eastern edge of Anna, forming a swollen lip of a dike that drops suddenly and sharply to Bowerman Meadows a thousand

Lake Anna Loop

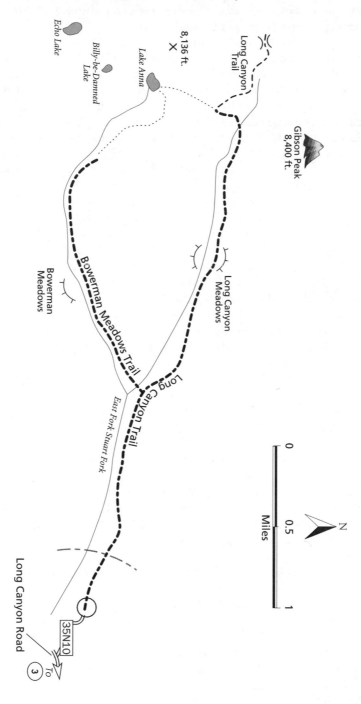

Echo Lake

Billy-be-Damned Lake

Lake Anna

8,136 ft. ✕

Long Canyon Trail

Gibson Peak 8,400 ft.

Long Canyon Meadows

Bowerman Meadows Trail

Bowerman Meadows

Long Canyon Trail

East Fork Stuart Fork

Long Canyon Road

35N10

To 3

0   0.5   1

Miles

N

feet below. The deep blue water (56 feet down and clear all the way) compels you to stay and linger for awhile. In fact, not a few of Anna's visitors have come here with great plans for further exploration, only to come under Anna's spell and never get beyond the basin.

A summer garden of wildflowers lines the inlet, which runs through a lush meadow a few hundred feet above the lake, then tumbles down a rocky cascade to the shore. The basin commands one of the best sunrise views in the Alps, with Mount Shasta in the picture if you climb up the west side of the cirque. Within easy day hiking distance are Billy-be-Damned and Echo Lakes, as well as Siligo Meadows and the Four Lakes Loop.

What's the catch? There's no trail to Lake Anna, and it's a steep haul from every side. Only hikers who are comfortable with route-finding and steep to very steep scrambling should attempt this hike. The loop route described here goes up Long Canyon, then off-trail up an unnamed gully to Lake Anna, and back through Bowerman Meadows. The off-trail descent from Anna to Bowerman Meadows is steep and rough. You can avoid it by returning the way you came. (The Long Canyon route is slightly longer but definitely easier.)

Start the hike at the Long Canyon Trailhead (see Hike 17 for a description of the Long Canyon Trail's first 4 miles). Leave the trail when you arrive at the base of a steep gully leading up the south wall of Long Canyon, about 4 miles from the trailhead. The gully is easy to identify because you cross from the north side of Long Canyon to the south side immediately before reaching its base. After crossing the creek at the bottom of Long Canyon, ascend switchbacks to the meadow hanging midway up the south wall of the canyon. A near-permanent snowbank fills the rocky bench gouged into the side of the canyon. The Long Canyon Trail jogs right and continues west, up the remainder of the drainage to Bee Tree Gap. The route to Lake Anna lies directly ahead, up the steep, rocky chute that leads out of Long Canyon and drops into Anna from above.

Cross the snowbank and head south up the gully (use caution: the stream running under the snow can undercut the seemingly stable field and leave it dangerously thin; the snow is easy to walk around). Once in the gully proper, traces of use trail and cairns may appear, but it's simply a matter of ascending the steep chute to the saddle about 500 feet and 0.5 mile above. Midsummer wildflowers on the grassy slope west of the streambed make this tough climb a delight.

Once you gain the ridge above Lake Anna, it's simply a matter of dropping into the deep blue water at your feet. The 4-acre lake sits at 7,550 feet, and you have to descend a couple of hundred feet to get there.

The red rock–blue water basin seems to hang on the side of the mountain so steep is the drop from Anna's outlet. The view, needless to say, is in keeping with the rest of the setting. Sit on the naked red rocks on a warm summer evening, watch the full moon breach the gap at your feet, and the name Anna will be stuck in your mind forever.

While at Anna, be sure to explore the upper basin (great sunrise view of Mount Shasta). Shallow, seldom-seen Billy-be-Damned Lake is directly over

View of Lake Anna, Lake Anna Loop.

the ridge to the south, just 15 minutes away. The shallow little (less than an acre) puddle is in a rock-lined basin with a red-rock dike that almost matches Anna's (the drop certainly does). You can reach Echo Lake via a steep talus slope southwest of Billy-be-Damned. The chute leads up to a narrow notch in the ridge, then down another steep slope on the other side (less than 0.5 mile between lakes.) No maintained trails lead between Anna, Billy-be-Damned, and Echo Lakes, but the routes are easy to follow in the near treeless basins (only Anna has a few sparse stands of any size).

To return to the trailhead via Bowerman Meadows, thread your way through the boulders above the northeast corner of Anna. Emerge on the shoulder of the ridge northeast of the steep outlet, then pick your way down the grassy, brushy slopes to the meadow nearly 1,000 feet below. I find that working your way east affords the most gentle grade. However, many Anna fans swear by the rocky route along the near-vertical outlet below the lake (I've done it that way too, and can attest that it's certainly not boring). Suffice it to say there are several routes down. Choose your medicine and proceed at your own risk.

Once at Bowerman Meadows (elevation 6,600 feet) you find yourself in an idyllic oasis of green grass and summer wildflowers. In fact, some visitors choose to approach Anna from this direction, basecamp in Bowerman Meadows, and day hike to the lakes and surrounding areas from here. This is a good option, but requires that you haul yourself up—instead of down—that steep hillside if you want to complete the loop through Long Canyon (I've also tried it that way and can attest that it's only for dedicated masochists).

From the meadow, pick up traces of use trail that lead southeast, downcanyon. Light use can leave the Bowerman Trail overgrown in places, but it's generally not hard to follow. Descend through *Sound-of-Music* meadows to the East Fork of Stuart Fork, then follow the river's north bank 2 miles to the junction with the Long Canyon Trail. The trail passes through open meadows, thick stands of alder, and shady groves of incense-cedar, cottonwood, pine, and fir. Crossing Long Canyon's creek can be difficult in high water. If you're concerned, it's easy to come down and take a look at the water level when you pass the junction on the way in (the creek crossing is less than a hundred yards from the junction). From here it's an easy stroll back to the trailhead, 1.3 miles away.

Options: The Four Lakes Loop is close to Lake Anna. Access it by following Long Canyon (Hike 17) to Deer Creek Pass and then the beginning of the loop (see Hike 18 for a description of the Four Lakes Loop). The 5.2-mile roller coaster of a path boasts more views-per-mile than just about any other trail in the Alps, with many good swimming, fishing, and camping opportunities along the way.

20 Swift Creek

Highlights:	An idyllic hike through a chain of sprawling meadows to the head of Swift Creek; good access to several lakes.
Type of hike:	Backpack; out-and-back.
Total distance:	18.8 miles.
Difficulty:	Moderate.
Elevation gain:	3,100 feet.
Maps:	USGS Siligo Peak, Covington Mill, Ycatapom Peak, and Caribou Lake quads; USDAFS Trinity Alps Wilderness map.

Finding the trailhead: From Weaverville, drive 30 miles north on California Highway 3, past Trinity Center, to the signed Swift Creek Trail turn-off on Forest Road 36N25 (just after crossing the Swift Creek bridge, and just prior to Wyntoon Resort). Turn left (west) and proceed 6 miles to the trailhead (bear left at the signed fork for Swift Creek) at the end of the road.

Parking and trailhead facilities: Ample parking at the trailhead (a good indication of the amount of use Swift Creek gets) and an outhouse. The closest campground is Preacher Meadow, on CA 3 near Trinity Center.

Key points:
- 0.0 Trailhead.
- 1.2 Granite Lake Trail junction.
- 2.3 Steer Creek.
- 3.4 Parker Creek.
- 3.5 Bear Basin–Parker Creek Trails.

Swift Creek

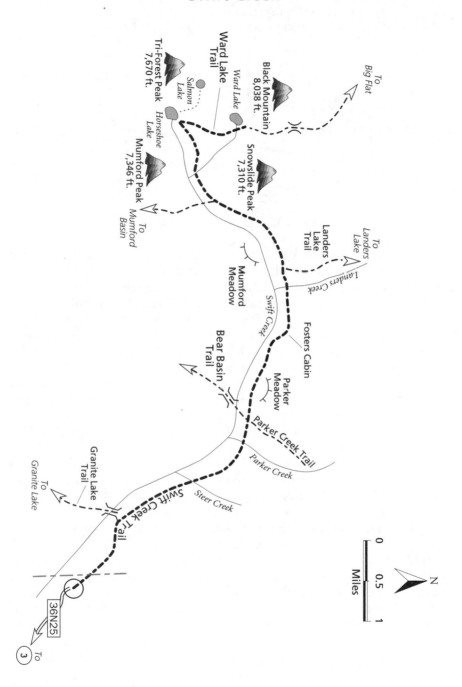

Tri-Forest Peak 7,670 ft.

Ward Lake Trail

Black Mountain 8,038 ft.

To Big Flat

Salmon Lake

Ward Lake

Horseshoe Lake

Snowslide Peak 7,310 ft.

Mumford Peak 7,346 ft.

To Mumford Basin

Landers Lake Trail

To Landers Lake

Mumford Meadow

Swift Creek

Landers Creek

Fosters Cabin

Parker Meadow

Bear Basin Trail

Parker Creek Trail

Parker Creek

Granite Lake Trail

To Granite Lake

Swift Creek Trail

Steer Creek

36N25

To 3

0
Miles
0.5
1

N

3.6 Parker Meadow.
4.7 Fosters Cabin.
5.5 Mumford Meadow–Landers Lake Trail.
8.0 Trail junction (spur trail to Horseshoe Lake).
8.3 Horseshoe Lake.
9.4 Ward Lake.

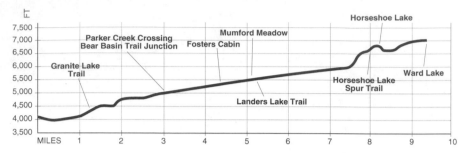

Profile data provided by TOPO! ©1999 Wildflower Productions (www.topo.com)

The hike: Horseshoe and Ward Lakes, each perched in a secluded basin at the upper end of Swift Creek drainage, attract a fair number of visitors with the lure of good swimming and great scenery. But the hike up Swift Creek is worth doing even if you never make it to the lakes. Parker and Mumford meadows, situated along the banks of the river, together form one of the most enchanting chains of greenery in the Alps. The lush meadows extend for more than 3 miles along the north bank of Swift Creek and offer such an inviting array of wildflowers in summer, it may be hard to pull yourself away. The forest fringes around Mumford Meadow are popular basecamping sites from which to explore the surrounding area. You can day hike easily up to the lakes, as well as into the more remote meadows hanging above Swift Creek (Bear Basin, Mumford Basin, and meadows along Landers, Sunrise, and Parker Creeks).

At the Swift Creek trailhead don't be discouraged if the parking lot is full of cars and horse trailers. The trailhead serves a number of destinations, and people tend to spread out fairly evenly (except at perpetually crowded Granite Lake).

The Swift Creek Trail (8W15) descends briefly from the trailhead and then levels out, heading northwest through a shady mix of ponderosa pine, Douglas-fir, and incense-cedar, and soon leads to a shelf along Swift Creek. The trail generally parallels Swift Creek from here all the way to the Landers Lake Trail junction. The path ascends gradually for the first mile, passing a number of incense-cedar and fir trees with old license plates nailed to them about 15 feet off the ground. (They are not remnants from some historic, catastrophic car accident. Rather, they help snow survey parties follow this route during the winter.) You also pass a small meadow on the right choked with California pitcher plants most of the summer. The rare insectivorous plants thrive in the Alps' wet meadows.

Soon the trail ascends moderately to a narrow ledge high above Swift Creek. Watch your step here—it's a long drop—but take the time to peer over the side, where Swift Creek cuts a dramatic gorge through solid rock.

110

Waterfalls, deep pools, and sheer cliffs await adventurous souls who want to explore the depths of the gorge. You can get down to river level both upstream and downstream from the ravine.

Just past the overlook, 1.2 miles from the trailhead, arrive at the junction with the Granite Lake Trail. The left fork at the signed junction leads down to a steel bridge crossing of Swift Creek, then 4.1 miles up to Granite Lake (Hike 21). To continue on the Swift Creek Trail, stay right at the fork and start climbing gradually on the shady path. The trail soon crosses an impressive swath of avalanche debris. Just under a mile from the Granite Lake junction, you cross the outlet stream from tiny Twin Lakes, a steep and brushy 0.5 mile up the hill on your right. Like some other misnamed lakes in the Alps, these two are just a couple of lilypad-choked puddles.

Steer Creek is the next major tributary you cross, but a number of smaller unnamed creeks with accompanying flower gardens cross the trail in numerous places. After climbing more steeply on moderate switchbacks, the trail veers away from Swift Creek to cross a pretty little stream and skirt a lush meadow decorated with gaudy orange leopard lilies in midsummer.

The trail crosses a gentle, forested flat after climbing above the meadow. Easy walking brings you to Parker Creek and the only significant stream crossing on the entire route. A bridge was built across Parker Creek in 1967, but only the concrete foundations now remain. Early-season high water could make this a difficult crossing, but usually it's just a matter of boulder hopping across. Across the creek a level path leads quickly to a three-way trail junction. Signs point southwest to Bear Basin (Hike 21), northwest to Fosters Cabin–Swift Creek, and north to Parker Creek–Deer Flat (Landers Lake Loop, Hike 22). Stay right and continue on the Swift Creek Trail toward Fosters Cabin.

The path hugs the southern edge of Parker Meadow from here, serving up a beautiful, leisurely stroll along lush fields of meadow grasses and summer wildflowers. Parker is the first in a remarkable series of meadows that dot the Swift Creek drainage from here to the head of the valley. At the top of Parker Meadow you come to Fosters Cabin, 4.7 miles from the trailhead.

The Forest Service restored Fosters Cabin in 1989, but the original structure dates from 1946. The ruins of an older horse barn remain across the trail from the restored structure. The site is named after Bill Foster, who built a cabin here for his cow hands sometime in the late 1800s. The cabin's wooden porch is a fine place to lean your pack if you want to get some water from the nearby spring, duck out of the rain (if need be), or just daydream about the old-timers who used to spend their summers in this beautiful place.

Proceed up the trail as it follows Swift Creek on a gradual bend to the west. As you enter the lower reaches of Mumford Meadow, pass the signed junction with the Landers Lake Trail (shortly after crossing Landers Creek), and continue west through wet, sometimes boggy terrain. Shake your boots off and continue on dry ground as the path skirts the south side of Mumford Meadow, passing a couple of well-used horse camps and a number of less visible campsites hidden in the stands of incense-cedar, fir, and pine between the trail and Swift Creek.

From here to the head of the canyon, enjoy walking the most pleasant couple of miles in the Alps. The trail alternates between shady forest cover and lush pockets of meadow. Flower gardens blooming with a rainbow of colors adorn the route, and sparkling little streams cross the path frequently. All the while, the trail ascends at a barely perceptible grade as gentle as a walk in the park, and across Swift Creek lies a largely untraveled wilderness where solitude is nearly guaranteed. Less than a mile before reaching the head of the canyon you pass an unmaintained route leading up to Mumford Basin and eventually over the ridge to Deer Creek. This trail is generally unmarked, hard to find, and seldom used—hence, a wonderful place to explore if you have the inclination.

Of course, there's a price for all that easy strolling. The last section of the trail climbs more than 1,000 feet on rocky, exposed switchbacks. Leave the meadows behind at the head of the drainage, where you enter a stand of fir and cross the outlet coming down from Horseshoe Lake. This stream and one more crossing midway up are the only sources of water on the steep climb (purify all water). In mid-July, the leopard lilies, shooting stars, and scarlet gilia at this second crossing are simply amazing.

Horseshoe Lake: At the top of the switchbacks, arrive at the signed junction for the Horseshoe–Ward Trails in a shady flat. Go left (south) to reach Horseshoe Lake, just 0.3 mile up the hill through granite ledges and scattered firs. Once on top of the dike, arrive at 6-acre Horseshoe Lake (elevation 6,850 feet). As the name implies, the sparkling body of water is wrapped neatly around an island of rock. Its clear water and sun-splashed slabs of granite look especially inviting after climbing those switchbacks on a summer afternoon. Watch your step on the rush to dive in.

Walk out on the ridge east of the lake to get a bird's eye view of the hike you just completed. On the northwest side of the lake you can scout an off-trail route up the barren, rocky slope to the divide between Horseshoe and Salmon Lakes, on the ridgeline just north of Tri-Forest Peak. The 7,670-foot peak, the ridge beneath it, and Salmon Lake are all good bets for further exploration. From the saddle, the view of Sawtooth Ridge and Caribou Mountain is breathtaking, and about 500 feet beneath your feet, little 1.5-acre Salmon Lake beckons when you want solitude. No trails lead to the shallow pond-cum-lake, and very few people make the effort to reach it. The off-trail route from Horseshoe to Salmon is steep but not technically demanding. Just aim for the saddle and start climbing.

Ward Lake: Back at the junction on the Swift Creek Trail (below Horseshoe Lake), turn right (north) to reach Ward Lake. The trail crosses a stream, then traverses the mountainside on a long contour to the northeast. Cross open, grassy slopes, a shady stand of fir, and finally ascend a couple of steep switchbacks that lead around a prominent bulge guarding the entrance to Ward Lake. Follow the outlet stream, which tumbles down a narrow green corridor at the southeast side of the basin, for the last few minutes. It's almost a surprise when you finally emerge at the lip of 5.5-acre Ward Lake, so protective are the steep ramparts around it. Ward sits at an elevation of 7,100 feet, 9.4 miles from the trailhead.

Red and gray cliffs hang over the basin, and an emerald meadow slopes steeply in from the north like a river of green grass. Like its neighbor, Ward also has a horseshoe shape that curves around a large prow of rocky terrain and stunted trees. For an excellent sunrise view, head for the ridge east of the lake. Use the Ward Lake Trail, which climbs to the saddle northeast of the lake, to reach the ridge (follow the trail nearly to the saddle, then head for the ridge when the angle seems right).

The Ward Lake Trail (Hike 32) originates at Big Flat and can be used as an alternate route to reach this area. It's typically less crowded than Swift Creek and is shorter by a few miles, but the trailhead is an hour farther drive and you miss out on Mumford Meadow.

Options: The Swift Creek Trail passes numerous paths with a bewildering array of options. A couple of the more obvious routes are described in other chapters (Bear Basin–Granite Lake Loop and Landers Lake Loop), or use the map to create your own.

21 Bear Basin–Granite Lake Loop

Highlights:	A scenic loop around 8,134-foot Seven Up Peak. Passes through seldom-seen Bear Basin and skirts popular Granite Lake; good access to Four Lakes Loop.
Type of hike:	Backpack; loop.
Total distance:	16.4 miles.
Difficulty:	Moderate.
Elevation gain:	3,500 feet.
Maps:	USGS Covington Mill, Siligo Peak, and Ycatapom Peak quads; USDAFS Trinity Alps Wilderness map.

Finding the trailhead: From Weaverville, drive 30 miles north on California Highway 3, past Trinity Center, to the signed Swift Creek Trail turnoff on Forest Road 36N25 (just after crossing the Swift Creek bridge, and just prior to Wyntoon Resort). Turn left (west) and proceed 6 miles to the trailhead (bear left at signed fork for Swift Creek) at the end of the road.

Parking and trailhead facilities: Ample parking (a good indication of the amount of use Swift Creek gets) and an outhouse. The closest campground is Preacher Meadow, on CA 3 near Trinity Center.

Key points:
- 0.0 Trailhead.
- 1.2 Granite Lake Trail junction.
- 3.4 Parker Creek–Bear Basin Trail junction.

Bear Basin–Granite Lake Loop

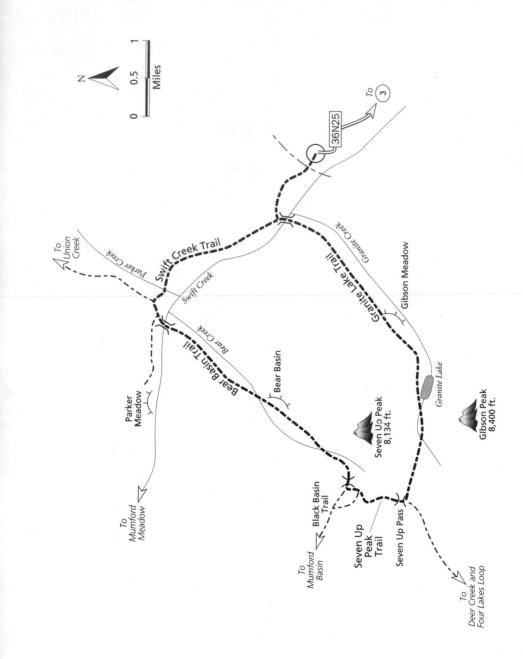

6.6	Bear Basin.
8.3	Seven Up Peak–Black Basin Trail junction.
9.3	Seven Up Pass.
11.1	Granite Lake.
11.6	Gibson Meadow.
15.2	Swift Creek Trail junction.
16.4	Trailhead.

Profile data provided by TOPO! ©1999 Wildflower Productions (www.topo.com)

The hike: This loop takes the scenic route to Granite Lake, a popular destination just 5.3 miles from the Swift Creek Trailhead. The lake sits in a dramatic granite cirque below Gibson Peak, and the short hike-to-spectacular scenery ratio draws the predictable weekend crowds. By taking this route around Seven Up Peak, you'll travel through the comparative solitude of Bear Basin, then drop into the Granite Lake basin from above. The loop can be done in either direction, but hiking it this way allows you to hike down (instead of up) the steep trail between Seven Up Pass and Granite Lake. You also have the option of taking a side trip to Deer Creek and the Four Lakes Loop (Hike 18).

See Swift Creek (Hike 20) for a description of the first 3.4 miles of trail to Parker Creek and the Bear Basin Trail junction. If you have your heart set on swimming in Granite Lake and want to get there the quickest way, just hang a left (southwest) at the Granite Lake Trail (1.2 miles from the trailhead) and you'll be doing the backstroke in a couple of hours. To hike the loop in the recommended direction, turn left (southwest) on the Bear Basin Trail (9W10).

The path quickly descends to a bridge crossing of Swift Creek, just upstream from the confluence of Swift and Bear Creeks. After crossing the bridge, begin a steady ascent into Bear Basin. The route into the thick-forested drainage is steep at first. The rocky trail passes several seeps and small tributaries as it climbs the west side of Bear Creek (the long-neglected trail was much improved by a trail crew in 1999, which constructed a causeway over a fragile wet meadow farther up the basin).

Slightly more than 2 miles from Swift Creek, the trail arrives at Bear Basin proper, where you skirt one of the prettiest meadows in all of the Alps. Mature incense-cedar and ponderosa pine fringe the idyllic setting. The trail passes on the west side of the meadow, on the new causeway built by the trail crew. California pitcher plants and a variety of wildflowers thrive in the lush environment. The wet meadow is a rare and fragile ecosystem—please be sure to observe Zero Impact practices (don't make new trails or campsites in the area).

Traveling southwest from the meadow, the trail continues to climb toward the ridge separating Swift and Deer Creek drainages. The ascent is much more gentle now, however, as the path traverses several smaller meadows in the upper basin. You cross and recross Bear Creek as you climb higher, so access to drinking water is never a worry (purify all water here and elsewhere on the hike).

The trail reaches the headwaters of Bear Creek about 7.5 miles from the trailhead. The path climbs up through fir and foxtail pine on the west side of the drainage, veering away from the creek and then coming level with the stream just a few hundred yards from the cirque at the head of the canyon. Here the trail turns right (west) and climbs a steep set of switchbacks to gain the ridgeline above. If you have time and inclination, leave the trail here and follow Bear Creek to its source. The near-permanent snowbank in upper Bear Basin is a great place to poke around (cross to the east side of the valley for a nice view of Mount Shasta).

The trail climbs 0.3 mile up a rocky hillside smothered in wildflowers in July and August. Red, yellow, and purple blooms take some of the sting out of the steep climb. Once you gain the ridgeline you arrive at a fork in the trail. A right (west) turn leads to a junction with the Black Basin Trail and routes to Deer Creek and Mumford Basin. To continue the loop, turn left (southeast) on the Seven Up Peak Trail (9W67). This path leads across the level basin on top of the ridge, and after 100 yards passes another trail junction. This short spur trail (on the right) also leads down to the Black Basin Trail, and is a slightly quicker route (by mere minutes) than the first fork, if your destination is Deer Creek.

The Seven Up Peak Trail continues south and east, climbing a short set of switchbacks to the ridgeline above Deer Creek drainage. On the way you pass an old mine shaft just to the side of the trail. Once the trail gains the crest of the ridge, it contours gently along through sparse tree cover and stretches of open terrain. The entire Deer Creek drainage drops away beneath your feet, with drop-dead views across the valley to Siligo Peak, Luella Lake, and the Deer Lake basin. If you're still on the fence about whether or not to drop down to Deer Creek and the Four Lakes Loop, this vista might help make up your mind.

After passing beneath the shoulder of 8,134-foot Seven Up Peak (named for a card game played by a couple of cowhands long ago, not the soft drink), the trail soon reaches a saddle where you run into the Granite Lake Trail (8W14). The gap in the knife-edge ridge commands an unbroken vista of both the Granite Creek and Deer Creek drainages, both of which drop steeply away at your feet. This is your last chance to add about 9 miles and the Four Lakes Loop to this hike (turn right, or west, to descend to Deer Creek on a set of switchbacks that zigzag down to the meadow 2 miles below).

Turn left (east) to descend into the headwaters of Granite Creek. The next 1.8 miles is a delightful descent through open meadows, wildflowers galore, and endless views up and down the wild canyon. The trail descends (steeply at first) on the north side of the drainage. After dropping down to meet Granite Creek, the trail passes through a junglelike profusion of corn lilies, leopard lilies, and monkshood. In late July this short section of trail can be head-high with wildflowers.

After crossing the creek a couple of times, the trail descends steeply again through forest cover to Granite Lake. Just before the second crossing, you traverse a rocky bench with excellent views of the lake below. The bench is just above a waterfall, and marks a good point for off-trail scramblers to set off for the ridge on the south side of the creek (great sunrises).

Granite Lake, tucked in a deep basin below 8,400-foot Gibson Peak, is a swimming and fishing haven. The basin is mostly forested on the east side, while the north side is lined with smooth slabs of gray granite and jumbled piles of rock. Like other beautiful wilderness destinations too close to the road for their own good, Granite Lake gets a high number of visitors on summer weekends.

To finish the loop, hike east on the Granite Lake Trail. The path traverses a rocky bench immediately east of the lake, then descends a short set of switchbacks to skirt the north side of Gibson Meadow. The route follows the course of Granite Creek the rest of the way, heading northeast on a gently descending grade in mostly shady forest cover. A number of small tributaries cross the path, so it's not necessary to fight your way through the brush along Granite Creek to get water. Arrive at a wood-and-steel footbridge that crosses Swift Creek, 4.1 miles from Granite Lake and just upstream from the Swift–Granite Creek confluence. Climb about 100 yards up the opposite bank and rejoin the Swift Creek Trail. Turn right and retrace your steps 1.2 miles to the trailhead.

Options: The best side trip off of this route is the Four Lakes Loop (Hike 18). Access the loop by turning right (west) at Seven Up Pass and descending to Deer Creek. From the trail junction at the bottom you can hike the Four Lakes Loop in either direction. The 5.2-mile roller coaster of a path boasts more views per mile than just about any other trail in the Alps, and offers many good swimming, fishing and camping opportunities along the way. Another good option is to head down the Deer Creek Trail (Hike 12), which connects to the Stuart Fork Trail (Hike 11).

22 Landers Lake Loop

<table>
<tr><td align="right">Highlights:</td><td>A scenic loop that leads up Swift Creek then down Parker Creek; beautiful Mumford Meadow and spectacular views of the Alps from the top of Red Rock Mountain.</td></tr>
<tr><td align="right">Type of hike:</td><td>Backpack; loop (repeat 3 miles on Swift Creek).</td></tr>
<tr><td align="right">Total distance:</td><td>16.4 miles.</td></tr>
<tr><td align="right">Difficulty:</td><td>Moderate.</td></tr>
<tr><td align="right">Elevation gain:</td><td>4,100 feet.</td></tr>
<tr><td align="right">Maps:</td><td>USGS Covington Mill, Ycatapom Peak, and Caribou Lake quads; USDAFS Trinity Alps Wilderness map.</td></tr>
</table>

Finding the trailhead: From Weaverville, drive 30 miles north on California Highway 3 to the signed Swift Creek Trail turnoff on Forest Road 36N25 (just after crossing the Swift Creek bridge, and just prior to Wyntoon Resort). Turn left (west) and proceed 6 miles to the trailhead (bear left at signed fork) at the end of the road.

Parking and trailhead facilities: Ample parking (a good indication of the amount of use Swift Creek gets) and an outhouse. The closest campground is Preacher Meadow, on CA 3 near Trinity Center.

Key points:

0.0	Trailhead.
1.2	Granite Lake Trail.
3.4	Parker Creek ford.
3.5	Bear Basin–Parker Creek Trails.
4.7	Fosters Cabin.
5.5	Mumford Meadow–Landers Lake Trail.
6.0	Sunrise Creek Trail.
7.0	Landers Lake spur trail.
7.7	Landers Lake.
9.6	Union Creek Trail.
10.5	Union/Parker Divide.
13.0	Swift Creek Trail.
16.4	Trailhead.

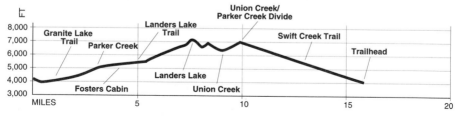

Profile data provided by TOPO! ©1999 Wildflower Productions (www.topo.com)

Landers Lake Loop

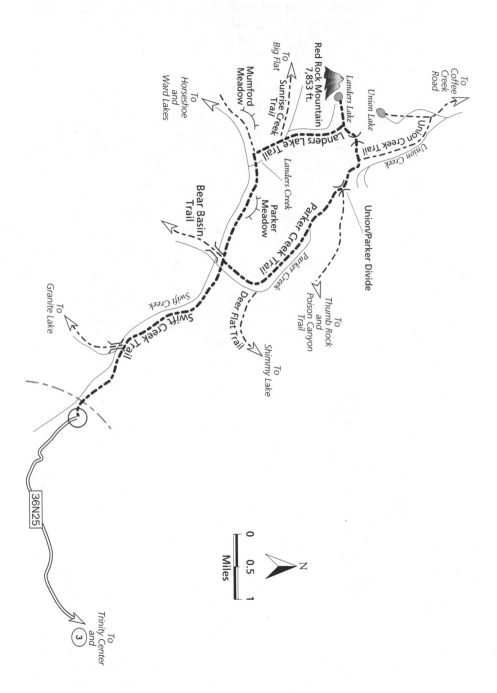

To Coffee Creek Road

Union Creek

Union Lake

Union Creek Trail

Union/Parker Divide

Landers Lake

Red Rock Mountain 7,853 ft.

Landers Lake Trail

To Sunrise Creek

To Big Flat

Mumford Meadow

To Horseshoe and Ward Lakes

Landers Creek

Parker Meadow

Parker Creek Trail

Parker Creek

To Thumb Rock and Poison Canyon Trail

Bear Basin Trail

Deer Flat Trail

To Shimmy Lake

Swift Creek

Swift Creek Trail

To Granite Lake

36N25

To Trinity Center and (3)

N

0   0.5   1

Miles

The hike: This route follows four different creeks on a loop through some of the Alps' most varied terrain—both physically and "socially." Shady forests, vast meadows, lush flower gardens, a secluded lake, and endless vistas come in rapid succession. On the social side, you have plenty of company on the Swift Creek Trail, but fellow hikers are few and far between on the rest of the route (especially along Parker Creek, a seldom-used trail despite its proximity to a popular trailhead).

Landers Lake, midway around the loop, isn't as spectacular as some lakes in Trinity, but its clear water and peaceful red-rock basin offer a nice change of pace from the more crowded areas in the Alps. Red Rock Mountain (7,853 feet) is an easy scramble west of the lake and offers one of the best 360-degree views in all the Alps. Side trips to Union, Foster, and Lion Lakes, as well as Shimmy and Lilypad, are within striking distance.

At the Swift Creek Trailhead, don't be discouraged if the parking lot is full of cars. The trailhead serves a number of destinations, and people tend to spread out fairly evenly (except at perpetually crowded Granite Lake). For the first segment of this hike (5.5 miles to the Landers Lake Trail junction) see the description in Swift Creek (Hike 20). On the way in take note of the Parker Creek Trail (3.5 miles in, just after crossing Parker Creek). This is the return route.

In the lower reaches of Mumford Meadow, look for the signed junction with the Landers Lake Trail (shortly after crossing Landers Creek). The wet meadow can become a mud bog here after numerous hikers and horses have stomped through it. Pick your way north along the eastern edge of the meadow (the trail is not always distinct) and pass a campsite on your right, just before heading steeply uphill on a well-defined trail (marked by cairns on the edge of the meadow and a conspicuous blaze on a huge pine).

Rough tread on steep switchbacks leads uphill 0.5 mile to the junction with the Sunrise Creek Trail, at the confluence of Sunrise and Landers Creeks. Bear right at the junction and descend to a crossing of Landers Creek, then continue north uphill as the trail hugs the east bank of Landers Creek.

Ascend to a beautiful meadow, punctuated by sparkling ponds, summer wildflowers, and a field of pitcher plants. The trail levels out to skirt the east side of the meadow, giving you a chance to catch your breath and enjoy the gardenlike setting.

A mile from the Sunrise Creek junction you arrive at another signed junction, this one with a spur trail that leads over the ridge to the Union Creek Trail (which you'll take on the way out). Bear left to continue up to Landers Lake. The trail again hugs the east side of a pleasant meadow, then starts the last steep climb up to the lake. Trees become more sparse and rocks more plentiful as you ascend the final 0.7 mile to Landers Lake.

Landers Lake sits at 7,100 feet in a starkly beautiful basin of red metamorphic rock. The Forest Service pegs the lake at 6 acres, but with little water trickling in from above, the lake usually shrinks back quite a bit by the end of summer. Black, water-stained rocks surround the shoreline and give the lake an eerie, lunar look. The lake is shallow and clear, ideal for

Landers Creek along Landers Lake Loop.

swimming when the water warms up. Grass-lined ponds and meadows northwest of the lake offer plenty of elbowroom.

Peak baggers will definitely appreciate the hike up to the top of Red Rock Mountain. The incline is gentle enough that you can get there any number of ways. A popular way to reach the summit is to cross the meadow at the lake's northwestern edge, then hike uphill to an obvious use trail that zigzags up the rocky slope to a gap on the basin's southern ridge. Once you gain the ridgeline, just follow the crest 0.5 mile to the peak. The rocky summit commands a view of just about everything there is to see in the heart of the Alps: To the west Sawtooth Mountain, Thompson Peak, and Caribou Mountain seem close enough to touch, while Mount Shasta dominates the horizon in the other direction. You'll also get a good view down into Sunrise Basin to the south. Another scenic diversion is to hike cross-country over the ridge between Landers and Union lakes (to the north). The off-trail route down to Union is steep but passable (though be forewarned that Union is a shallow, murky, brush-lined lake).

To continue the loop from Landers, head back down the trail to the junction with Landers Lake spur trail at the southeast end of the meadow 0.7 mile below the lake (signed Union Creek). Turn left (northeast) and climb moderately to a saddle on the ridge dividing Landers and Union Creeks. From the gap it's a steep mile down to the floor of the valley below. Descend on rough switchbacks at first, then proceed more gradually on a gentle grade that leads east into the heart of a large, wide meadow at the head of Union Creek. Cross the clear-running creek just before the path you're on dead-ends at the junction with the Union Creek Trail in a clearing marked by a dead tree.

A left turn here (northwest) leads downstream to many good campsites along uncrowded Union Creek (Hike 30), while a right turn (southeast) takes you up and over the divide to Parker Creek and eventually back to Swift Creek.

Fill up on water before heading uphill (it's a steep haul to the saddle). Enjoy pleasant going as you ascend moderately through the lush headwaters of Union Creek. Long, moderate switchbacks take you the rest of the way up to the saddle through sparse tree cover and open slopes. The top of the Union/Parker divide is just under a mile from the junction in the meadow below. There's not much on the nearly 7,000-foot saddle to impede your view down the two pristine drainages.

A signed trail junction on the saddle indicates the Thumb Rock–Poison Canyon Trail heading east along the ridgeline (accessing Lilypad and Shimmy Lakes). The Parker Creek Trail, the route back down to Swift Creek, plunges southeast down the Parker Creek Canyon. This is one of the least-traveled trails in the region, and if you appreciate backcountry solitude you should particularly enjoy the hike along Parker Creek. The upper canyon is distinguished by sloping, wide-open meadows and intermittent stands of fir and pine, while the lower canyon becomes more forested and rocky. In late summer you walk through fields of knee-high grass that all but hide the little-used trail. The path crosses the headwaters of Parker Creek from east to west after passing the last big meadow, then descends the rest of the way on the creek's west bank. Stay right (south) at the junction with the Deer Flat Trail (it crosses Parker Creek and heads east). Rocky tread on a steep bank above the creek leads the rest of the way down to the junction with the Swift Creek Trail (2.5 miles from the saddle). The path levels out next to the campsite at the three-way junction on Swift Creek. Turn left (southeast) on the Swift Creek Trail and retrace your steps 3.5 easy miles to the trailhead.

Options: You can make forays into the Swift Creek, Sunrise Creek, Union Creek, and Poison Canyon drainages while on the Landers Lake Loop. The best bet is to spend a night in Mumford Meadow or along Union Creek, then day hike to one of the nearby lakes.

---

23 Poison Canyon

Highlights:	A beautiful, secluded hike through one of the Trinity Alps' hidden corners; no big lakes, just big solitude.
Type of hike:	Day hike or backpack; semi-loop.
Total distance:	11.2 miles.
Difficulty:	Moderate.
Elevation gain:	4,000 feet.
Maps:	USGS Ycatapom Peak quad; USDAFS Trinity Alps Wilderness map.

Poison Canyon

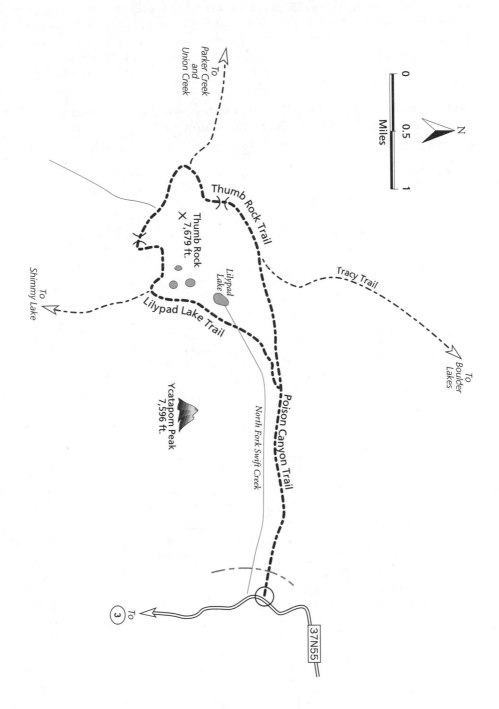

To Parker Creek and Union Creek

Thumb Rock Trail

Thumb Rock
✕ 7,679 ft.

Lilypad Lake

Tracy Trail

To Shimmy Lake

Lilypad Lake Trail

Ycatapom Peak
7,596 ft.

North Fork Swift Creek

Poison Canyon Trail

To Boulder Lakes

0   0.5   1
Miles

N

To 3

37N55

Finding the trailhead: From Weaverville, drive 30 miles north on California Highway 3, past Trinity Center, to the signed Swift Creek Trailhead turnoff on Forest Road 36N25 (just after crossing the Swift Creek bridge, and just prior to Wyntoon Resort). Turn left (west) and proceed 1.4 miles to the signed right turn (north) for the Poison Canyon–Lake Eleanor trails. Immediately take the next right (signed Poison Canyon) on Forest Road 37N55, which heads west and then north as it climbs 8 miles to the trailhead. Stay right at an unmarked junction at 5.1 miles.

Parking and trailhead facilities: Ample roadside parking, but no water or other facilities; closest Forest Service campground is at Preacher Meadow, 2 miles south of Trinity Center on CA 3.

Key points:
- 0.0   Trailhead.
- 2.7   Lilypad Lake Trail junction.
- 3.5   Tracy Trail junction.
- 4.7   Thumb Rock Trail junction.
- 6.5   Lilypad Lake Trail junction.
- 7.7   Lilypad Lake.
- 8.5   Poison Canyon Trail junction.
- 11.2 Trailhead.

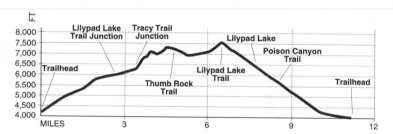

Profile data provided by TOPO! ©1999 Wildflower Productions (www.topo.com)

The hike: Maybe it's the ominous sounding name, or maybe it's the fact that the only lake here is covered with lilypads by midsummer, but for some reason Poison Canyon gets very few visitors. Though it's just one ridge away from Boulder Lake, one of the most popular day hiking destinations in the Trinity Alps, Poison Canyon exists in its own quiet solitude. As they say, one person's loss is another's gain. Hikers who find their way into this beautiful canyon will be happy indeed.

Poison Canyon is one of those hidden backcountry corners where wilderness with a capital W still reigns. Unlike most such places, however, you don't need to work all that hard to get here. The canyon is just 3 miles from the trailhead. But without a deep lake to draw water and trout lovers, Poison Canyon remains off the radar of most Trinity Alps visitors. What it does have is excellent solitude, beautiful hanging meadows and flower gardens, perfect views of Mount Shasta, and a chance to scramble up 7,596-foot Ycatapom Peak.

From the trailhead, the Poison Canyon Trail (8W10) follows the North Fork Swift Creek in a westerly direction, with the first mile zigging and zagging steeply uphill. The route is mostly shaded by fir and pine and the trail passes a profusion of berry bushes (most not edible) on the way to higher elevations. With the cascading North Fork and a number of sparkling tributaries feeding the canyon's lush undergrowth, it feels like you're walking through an enchanted forest at times (though if it was truly a fairyland it wouldn't be steep, would it?).

A 2.7-mile ascent brings you to the junction with the Lilypad Lake Trail (8W21) in a flat on the north side of the North Fork. Look for ducks or a sign on a tree at the trail junction, as the path itself is often overgrown. Go left (southwest) to reach Lilypad Lake. The Poison Canyon Trail continues straight (west), climbing along the canyon's north wall. From here you can make a 5.8-mile loop around Thumb Rock. If you're day hiking, I recommend staying right and making the loop in a counter-clockwise direction. If you're backpacking, you may want to hike a mile into the Lilypad Lake drainage to set up camp, then make your loop from there.

A mile up the Poison Canyon Trail, pass the junction with the Tracy Trail (8W26) on an open bench. The Tracy Trail leads north over the ridge to Boulder Lakes (Hike 25), less than 2 miles away. Continue west past the junction, climbing higher above Poison Canyon and gaining ever more spectacular views across the drainage—views of Mount Shasta to the east, Ycatapom Peak to the southeast, and Thumb Rock directly south. After gaining the ridgeline, the trail winds around the back side of Thumb Rock, skirting the head of the canyon above Cub Wallow (if you ever want to disappear from the world, head down there), then descends slightly to the junction with the Thumb Rock Trail (8W16). The unsigned junction, on an exposed, rocky ridge on the west side of Thumb Rock, is easy to miss. Look for the trail soon after you round the base of Thumb Rock and start descending the spine of the ridge; turn left (southeast).

The Thumb Rock Trail doubles back to the southeast, leading down into wild, overgrown Sandy Canyon, then up to the forested ridgeline on the south side of Thumb Rock. Dip down to a junction with the Lilypad Lake Trail and go left (north) to head back into Poison Canyon and descend to Lilypad Lake. A right (south) turn here leads downhill to Deer Flat and Shimmy Lake (slightly over a mile away; see Hike 24).

The descent from ridgeline to canyon bottom on the Lilypad Lake Trail is one of the most beautiful hikes in the Trinity Alps. The path leads down across hanging terraces of emerald green grass, sparkling snowmelt tarns, clear running streams, and view upon vista upon overlook. Amazingly, you could probably spend a week here in the middle of summer and not see a soul. Experienced mountaineers planning to climb Ycatapom Peak (the name is generally attributed to the Wintu word which means "mountain that leans") should start their climb before getting too comfortable on one of these idyllic terraces.

Due to lack of use, the route down to Lilypad Lake is not obvious. Cairns are sometimes visible, but you may have to use some common sense to pick your way down and across the rocky ledges between you and the lake.

Lilypad Lake along Poison Canyon Loop.

From the junction with the Thumb Rock Trail, the Lilypad Lake Trail descends north into the upper reaches of Poison Canyon. The path soon crosses a hanging meadow that holds two shallow, unnamed ponds surrounded by lush fields of grasses, corn lilies, and asters. The trail zigzags from west to east across the meadow, then descends steeply along the east side of the ponds' outlet stream. The short but steep descent brings you to another, smaller bench hanging above the canyon. Cross the rocky shelf and look for good views of Mount Shasta in the east and Lilypad Lake at your feet. Follow the last set of switchbacks down to the lake, 1.2 miles from the last trail junction.

From the lilypad-covered lake, the last mile of trail meanders through a parklike setting of mixed conifers and grassy glades. The mostly level path is easy to follow as it heads northeast to the junction with the Poison Canyon Trail. From here retrace your steps 2.7 miles to the trailhead.

Options: Nearby destinations include Boulder Lakes and Shimmy Lake. You can make a longer foray into the Union Creek drainage by following the Poison Canyon Trail down to the Parker Creek–Union Creek divide. You can add a 20-mile loop to this hike by linking the Union Creek, Foster Lake, Boulder Creek, and Boulder Lake Trails (see Hike 27, which describes most of the route in reverse).

24 Eleanor and Shimmy Lakes

Highlights:	A short hike to small and scenic Shimmy Lake, with lilypad-covered Lake Eleanor thrown in for good measure.
Type of hike:	Day hike or backpack; out-and-back.
Total distance:	7.2 miles.
Difficulty:	Easy.
Elevation gain:	1,550 feet.
Maps:	USGS Covington Mill and Ycatapom Peak quads; USDAFS Trinity Alps Wilderness map.

Finding the trailhead: From Weaverville, drive 30 miles north on California Highway 3, past Trinity Center, to the signed Swift Creek Trail turnoff on Forest Road 36N25 (just after crossing the Swift Creek bridge, and just prior to Wyntoon Resort). Turn left (west) and proceed 1.4 miles to the signed turn (north) for the Lake Eleanor–Poison Canyon Trails. Continue on Forest Road 36N24, following the main route (stay straight at 1.9 miles, left at 3.4 miles, right at 4.6 miles, left at 6.3 miles, and right at 7.6 miles). The trailhead is 7.8 miles from the highway.

Parking and trailhead facilities: Parking for a few cars; however, more parking is available a few hundred yards farther up the road (if the Forest

Eleanor and Shimmy Lakes

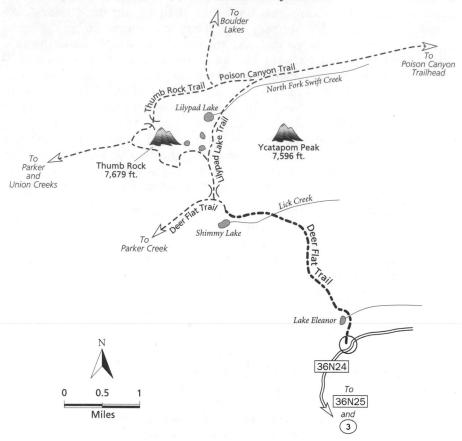

Service gate is open), and in pullouts along the road. No facilities. The closest developed campground is at Preacher Meadow (CA 3 near Trinity Center).

Key points:
0.0	Trailhead.
0.3	Lake Eleanor.
3.1	Lick Creek crossing.
3.6	Shimmy Lake.

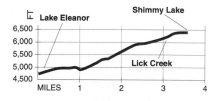

Profile data provided by TOPO!
©1999 Wildflower Productions (www.topo.com)

The hike: The route to Shimmy Lake rises moderately through mixed conifers and open slopes of ceanothus bushes, with sweeping views east over Trinity Lake. The trail skirts marshy, lilypad-covered Lake Eleanor almost immediately (a good destination for families with small children), then climbs to little Shimmy Lake, a lightly used pond at the base of a rocky ridge.

From the trailhead, the path (8W13) jogs west then heads north through incense-cedars, ponderosa pine, and other conifers. In a few minutes you

Shimmy Lake in late fall with new snow.

cross the access road FR 36N24 (it's possible to drive this far if the gate is open, but it saves very little walking). The trail continues north on the other side of the road, climbing gently through rocky, sparsely forested terrain to a slight rise, then dropping to the shore of Lake Eleanor (0.3 mile from the trailhead). The shallow lake is in a forested basin, with a wet meadow sprinkled with insectivorous pitcher plants near the inlet and grassy margins along most of the shoreline. The lake supports a lush supply of lilypads, but pay a visit to nearby Lilypad Lake (Poison Canyon, Hike 23) if that's what you're after.

Lake Eleanor is visited mostly by day users and anglers looking for a short hike. The lake's low elevation (4,950 feet) and easy access make it a good destination in early and late season.

To continue to Shimmy Lake, follow the trail around the east side of Lake Eleanor, then head north/northwest away from the lake. The next 3 miles are a straightforward, moderate ascent through mixed forest (white fir, pine, and incense-cedar), with some sunny, open sections that command good views of Trinity Lake. The trail is marked with red ribbons and/or cairns where it crosses old logging roads in the first mile after Lake Eleanor.

The trail follows a northwest route through gentle terrain, passing a tiny pond, then crosses Lick Creek 3.1 miles from the trailhead. A pleasant meadow slopes uphill from the easy creek crossing. The trail plunges back into the forest again, then climbs the final short ascent to the eastern edge of Shimmy Lake. The little lake (1.5 acres, 10 feet deep) sits in a grassy bowl at the base of a jagged rock outcropping. Shimmy's small size and relative lack of notoriety make it a good place to find solitude without going on a long hike.

Options: From Shimmy Lake, you can easily access Poison Canyon (Hike 23) and Parker Creek (Hike 22, Landers Lake Loop), with extended journeys possible.

25 Boulder Lakes

Highlights:	This short hike delivers maximum scenery for minimum effort, making it one of the Alps' busiest trails; great route for families with young children and other hikers who want an easy outing.
Type of hike:	Day hike or backpack; out-and-back.
Total distance:	3.8 miles.
Difficulty:	Easy.
Elevation gain:	800 feet.
Maps:	USGS Ycatapom Peak quad; USDAFS Trinity Alps Wilderness map.

Finding the trailhead: The road to Boulder Lake Trailhead is located 0.3 mile south of Coffee Creek. From Weaverville, drive 40 miles north on California Highway 3 and turn left (west) at the signed junction for Boulder Lakes Trailhead. Proceed 11 miles up the well-signed dirt road to the trailhead. (Follow Forest Road 37N52 for 3.5 miles to a right turn on Forest Road 37N53, stay left at 4.7 and 9.7 miles, and continue to the trailhead.) Ignore the logging roads that diverge from the main track.

Parking and trailhead facilities: Ample parking at the dead-end trailhead. No facilities, but several Forest Service campgrounds are located on nearby CA 3.

Key points:
  0.0   Trailhead.
  1.4   Little Boulder Lake Trail Junction.
  1.9   Boulder Lake.
  1.9   Little Boulder Lake.

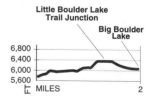

Profile data provided by TOPO!
©1999 Wildflower Productions
(www.topo.com)

The hike: Depending on your point of view, Boulder Lake is either one of the best or one of the worst destinations in the Trinity Alps. If you like maximum scenery for minimum effort, this is your spot. If, on the other hand, you cherish solitude more than an easy stroll, keep on walking. (Past Boulder Lake you find small and uncrowded Found and Tapie lakes, and farther still the lonely meadows of Poison Canyon. See Hike 26 for Tapie, Found, and Lost Lakes, Hike 23 for Poison Canyon.)

Boulder didn't always draw such large numbers. The original route to the lake started on Coffee Creek Road and climbed 7 quad-burning miles up Boulder Creek and over the ridge to Boulder Lake. But that was years ago.

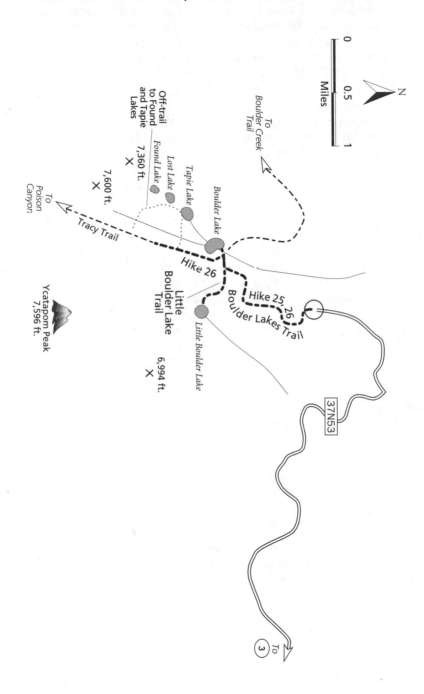

N

0   0.5   1

Miles

To
Boulder Creek
Trail

Off-trail
to Found
and Tapie
Lakes

Found Lake
Lost Lake
7,360 ft.
X

7,600 ft.
X

Tapie Lake

Boulder Lake

To
Poison
Canyon

Tracy Trail

Hike 26

Little
Boulder Lake
Trail

Hike 25, 26
Boulder Lakes Trail

Little Boulder Lake

Ycatapom Peak
7,596 ft.

6,994 ft.
X

37N53

To
3

Now it's an easy 1.9-mile hop, skip, and jump from the new Boulder Lakes Trailhead. The new trail really isn't new anymore, but it has caught some Trinity old-timers off guard. It wasn't long ago that a couple of hikers I know (okay, my parents) unwittingly slogged up the Boulder Creek Trail thinking it was the only way in. They didn't see any other cars at the trailhead or other people on the trail, so they became rather smug with the knowledge they'd have Boulder Lake all to themselves. Imagine their surprise when they found the lake crowded with families with little kids, big ice chests, and loud dogs.

But like most places that attract a crowd, Boulder Lake has its charms: an easy hike in (go ahead and bring those steaks), lilypad-lined shores, good fishing, shady campsites, granite cliffs, and numerous opportunities for day hikes. On the downside, early-season mosquitoes far outnumber the people, and the crowds on summer weekends can be thick as bugs.

The disclaimer about crowds aside, I must admit I've spent a delightful summer night at Boulder Lake with no company at all, awoke to a peaceful morning mist blanketing the basin, and never would have guessed I was a mere 45 minutes from the trailhead.

The trailhead itself is a parking lot-size clearing at an elevation of nearly 6,000 feet, which means you only have to climb about 600 feet over a ridge and down the other side to reach the lake's 6,070-foot level.

The trail starts on a wide track heading south up the ridgeline. Fir and sugar pine are scattered to either side, but the first quarter mile is mostly open and exposed. While the ridgeline is still open, look backward for your first of many Mount Shasta views on this hike.

After a small, level landing, the wide track gives way to trail and you start climbing more steeply through forest cover (mostly fir). The walking is pleasant and shady on soft duff. Continue the gradual ascent to an obvious switchback, then climb northwest to the crest of the ridge, just over a mile from the trailhead.

After gaining the crest, the trail continues south at a nearly level grade. Good views of the drainages ahead and to the west open up. Arrive at the signed junction to Little Boulder Lake a few minutes after hiking along the ridgecrest. A left (southeast) turn here leads to Little Boulder Lake; stay right (south) for Boulder Lake.

Boulder Lake: Start descending into Boulder Lake basin on moderate switchbacks. Before dropping into the firs, get a glimpse of the upper reaches of the basin, where Found and Tapie lakes are tucked away out of sight. The trail is rocky but well worn.

Don't worry if it feels like you're walking past the lake. The trail traverses nearly all the way across the basin before spitting you out on the north side of the lake, just before the outlet (1.9 miles from the trailhead). Arrive at a three-way trail junction next to a large campsite. The junction is signed: Boulder Lake Trail; Poison Canyon–Tracy Trail; and the Foster–Lion Lake Trail. A right turn (north) here leads across the outlet stream and eventually to the Boulder Creek Trail and options of going up to Foster and Lion lakes or down to Coffee Creek Road. A left turn (south) leads around Boulder Lake and climbs up and over the ridge to Poison Canyon. The Tracy Trail is also the way to start a cross-country hike to Found and Tapie Lakes (Hike 26).

Boulder Lake is a medium-size lake (8 acres) at an elevation of 6,070 feet. One of the reasons the lake is so popular (besides the easy hike in) is the pleasing mixture of terrain: forest, meadow, water, lilypad, and granite seem to be in perfect harmony. Forest cover (mostly fir with a smattering of lodgepole pines) dominates the shoreline, but there's also a lush wet meadow on the south side at the inlet. A picturesque ring of lilypads hugs much of the water's edge, and a jumble of craggy granite hangs over the upper basin (saving the scene from an overdose of gentleness). The water is tinged slightly green with algae, but not enough to put a damper on swimming. Using the Tracy Trail and an obvious use path on the west shore, it's possible to circumnavigate the entire lake.

Boulder Lake is an ideal basecamp for staging hikes into the surrounding areas, a fine place to stop for the night on your way coming or going on either the Poison Canyon or Foster–Lion Lakes trails, or a good destination for families with young children (big ice chests not required).

Side trip to Little Boulder Lake: Though only 0.5 mile (as the bird flies) and a few hundred feet in elevation separate Boulder and Little Boulder lakes, the neighbors are surprisingly different in nature. Little Boulder is gouged into the flank of Peak 6994, with not much room for more than the lake itself and a few campsites.

A steep granite slope plunges into the Little Boulder Lake's south shore. Except for the forested shelf where a few campsites are tucked away in the trees, the north shore falls away steeply as well, so there are fewer opportunities for exploring than at Boulder Lake. Still the pretty little lake makes a fine destination as either a day hike or overnight (though beware—there's less room for crowds on busy weekends). Early-season azaleas decorate the perimeter of the north shore.

To reach Little Boulder from the junction, take the left fork and head southeast uphill along the crest of the ridge between the two lakes. Climb gradually in fir and manzanita for a quarter mile, then start an easy descent (east) toward the lake. The trail emerges from tree cover onto a rocky, exposed slope before arriving at the southwest corner of the basin, still high above the lake. Look for great views of Mount Shasta as you descend rocky tread along the west side of the lake. The path bends right (east) at the bottom of the basin and traverses the shelf along the north shore. The elevation is 6,350 feet. All water should be purified.

Options: Explore the upper reaches of the Boulder Lakes drainage, where you can hike to Tapie and Found lakes via a moderate cross-country route (Hike 26). Or use the Tracy Trail to reach nearby Poison Canyon (Hike 23), a secluded drainage with good opportunities for solitude.

26 Tapie, Found, and Lost Lakes

See Map on Page 131

Highlights: A cross-country trek to three pretty little lakes in the rugged basin above Boulder Lake; some minor scrambling over granite and talus slopes.

Type of hike: Day hike or backpack (1–2 nights); out-and-back.

Total distance: 6.6 miles.

Difficulty: Strenuous (off-trail scrambling, route-finding skills required).

Elevation gain: 1,600 feet.

Maps: USGS Ycatapom Peak quad; USDAFS Trinity Alps Wilderness map.

Finding the trailhead: The road to Boulder Lakes Trailhead is located a third of a mile south of Coffee Creek. From Weaverville, drive 40 miles north on California Highway 3 and turn left (west) at the signed junction for Boulder Lakes Trailhead. Proceed 11 miles up the well-signed dirt road to the trailhead. (Follow Forest Road 37N52 for 3.5 miles to a right turn on Forest Road 37N53, stay left at 4.7 and 9.7 miles, and continue to the trailhead.) Ignore the logging roads which diverge from the main track.

Parking and trailhead facilities: Ample parking but no facilities at the dead-end trailhead. The closest developed campground is Trinity River on CA 3.

Key points:

0.0	Trailhead.
1.4	Little Boulder Lake Trail Junction.
1.9	Boulder Lake.
1.9	Tracy Trail.
2.8	Tapie Lake.
3.3	Found Lake.

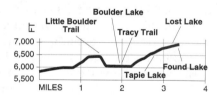

Profile data provided by TOPO!
©1999 Wildflower Productions(www.topo.com)

The hike: Though just an hour's hike above popular Boulder Lake, Tapie, Lost, and Found Lakes get hardly any traffic. Reaching the tiny lakes requires a cross-country scramble that deters most visitors, leaving the lakes in relative obscurity next to one of the Alps' most-traveled trails.

The three little bodies of water tucked into the rugged upper basin challenge the notion of what, exactly, constitutes a lake in the Trinity Alps. Obviously, mapmakers can't agree. My preferred definition of a lake is anything I can skip a rock across. By my standards then, the little beauties above Boulder qualify as lakes.

There are several options for reaching these lakes. One way is to scramble up the granite above the southwest corner of Boulder Lake. Though possible, it's not the recommended route. A better way is to hike up the Tracy Trail along Boulder's inlet, then contour northwest to the lakes after ascending

134

above the brushy slopes and gullies that present a formidable barrier around the headwall of the upper basin.

Start at the three-way trail junction on Boulder Lake's north shore (see Hike 25 for description of the hike from the trailhead to this point). Head south on the Tracy Trail (toward Poison Canyon) along the lake's east shore, then start climbing as the path parallels the inlet. The trail ascends through intermittent stands of fir and lodgepole pine, and crosses several small but scenic meadows. These isolated flower gardens are spectacular in July and August.

On the way up you pass an obscure use trail that leads up a gully to the west. Be patient and stay on the Tracy Trail as it switchbacks steeply up toward the ridgeline. Save the bushwhacking for the descent, if you want to try that route.

The path crosses the sparkling inlet creek several times on the way up. The refreshing stream runs even in late summer (and should be purified before drinking, no matter how pristine it looks). Near the headwaters of the stream, a couple of hundred feet below the Poison–Boulder divide, the trail bends east and climbs the last few steep switchbacks to the ridgeline. Jump off the trail here and pick your way west across the creek; the easiest crossing is near the bottom of a small meadow. (This point is just over 0.5 mile from Boulder Lake.)

After leaving the trail, contour northwest around Tapie Peak and work your way over to the upper basin. You should end up below Lost Lake and above Tapie. If you want a good look at the route before setting off, climb up to the divide and look back toward Boulder Lake. A slice of Tapie Lake is visible beyond a shoulder of granite and gives you a good view of the route across sunny, treeless slopes of granite and talus. (The climb to the ridgeline is only a few minutes' extra hiking and, as a bonus, you get yet another great view of Mount Shasta.)

From the west side of the inlet creek, pick your way through the bushes and out onto the open slopes. A few ducks are scattered here and there, but the route is fairly straightforward: stay as high as you can (a sheer cliff band prevents you from going too high, and steep brushy slopes await below) and make your way northwest across the granite and talus. The rock hopping is fun, but watch your footing—the sharp-edged granite can cut like a knife.

Once you make it around to the middle of the drainage on the northwest side of Tapie Peak, you have the option of going up a quarter mile to Lost or down the same distance to Tapie. Found Lake lies 100 yards beyond Lost.

Found Lake is hidden in the uppermost reaches of the basin. It's nearly invisible until you're practically swimming in it. It's a small, charming lake with a spectacular backdrop of granite and truly wild country. The shoreline is rocky, with just a few stunted trees and grass fringes.

A short walk up the ridge northwest of Found Lake leads to a ridgetop with a magnificent view. It commands an unbroken vista of upper Boulder Canyon and Cub Wallow. If you want a private slice of paradise in the Trinity Alps without going on a long trek, it's hard to find a better place than Found Lake.

To reach Tapie Lake, head back downhill (northeast) and skirt the edge of Lost Lake, which dries up to a puddle in late summer (all three lakes in the

Found Lake (upper lake).

basin are fed by snowmelt only, so they tend to shrink over the course of the summer).

Continue down the slope above Tapie by staying left (northwest) of the main gully below Lost. Zigzag down a series of granite benches to reach the south end of the narrow 2-acre lake. Thick stands of pine and fir crowd the west shore of Tapie, and a rocky bluff hems in the east side, enfolding the quiet little lake in an isolated cleft.

Options: Options for the return trip include going back the way you came; following a rough route down Tapie's outlet to Boulder Lake (steep); and picking your way down the gully southeast of the lake (also steep, but rock ducks show most people prefer this route). The outlet route deposits you on Boulder's west shore, while the gully route returns you to the Tracy Trail.

Another good side trip from here includes Poison Canyon, which lies just over the ridge to the south, along the Tracy Trail.

27 Foster Lake Loop

Highlights:	A charming lake worth the steep ascent.
Type of hike:	Backpack; loop.
Total distance:	22 miles.
Difficulty:	Strenuous.
Elevation gain:	5,600 feet.
Maps:	USGS Ycatapom Peak quad; USDAFS Trinity Alps Wilderness map.

Finding the trailhead: The road to Boulder Lakes Trailhead is located 0.3 mile south of Coffee Creek. From Weaverville, drive 40 miles north on California Highway 3 and turn left (west) at the signed junction for Boulder Lakes Trailhead. Proceed 11 miles up the well-signed dirt road to the trailhead. (Follow Forest Road 37N52 for 3.5 miles to a right turn on Forest Road 37N53, stay left at 4.7 and 9.7 miles, and continue to the trailhead.) Ignore the logging roads which diverge from the main track.

Parking and trailhead facilities: Ample parking but no facilities at the dead-end trailhead. The closest campground is Trinity River on CA 3.

Key points:

0.0	Trailhead.
1.9	Boulder Lake.
2.0	Cross Boulder Lake outlet.
4.4	Boulder Creek crossing.
4.6	Lion Lake Trail junction.
6.5	Conway Lake Trail and Lion Lakes Trail junction.
8.0	Foster Lake.
9.5	Union Creek crossing.
12.0	Poison Canyon Trail.
13.8	Thumb Rock Trail.
15.7	Lilypad Lake Trail.
16.8	Lilypad Lake.
17.7	Poison Canyon Trail.
18.7	Tracy Trail.
20.1	Boulder Lake.
22.0	Trailhead.

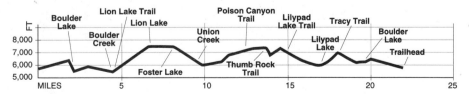

Profile data provided by TOPO! ©1999 Wildflower Productions(www.topo.com)

Foster Lake Loop

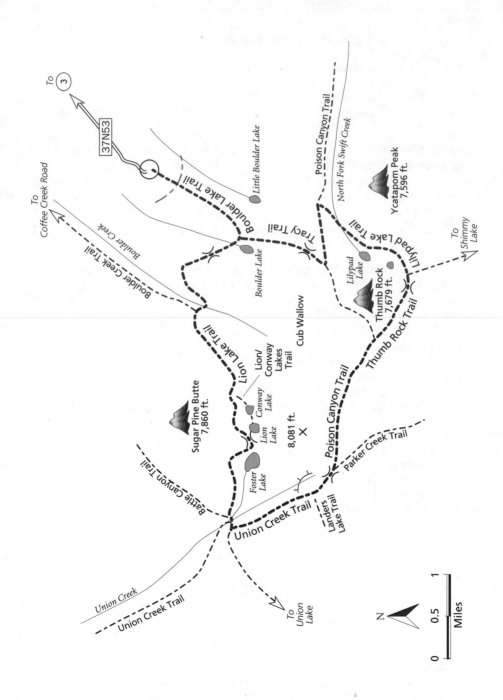

The hike: This loop combines spectacular scenery (Foster Lake) with spectacular solitude (Poison Canyon). It's an up and down journey, with three deep canyons en route, but there's ample compensation for your effort. If you only want to go to Foster Lake, just retrace your steps instead of completing the loop, or consider one of the other routes mentioned below.

The two alternate ways to approach Foster Lake are both good options, but the route from Boulder Lake offers the most variety and the best loop. The alternative trailheads are Boulder Creek (Hike 28) and Union Creek (Hike 30). On the plus side, using one of these trailheads means you won't have to wade through the summertime crowds at Boulder Lake. All three routes require about the same distance and difficulty to reach Foster Lake.

The first part of this route is on the easy 1.9-mile trail to Boulder Lake (see Hike 25). Follow the path to the signed three-way junction near the outlet at Boulder Lake. Boulder or Little Boulder make nice stopovers if you need an extra night coming or going (though keep in mind that both lakes are sure to be crowded on summer weekends).

The junction at the north end of Boulder Lake is signed "8W20 Coffee Creek Road" to the north (this is the trail to Foster and Lion Lakes) and "8W26 Poison Canyon–Lilypad Lake" to the south. The route to Foster Lake is north, but if you're contemplating the loop via Thumb Rock, then you return on the other trail.

Head north and descend slightly to cross the outlet of Boulder Lake. Fill up here if you need water; the next available water is just over 2 miles away in Boulder Creek. Purify water here and at all other sources on the hike.

After crossing the outlet, the trail descends gradually to round the shoulder of the ridge between you and the Boulder Creek drainage. The descent is shady under a canopy of mixed fir and pine. This pleasant new trail (built in 1995) is not shown on the 1986 USGS quadrangle, which instead displays an older path that dipped down to an out-of-use jeep road before climbing steeply to the ridgeline. Look for a good view of Mount Shasta just before crossing the crest of the ridge.

The trail nearly doubles back on itself after crossing the ridgeline. Head southwest now on a long but gradual descent to Boulder Creek. Mixed conifers shade the path all the way down to the bottom of the canyon—a drop of nearly 1,000 feet. Before rushing down, take a moment to admire the efforts of the crew that built this section of trail. The traverse strikes the perfect grade: gentle on your knees and gentle on the soil.

At the bottom of the drainage, cross a small meadow splashed with summer wildflowers; look for the bright purple of monkshood in the lush little glen. Arrive at Boulder Creek after crossing the little meadow. Alders and willows line the banks in most places, but the sparkling clear stream is generally easy to cross (except very early in the year) and plenty of large, smooth boulders are strewn about if you want to put your feet up. The creek crossing is slightly more than halfway to Foster Lake—and much of the remainder is uphill—so it's a logical place to take a break. In any case, be sure to replenish water supplies before heading off. The rest of the way is steep and hot on a summer afternoon (a few small tributaries do cross the trail, but keep water bottles topped off to be prudent).

The main trail proceeds downstream (southeast) less than a quarter mile to the junction with the Lion Lake Trail. The junction is marked by ducks and a sign on a fir tree. The Boulder Creek Trail (8W08) continues northeast (downstream) to Goldfield Campground and Coffee Creek Road, and the Lion Lake Trail (8W12) turns sharply uphill (west) and climbs out of the drainage on a rocky path.

The first leg out of the drainage is as steep as any trail in the Trinity Alps. It's the exact opposite of the trail you just descended—so if you didn't appreciate the gentle grade on the way down, you will now. Climb through mixed fir, pine, and incense-cedar, occasionally crossing small meadows filled with a variety of summer flowers. The trail alternates steep pitches with more moderate grades as it ascends a series of benches on the canyon wall, heading southwest toward the pass between Lion and Foster lakes. As you gain elevation, look for good views up the Boulder Creek drainage. The headwaters of the creek are in a trailless, seldom-visited wilderness called Cub Wallow. If you plan on returning via Thumb Rock, your path traverses the divide just south of Cub Wallow, above Parker Creek.

Side trip to Conway and Lion Lakes: Almost 2.5 miles from the Boulder Creek crossing, arrive at the junction with the Lion–Conway Lakes trail. A left turn at this fork brings you first to Conway Lake (a pretty, but small, lilypad-choked puddle). Conway is surrounded by lush, wet meadows on a shelf high above Boulder Creek.

To reach Lion, merely follow Conway Lake's inlet creek uphill to its source. The water tumbling down the granite slope west of Conway leads directly to spectacular and deep Lion Lake (elevation 7,000 feet). Scramble up the south side of the creek for the easiest path to the lake. The 3-acre lake sits in a glacier-gouged basin behind a granite dike. The water is clear, blue, and incredibly refreshing on a summer afternoon. A sheer granite wall rises on Lion's north shore, where a rockslide has deposited a pile of debris that reaches nearly to the water's surface. The other sides of the lake aren't much less steep—creating a dramatic setting. A few stunted firs grow on the lake's west side. The contrast between sheer-sided Lion and meadow-lined Conway makes the two-lake basin a nice place to spend a day or two exploring.

Foster Lake: To continue on the main trail to Foster Lake, take the right fork at the junction with the Lion–Conway Lake trail and keep climbing. The path zigzags up the canyon wall to a rocky, exposed shelf above Lion Lake. The route traverses the steep hillside directly above the lake, offering great views of Lion's brilliant blue water (and a few narrow sections where it's wise to watch your step). The trail reaches the divide between Lion and Foster in 0.5 mile, on a rocky pass with a good vantage point down both drainages and a perfect view of Mount Shasta.

From the saddle above Foster Lake, you can look down and see the 5.5-acre body of water filling an oblong basin carved into steep granite slopes. The north-facing lake stays fairly cold through the summer, with snow often remaining on the south side of the cirque in August. The trail descends through boulders on the lake's northeast side, then switchbacks down to cross the outlet. The west shore has plenty of room to spread out, shady firs and mountain hemlocks, and a couple of lilypad-lined ponds.

A rounded, rocky bluff west of the lake commands an awesome view of the western horizon and, far below, the Union Creek drainage. Get an early seat here for one of the best sunset shows in the Alps. Golden light fills the basin behind you as the sun sinks into a sea of mountains on the horizon. You also get a good look at the endless switchbacks leading down to Union Creek—a good sight to ponder before leaving your high perch for the valley below. Foster's elevation is 7,245 feet.

To continue on the loop, descend those formidable switchbacks to Union Creek, 1.5 miles and nearly 1,500 feet below (pass the trail to Sugar Pine Lake just before reaching the bottom of the drainage). Cross Union Creek and turn left (southeast) at the trail junction 100 yards up the slope on the other side, at the lower end of a wide meadow. Follow the Union Creek Trail (9W07) southeast, toward the Parker–Union Creek divide.

A pleasant 2.5-mile climb leads through the upper end of the canyon (passing the spur trail to Landers Lake) and then brings you, more steeply on the final push, to the saddle between Union and Parker Creeks. Be sure to replenish water before leaving Union Creek. From the divide, turn left (east) on the signed trail to Thumb Rock–Poison Canyon (if you continue along Parker Creek you'll descend to Swift Creek). From here you're on a trail that sees very few boot prints. Enjoy great views of Swift Creek drainage and Cub Wallow as you climb the ridgeline toward Thumb Rock. Just before reaching the base of Thumb Rock, bear right on the Thumb Rock Trail (8W16) at an unsigned junction in an open, rocky area on the ridgeline. The trail descends southeast toward Shimmy Lake and the Lilypad Lake Trail. The left fork contours around Thumb Rock to the east and then north, before descending into the head of Poison Canyon and arriving at the Tracy Trail, which leads back to Boulder Lake (take the left fork if you're in a hurry; otherwise stay on the recommended route).

For a detailed description of this portion of the loop, see Hike 23. The short version is this: Take the Lilypad Lake Trail (8W21) at mile 15.7 and descend north, across a series of gorgeous hanging meadows with great views of Ycatapom Peak and Mount Shasta. Skirt Lilypad Lake and continue northeast to the Poison Canyon Trail, then turn left (west) and ascend 1.0 mile to the Tracy Trail (8W26). Turn right (north) on the Tracy Trail and proceed over the ridge to the Boulder Lake basin. From here it's an easy mile-long descent to the three-way junction at Boulder Lake where you started the loop. Retrace your steps 1.9 miles to the trailhead.

Options: From Union Creek, take side trips to Union Lake or Landers Lake (Hikes 30 and 22), or tackle the steep climb up Battle Canyon Trail and visit Sugar Pine Lake (Hike 29). The Foster Lake Loop passes numerous trail junctions, allowing you to create custom side trips that suit your needs.

28 Boulder Creek

Highlights:	Moderately used trail that connects with trails to Foster and Lion Lakes and Boulder Lakes. Can be used to create a longer loop using the Sugar Pine Lake Trail.
Type of hike:	Day hike or backpack; out-and-back.
Total distance:	8.6 miles.
Difficulty:	Moderate.
Elevation gain:	2,150 feet.
Maps:	USGS Ycatapom Peak quad; USDAFS Trinity Alps Wilderness map.

Finding the trailhead: From Weaverville, drive 40 miles north on California Highway 3 and turn left (west) on Coffee Creek Road. Proceed 5 miles up the paved road to the signed turnoff for Goldfield Campground/Boulder Creek Trailhead. Turn left and continue 0.5 mile on the dirt road to the trailhead (on the right, just before the road crosses Boulder Creek).

Parking and trailhead facilities: Limited parking at the trailhead (more is available at the creek crossing and back at Goldfield Campground). The campground has an outhouse but no potable water.

Key points:

  0.0   Trailhead.
  4.1   Junction with Foster/Lion lakes trail.
  4.3   Boulder Creek ford.

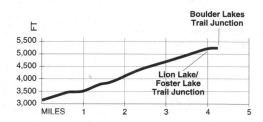

Profile data provided by TOPO!
©1999 Wildflower Productions(www.topo.com)

The hike: The Boulder Creek Trail ascends gradually along its namesake creek, climbing steadily but not steeply through oak, madrone, incense-cedar, and fir. The path can be used a number of ways: it makes for a pleasant day hike for campers staying at Goldfield Campground; it's a good place to start a trip to Foster or Lion Lakes (less crowded than starting at Boulder Lakes, but less scenic variety and it's all uphill on the way in); or use it and the Sugar Pine Lake Trail to create a spectacular 20-mile loop (requires a 3-mile walk on Coffee Creek Road; see Hike 29). Unless you're a glutton for punishment, don't use the Boulder Creek Trail to reach Boulder Lakes. It's more than twice as far as the route from the Boulder Lakes Trailhead (Hike 25), quite a bit steeper, and your reward is cooler-carrying crowds at Boulder Lake.

The first part of the route is on an old track blocked by a metal gate. Go around the gate and head uphill on the Boulder Creek Trail (8W08). The wide dirt track gives way to trail soon after the initial ascent and continues climbing southwest at a moderate grade. Forest on both sides of the trail consists mostly of young incense-cedars, oaks, fir, and madrone. The path ascends gradually up

Boulder Creek

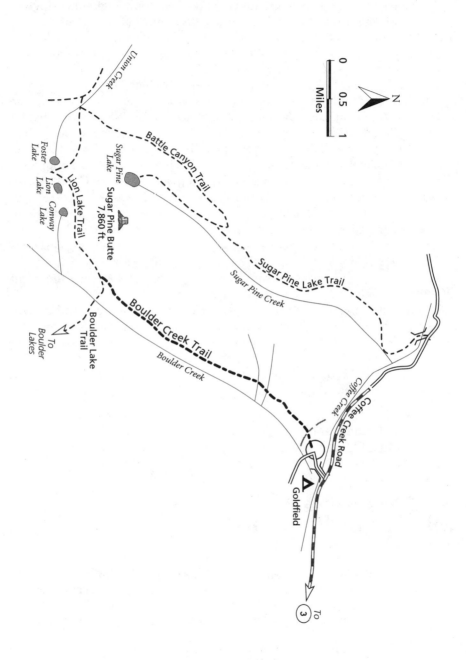

the side of Boulder Creek Canyon, without benefit of switchbacks, so the elevation gain has a way of sneaking up on you. Soon enough, you find yourself high on the canyon wall, the creek now tumbling quietly by far below.

Madrones give way to oak and fir as the trail contours higher and higher. Cross two strong tributaries of Boulder Creek in quick succession 1.5 miles from the trailhead. The water is clear, cold, and dependable, but should be purified. Water along the trail alleviates the need to fill water bottles at every tributary. Look for good views of Billys Peak behind you as the canyon opens up a short distance after the creek crossings.

The first (and only) switchback appears after 3 miles, but it's a false alarm. The trail continues its moderate ascent, dipping occasionally to run alongside Boulder Creek, through a couple of small but lush meadows. Just before the trail reaches Boulder Creek (less than a quarter mile) is the junction with the Lion Lake Trail. The signed junction is 4 miles from the trailhead. A wooden sign on a fir tree is marked 8W08 (back to Coffee Creek Road); 8W20 (to Boulder Lakes); and Foster–Lion Lakes. The trail to Foster and Lion (and little Conway) heads steeply uphill to the west. The trail to Boulder Lakes continues upstream for less than a quarter mile, than crosses the creek before climbing the opposite side of the canyon and heading east over the ridge. An obvious use trail at the creek crossing leads west a short distance to a small, pleasant campsite. Even if you're not spending the night here, it's a fine lunch stop coming or going.

If you're heading on up to Lion or Foster Lakes, take a break and replenish water supplies before tackling the steep route. From the junction with the Boulder Creek Trail, it's a long haul uphill (see Hike 27). If you want to make a loop using the Sugar Pine Trail, continue past Foster Lake to Union Creek, then use the Battle Canyon Trail to reach the Sugar Pine Lake Trail and Coffee Creek Road (this route is described in Hike 29 in reverse).

Options: Most people on this trail are heading for Lion or Foster Lakes, just over 7 miles from the trailhead. You could also make a long loop connecting the Union Creek, Poison Canyon, and Boulder Lakes Trails.

29 Sugar Pine Lake

Highlights:	A steep hike to an isolated granite cirque sheltering Sugar Pine Lake; optional loop with incredible views.
Type of hike:	Backpack; out-and-back with optional loop.
Total distance:	12.4 miles (Sugar Pine Lake only); 21.7 miles (optional loop).
Difficulty:	Moderate (to Sugar Pine Lake only); strenuous (optional loop).
Elevation gain:	3,400 feet (lake only); 6,500 feet (optional loop).
Maps:	USGS Ycatapom Peak and Caribou Lake quad; USDAFS Trinity Alps Wilderness map.

Sugar Pine Lake

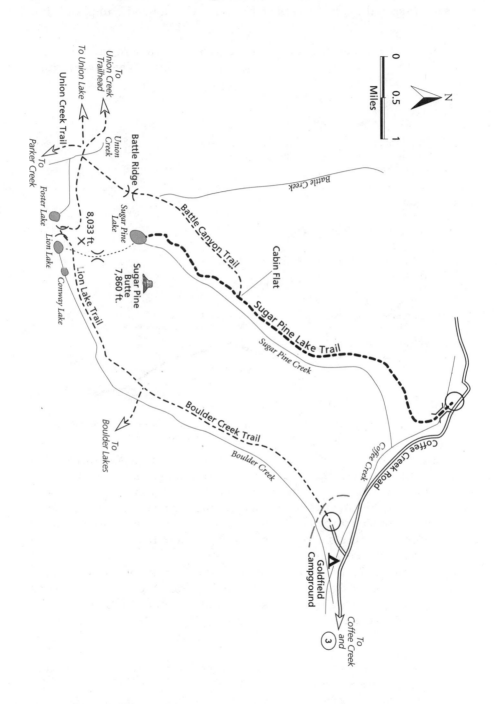

Finding the trailhead: From Weaverville, drive 40 miles north on California Highway 3 to Coffee Creek Road and go left (west). Follow this road 8 miles to the signed trailhead on the left (Coffee Creek Road is unpaved after first 5 miles).

Parking and trailhead facilities: Ample parking both here and across the road at East Fork Coffee Creek trailhead but no facilities. The closest campground is Goldfield, 3.5 miles east on Coffee Creek Road.

Key points:
- 0.0   Trailhead.
- 1.1   Junction with Old Sugar Pine Trail (unmarked).
- 4.0   Cabin Flat–Battle Canyon Trail junction.
- 6.2   Sugar Pine Lake.
- 10.9 Battle Ridge.
- 12.1 Union Creek.
- 13.5 Foster Lake.
- 14.3 Off-trail route to Sugar Pine Lake.
- 15.5 Sugar Pine Lake.
- 17.7 Cabin Flat–Battle Canyon Trail junction.
- 21.7 Trailhead.

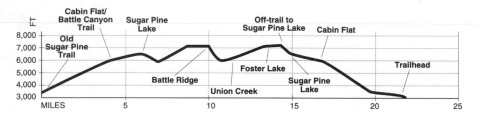

Profile data provided by TOPO! ©1999 Wildflower Productions(www.topo.com)

The hike: Despite being at the head of a beautiful drainage and surrounded by impressive granite cliffs, Sugar Pine Lake doesn't get as many visitors as one might expect. The lake isn't really on the way from anywhere, so it tends to get less hike-by traffic than some other Trinity Alps' destinations. Add a steep approach (the trail climbs more than 3,500 feet, most of it in the first 4 miles) and more steep hiking to go anywhere beyond the lake, and you get a rather lonely outpost.

A new bridge, completed in 1999, leads to the start of the Sugar Pine Lake Trail (the old bridge, located downstream from the new site, washed away in 1996). The new trailhead adds about 1.1 miles to the route. The additional distance is mostly an easy contour along Coffee Creek, then you meet the old trail and it's uphill to Cabin Flat. The last 2.2 miles to Sugar Pine Lake are a walk in the park.

You have several options on the Sugar Pine Lake Trail. You can simply hike up to the lake and back, which makes a pleasant route by itself. Ambitious hikers, however, can use the Battle Canyon Trail to create a spectacular loop through Union Creek and past Foster and Lion Lakes. Complete the loop by returning via Sugar Pine Lake, which requires a short but steep off-trail hike, or by using the Boulder Creek Trail to reach Coffee Creek Road at Goldfield Campground (this alternative lands you about 3.5 miles east of the Sugar Pine trailhead). The route described here is the off-trail version.

From Sugar Pine Trailhead, cross Coffee Creek on the new steel bridge and climb gently southeast as the trail contours downstream to meet the old trail. The low-elevation forest consists mostly of oak, madrone, and Douglas-fir. As you gain altitude, white fir, incense-cedar, and several varieties of pine begin to appear. In midsummer, expect hot hiking on this initial ascent. And though the map shows Sugar Pine Creek near the trail, it's really too far away to be useful. Stock up on water and refill at tributaries. Be sure to purify all water.

Sugar Pine Lake Trail, though steep, doesn't employ many switchbacks—just a long southward climb. The ascent eases at Cabin Flat, 4 miles from the trailhead. There, amid a welcome meadow of lush grass and corn lilies, you find the junction with the Battle Canyon Trail (9W59). A sign indicates that's the way to Union Creek. To reach Sugar Pine Lake, continue southwest on the Sugar Pine Lake Trail. The 9-acre lake lies 2.2 miles away at the head of the drainage, in a granite cirque with the usual cast of alpine charms. This last section of trail is a pleasant walk through lush meadows and shady forest, ending abruptly at the shore of Sugar Pine Lake.

If you're not hiking the loop beyond Sugar Pine Lake, just retrace your steps back to the trailhead from here. If you want to make the 9.3-mile loop by way of Battle Canyon, Union Creek, and Foster Lake, you have the choice of starting at Sugar Pine Lake and going clockwise or returning to Cabin Flat and hiking counterclockwise. The description here is counterclockwise, so hikers who prefer not to do the off-trail portion can follow the route to Lion Lake, then keep going on maintained trails.

Back at Cabin Flat, go west on the Battle Canyon Trail (signed Union Creek). The little-used trail is not obvious until you start climbing away from the meadow. Veer right (northwest) from the trail sign. You pick up the path as you leave the meadow's western edge. Once you clear the lower canyon, the trail becomes distinct again as it climbs steeply west and south (gaining 1,000 feet in 1 mile). Then enjoy a more moderate grade as the trail winds along the open ridge separating Battle and Sugar Pine Creeks. This portion of the route is blessed with beautiful views and wildflower gardens of aster, angelica, monkshood, lupine, and other blooms. It also passes an interesting array of knob-like rock formations—The Battleship.

Amid open terrain and great views, the trail dips down into the head of Battle Canyon before making yet another steep climb (about 700 feet) up to the saddle between Battle and Union Creeks. The trail may be overgrown and indistinct at times as you traverse the head of Battle Canyon. Set your sights on that low gap to the south and you should have no problem. The view from the saddle is a near 360-degree jaw-dropper that encompasses Mount Shasta, Caribou Mountain, Sawtooth Mountain, and a number of lesser peaks.

The way down to Union Creek, 1,500 feet below, is literally at your feet. The trail plummets the whole way in about 1.2 miles. Midway down, the

Sugar Pine/Cabin Flat trail sign.

trail appears to peter out in a grassy bench. It's there, just look for it on the meadow's southwest side. The rest of the descent is straightforward, leading to a three-way junction with the Lion Lake Trail (8W12) and Union Creek Trail (9W07). A right (west) turn leads to Union Creek, with numerous exploring and camping options (see Hike 30).

To continue the loop, turn left (east) and follow the Lion Lake Trail. The path makes a steep, nearly 1,500-foot, 1.5-mile ascent to Foster Lake. The deep blue lake is tucked into a granite shelf with one of the most beautiful sunset views in the Alps. The approach to Foster is a straightforward climb up the north side of the drainage, alongside an impressive avalanche gully and with ever-better views as you climb out of the forest cover. Traverse a series of smooth granite slabs just before arriving at lake level. (See Hike 27 for a description of Foster Lake and the surrounding area.)

The trail climbs above the lake on rocky tread to an obvious saddle between Foster and Lion Lakes (and another great view of Mount Shasta). Once over the saddle, descend northeast on a rocky path that literally hangs over the west edge of Lion Lake. After passing the lake, look for the low gap on the ridge to the northwest. That's the off-trail route back to Sugar Pine Lake. The 1.2-mile hike is not exceptionally difficult, but it does require some rough scrambling and good route-finding skills. To return via maintained trails, continue down to the Boulder Creek Trail and hike out to Coffee Creek Road, then walk back to Sugar Pine Lake Trailhead on the road. It's about 10 miles back to the trailhead via this route (consult Hikes 27 and 28, which describe Lion Lake and Boulder Creek Trails in reverse).

The most difficult part of the off-trail hike to Sugar Pine Lake is picking your way through fields of manzanita when you first leave the trail. It's a tradeoff between staying high (more manzanita) and dropping lower before leaving the trail (less manzanita but more elevation gain). Choose your medicine and shoot for the saddle south of Sugar Pine Butte.

Once on the saddle, it's a simple matter of picking your way down to Sugar Pine Lake. Granite benches lead down into the basin like a series of huge stone steps. Once at the lake, make your way over to the outlet and resume hiking on the Sugar Pine Lake Trail. Retrace your steps to the trailhead.

Options: Use the Union Creek Trail (Hike 30) to connect with the Landers Lake Loop (Hike 22) and Bullards Basin (Hike 31).

30 Union Creek

Highlights:	An often-overlooked trail to one of the Alps' most underrated valleys.
Type of hike:	Day hike or backpack; out-and-back.
Total distance:	12.4 miles (to Union Lake), plus optional 10-mile loop.
Difficulty:	Easy.
Elevation gain:	1,700 feet.
Maps:	USGS Caribou Lake and Ycatapom Peak quad; USDAFS Trinity Alps Wilderness map.

Finding the trailhead: From Weaverville, drive 40 miles north on California Highway 3 to Coffee Creek Road and go left (west). Follow this road 11 miles to the signed trailhead (trail is on the left, parking on the right). Coffee Creek Road is unpaved after first 5 miles.

Parking and trailhead facilities: Adequate parking, but horse trailers sometimes take up a lot of room; no facilities. The closest campgrounds are Goldfield and Big Flat.

Key points:

0.0	Trailhead.
2.5	Union Creek bridge.
3.0	Pin Creek crossing.
5.0	Dorleska Mine Trail junction.
5.5	Union Lake Trail junction.
6.2	Union Lake.

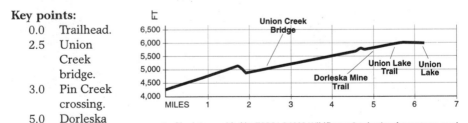

Profile data provided by TOPO! ©1999 Wildflower Productions(www.topo.com)

The hike: Other destinations in the Trinity Alps are more spectacular. Other creeks are bigger, other drainages longer. But for a pleasant place to spend a

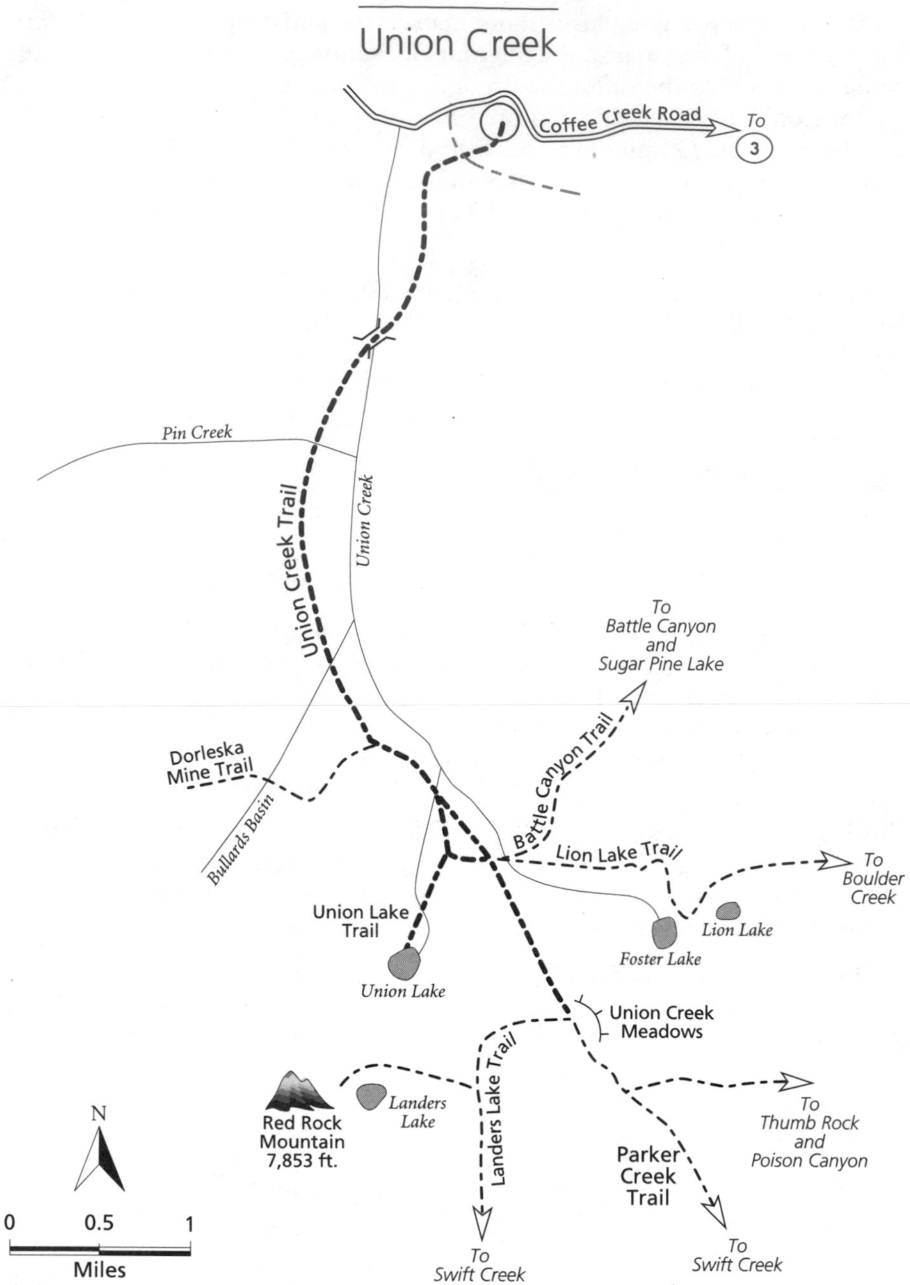

Union Creek

Coffee Creek Road
To 3

Pin Creek

Union Creek Trail

Union Creek

To
Battle Canyon
and
Sugar Pine Lake

Dorleska
Mine Trail

Bullards Basin

Battle Canyon Trail

Lion Lake Trail
To
Boulder
Creek

Union Lake
Trail

Foster Lake

Lion Lake

Union Lake

Union Creek
Meadows

N

Red Rock
Mountain
7,853 ft.

Landers
Lake

Landers Lake Trail

To
Thumb Rock
and
Poison Canyon

Parker
Creek
Trail

0   0.5   1
Miles

To
Swift Creek

To
Swift Creek

few days immersed in mountain splendor, it's hard to beat Union Creek. The approach is more like a walk in the park than an alpine hike. After 6 gently ascending miles, you find yourself in a sprawling meadow at the heart of a perfectly proportioned valley: a sparkling creek here, a sweet-smelling forest of Jeffrey pines there, a field of wildflowers over here.

There's plenty of elbowroom along Union Creek and its secluded little glades, but what makes this hike truly attractive is the variety of side trips available. From a half-mile stroll to low-lying Union Lake to a leg-burning 1,500-foot climb to Foster Lake, there's something for everyone. Connecting trails make it possible to extend this hike by several days.

At the trailhead, start hiking south up the old roadbed (signed Union Creek). The Union Creek Trail (9W07) follows this wide track for the first 1.5 miles. Immediately pass a locked Forest Service gate, then head east until a sharp switchback sends you on a long traverse to the southwest. Don't be alarmed by the initial climb, which rises steadily above a boulder field on a sunny, exposed slope. The path levels out as soon as you round the nose of the ridge above Union Creek proper. From there it's an easy hike, downhill at times, to a bridge crossing at 2.5 miles. There's plenty of water along the way, and mature stands of Douglas-fir, white fir, and mixed pines shade the trail. In early summer, look for a lush and fragrant stand of azalea bushes at about 1 mile (near a small pond beside the trail).

After crossing Union Creek, the trail follows the west side of the drainage, climbing gently through alternating thickets of mixed conifers and pretty green glades of meadow grass, alders, and wildflowers. At 3 miles, the trail crosses Pin Creek on a cement-lined creekbed. Watch your step if the water is high in early season.

More gentle hiking leads to the next creek crossing, a wide braid of water that flows out of Bullards Basin. The ford, upstream from the creek's confluence with Union Creek, can be difficult in early season. A log across the water provides a dry crossing upstream from the trail (pick your way through a stand of alders to find the log).

The next mile climbs more earnestly as the trail winds around to the southeast, following the bending course of the drainage. At 4.8 miles, just before the junction with the Dorleska Mine Trail, you skirt the lower end of a beautiful, emerald green meadow filled with corn lilies. A sparkling little stream flows across the west side of the meadow, nourishing a small field of California pitcher plants that thrive in the wet environment.

At the east end of the meadow, continue on the Union Creek Trail and soon arrive at the junction with the Dorleska Mine Trail (9W65). To the right (west), 2 miles away, lie the remains of the Dorleska Mine, tucked away on a bench overlooking the rarely visited Bullards Basin (see Hike 31). The Union Creek Trail continues southeast. After another jaunt through easygoing terrain, cross Union Lake's outlet and arrive at the junction with the Union Lake Trail (9W64). This junction marks the northwest corner of a triangle formed by three trail segments that intersect in the Union Creek drainage. A glance at the map will show that these short segments (about a half-mile each) are the two spur trails to Union Lake, along with the main Union Creek Trail. In the past, poor or missing trail signs at the southeast corner of the triangle have made the junction confusing.

From this first junction to the head of the Union Creek drainage, 2 miles upstream, you find expansive meadows, views of the surrounding peaks, towering ponderosa and white pines, and plenty of places to pitch a tent in perfect solitude.

Turn right (south) on the Union Lake Trail to reach the shallow, low-lying (6,200 feet) lake. Go straight, then left (northeast) on the Lion Lake Trail

(8W12) to reach Foster Lake and the trail to Sugar Pine Lake. Continue southeast on the Union Creek Trail to reach the junctions for Landers Lake and Parker Creek.

Either use Union Creek as a basecamp and explore the surrounding area by day, or, if you have more time, consider making a longer loop out of this (see options below). Retrace your steps to the trailhead.

Options: Use Landers Lake, Sunrise Creek, and Bullards Basin to make a 10-mile loop around Red Rock Mountain (ending at the Dorleska Mine and Union Creek trail junction; see Hike 31), or use Parker Creek to make a loop through Swift Creek and ending at the Landers Lake–Union Creek trail junction (Hike 22). More ambitious hikers might consider a loop around Sugar Pine Lake, using Battle Canyon Trail, Lion Lake Trail, and an off-trail route to Sugar Pine Lake (Hike 29).

31 Bullards Basin– Sunrise Creek Loop

Highlights:	A lightly used route through gentle terrain of lush meadows and broad valleys; passes near several lakes and an easily climbed peak.
Type of hike:	Backpack; loop.
Total distance:	15.5 miles.
Difficulty:	Moderate.
Elevation gain:	4,600 feet.
Maps:	USGS Caribou Lake and Ycatapom Peak quads; USDAFS Trinity Alps Wilderness map.

Finding the trailhead: From Weaverville, drive 40 miles north on California Highway 3 to Coffee Creek Road and go left (west). Follow this road 20 miles to an obvious fork (Coffee Creek Road is unpaved after first 5 miles). Go left (east) at the signed fork. The signed entrance to Big Flat Trailhead and campground is located 0.8 mile beyond the fork, on the right.

Parking and trailhead facilities: Ample parking at Big Flat Trailhead. The campground (no fee) is a popular, pleasant, creekside camp; outhouse available, but no potable water.

Key points:
- 0.0   Trailhead.
- 2.0   Yellow Rose Mine.
- 2.1   Dorleska Trail junction.
- 3.4   Dorleska Mine.
- 4.4   Union Creek Trail junction.
- 5.1   Union Lake Trail junction.

Bullards Basin–Sunrise Creek Loop

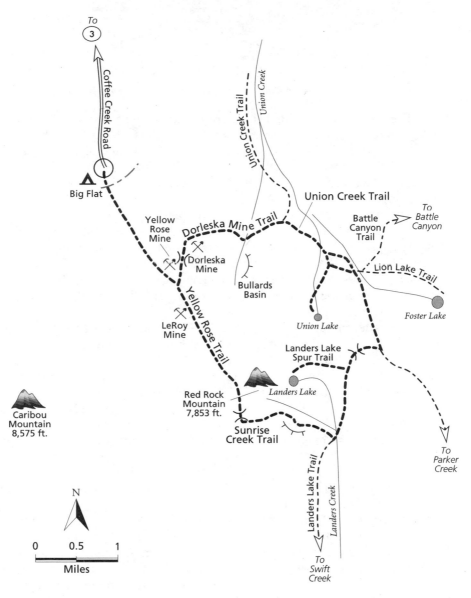

5.5   Lion Lake Trail–Battle Canyon Trail junction.
6.6   Landers Lake Trail junction.
7.8   Landers Lake Spur Trail junction.
8.6   Sunrise Creek Trail junction.
13.5   Yellow Rose Mine.
15.5   Trailhead.

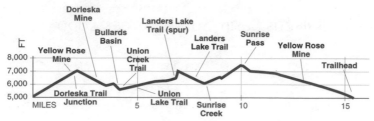

Profile data provided by TOPO! ©1999 Wildflower Productions(www.topo.com)

The hike: This leisurely loop is ideal for hikers who place stargazing above peak bagging. Expect lots of meadows, sparkling streams, and idyllic creekside camps. The trail passes within casting distance of several lakes, and Red Rock Mountain is within easy reach for anyone who decides to bag a peak along with a few million stars. You also pass three historic mine sites on the way.

The trailhead is directly across the road (east) from the parking area at Big Flat. A sign on the left, just beyond the locked gate, indicates that Yellow Rose Mine is 3 miles away (slightly exaggerated). Start ascending steadily but moderately to the southeast on a well-defined track. Mixed forest of fir and pine provides plenty of shade, and outstanding views of Caribou Mountain appear when you break out of the forest. Plenty of water is available in creeks along the way (purify all water).

Scattered debris and a decrepit old shack signal your arrival at Yellow Rose Mine, 2 miles from the trailhead. Just beyond the mine, arrive at the junction with the Dorleska Mine Trail (9W65). The path ahead continues to Sunrise Creek Trail (the way you return). To hike the loop in the direction described, turn left (east) on the Dorleska Mine Trail and continue uphill to the northeast. Half a mile later you top out on the ridge, with panoramic views of the Union Creek drainage spread out beneath your feet.

Descend through open, grassy terrain sprinkled with yarrow and asters. Half a mile below the ridgeline arrive at a bench littered with ancient, rusted machinery—the first signs of Dorleska Mine. The mine was a bustling operation during the first 30 years of the twentieth century. Dorleska was the name of the mine owner's wife.

A quarter of a mile downhill from the first mine relics, look for a faint trail leading off to the right (south). This unmarked, unmaintained path leads a few hundred yards over a rise to a little gem of a pond perched on a knoll above Bullards Basin. The nameless pond is well worth the detour.

The Dorleska Mine Trail continues a steep descent into the bottom of the canyon, descending into a dense forest distinguished by enormous incense-cedars, then crossing the creek at the heart of the canyon. Upstream lies Bullards Basin, one of those rarely visited drainages, with neither lake nor trail to attract crowds, that's guaranteed to delight lovers of true wilderness. Anyone looking for an adventure can follow the basin south, up a steep headwall of unstable talus, and onto the northern shoulder of Red Rock Mountain. A little snowmelt pond up there probably only sees a handful of visitors each year. Above the pond a gap in the ridgeline allows access to the

154

summit of Red Rock Mountain, as well as the entire Landers Lake basin. This off-trail route is not for the faint of heart.

After crossing the stream in Bullards Basin, descend northeast, contouring along the base of a spur ridge. Skirt the top of a lush corn lily meadow just before dropping down to the junction with Union Creek Trail (9W07), 4.4 miles from the trailhead.

Turn right (southeast) on the Union Creek Trail (a left turn leads back to a trailhead on Coffee Creek Road; see Hike 30). Half a mile up Union Creek, cross the outlet stream from Union Lake and enter the wide, welcoming valley of Union Creek proper. The broad valley ahead offers a number of trail junctions, plus a wealth of inviting meadows if you don't want to go anywhere at all. Altogether, Union Creek is easily the area's most overlooked drainage.

Union Lake lies a mile south of the first junction (signed Union Lake to the right). The low-elevation, shallow lake warms up considerably by midsummer, but a mucky bottom puts most swimmers off. Anglers have no complaints. The lake sits on the east side of a wide basin, with extensive meadows that make the site popular with horsepackers. As in Bullards Basin, a steep off-trail scramble up the cirque's southern headwall will land you on the shores of an idyllic pond high on the shoulder of Red Rock Mountain. A grassy slope as smooth as a putting green and steep as a waterfall leads over the divide to Landers Lake. Wildflowers are glorious in late July.

Back along Union Creek, a three-way junction lies half a mile southeast of the last one. Arriving along Union Creek Trail, you'll face: to the right (west), a connecting path to Union Lake (a spur trail, 9W64A); to the left (east) Lion Lake Trail (8W12), which also connects to Battle Canyon Trail–Sugar Pine Lake Trail (9W59); and straight (southeast), the Union Creek Trail continues up the drainage.

Foster Lake lies 1.5 miles and 1,500 feet up the Lion Lake Trail. It's higher, deeper, and much clearer than Union Lake. It's also colder, but makes a great swimming lake on a hot day (see Hike 27 for Foster Lake Loop; Hike 29 for Sugar Pine Lake).

To continue the loop, hike southeast from the three-way junction on the Union Creek Trail and make your way 1.3 miles up the gently rising valley to the head of the canyon. In a treeless, flower-sprinkled meadow, arrive at the Landers Lake Trail junction, signed on a snag next to the trail. Turn right (west) to reach Landers Lake and Sunrise Creek. The Union Creek Trail continues southeast, ascending to a saddle on the ridge ahead and connecting with the Parker Creek and Thumb Rock Trails (detailed in Hikes 22 and 23).

The Landers Lake Trail (9W09) crosses the high meadow, then climbs west and south through open forest to a saddle on the ridge above Landers Creek. An easy descent, accompanied by superlative views of Red Rock Mountain, Swift Creek drainage, and Snowslide Peak, brings you to the Landers Lake Spur Trail (9W09A), 1.2 miles from Union Creek. The junction is at the bottom of a wet meadow dotted with incredibly clear pools of water.

Turn right (north) to reach Landers Lake, just under 1 mile farther up the canyon. That's also the way to go for the easiest ascent of Red Rock Mountain,

Dorleska Mine relic along Bullards Basin–Sunrise Creek Loop.

with one of the best views in the Trinity Alps. (See Hike 22 for a description of Landers Lake and Red Rock Mountain.)

Turn left (south) to descend to the junction with the Sunrise Creek Trail (9W15), 1.1 miles away. The hike down to the junction is a pleasant stroll along the east side of Landers Creek, with more wet meadows thick with California pitcher plants and flower-lined borders.

Cross Landers Creek just below the confluence of Landers and Sunrise Creeks, and just before the trail junction. Turn right (west) on Sunrise Creek Trail. The Landers Lake Trail continues down to Mumford Meadow and Swift Creek (see Hike 20).

Heading west on Sunrise Creek Trail, climb moderately along the south side of the creek. Mixed forest of white fir, pine, and incense-cedar provides shade for the first push, but you soon break into open, grassy terrain as the valley widens and the trail levels out. Look for colorful fields of Indian paintbrush, yarrow, and asters when you cross to the north side of the creek. The drainage gets relatively few visitors and is well worth some extra exploring time. (Don't worry, that high-tech contraption in the meadow isn't spying on you. It's a snow-level gauge with a solar panel on top.)

After crossing the stream, the trail climbs steeply again as you tackle the canyon's headwall. Water may not be available above the lower canyon, so be sure to refill while you can. The path is faint at times, but the route sticks dependably to the center of the drainage—just hike up to the saddle if you lose the trail. Blue gentians, yellow lupine, and lilies grow along the way.

Once you gain the saddle (after a deceptively strenuous climb), the red meta-igneous rocks of Red Rock Mountain are off to the north (the summit can be easily reached from here). Caribou Mountain in all its glory is directly across the valley to the west.

The view hardly changes as you descend into the open basin, contouring northwest along the canyon wall. The hike from here is a pleasant downhill stroll on the Yellow Rose Trail, the path on which you started. Pass the Le Roy Mine, then the Yellow Rose Mine, then arrive at the trailhead, 5 miles from the saddle above Sunrise Creek.

Options: Besides making jaunts to various lakes (Union, Foster, Lion, Sugar Pine, Landers), you can make the loop longer by using the Swift Creek Trail (Hike 20) to return to Big Flat via Ward Lake (Hike 32).

32 Ward Lake Loop

Highlights:	Great views of Caribou Mountain, good swimming in Ward and Horseshoe Lakes, and more meadows than you can shake a corn lily at.
Type of hike:	Backpack (2–4 nights); loop.
Total distance:	18.7 miles.
Difficulty:	Moderate.
Elevation gain:	4,600 feet.
Maps:	USGS Caribou Lake, Siligo Peak, and Ycatapom Peak quads; USDAFS Trinity Alps Wilderness map.

Finding the trailhead: From Weaverville, drive 40 miles north on California Highway 3 to Coffee Creek Road and go left (west). Follow this road 20 miles to an obvious fork (Coffee Creek Road is unpaved after the first 5 miles). Go left (east) at the signed fork. The signed entrance to Big Flat Trailhead and campground is located 0.8 mile beyond the fork, on the right.

Parking and trailhead facilities: Ample parking at Big Flat Trailhead. The campground (no fee) is a popular, pleasant, creekside camp. An outhouse is available, but no potable water.

Key points:
- 0.0 Trailhead.
- 0.3 Old Caribou Trail junction and creek crossing.
- 0.4 Tri-Forest Peak Trail junction.
- 2.7 Carters Road crossing.
- 3.6 Ward Lake Trail.
- 6.5 Kidd Creek divide.
- 6.9 Ward Lake.
- 8.9 Horseshoe Lake.
- 11.2 Landers Lake Trail.
- 12.0 Sunrise Creek Trail.
- 16.2 Yellow Rose Mine.
- 18.7 Trailhead.

Ward Lake Loop

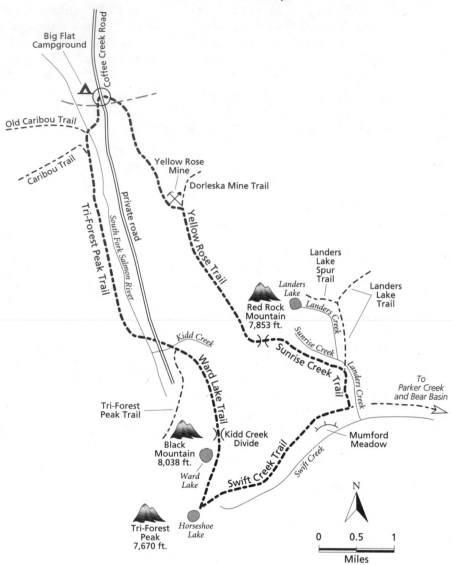

The hike: If Goldilocks were a hiker, she'd pronounce this loop just right: just the right amount of steeps (great views without killing yourself); just the right amount of lakes (three, with remarkably different settings); and just the right amount of easy meadow walking (lots). Traffic can be high along Swift Creek, but the other drainages offer an excellent chance for solitude. This is also the shortest way to reach Ward Lake, so a lot of people just go there and turn around. There's no compelling reason to hike this loop in either direction, but I like counterclockwise because you go down instead of up the steep, exposed hill at the head of Swift Creek.

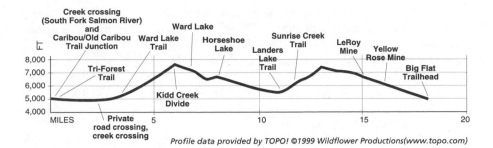

Start at the Big Flat Trailhead and follow signs to Kidd Creek and Caribou Lake trailheads. A sign by the trailhead parking area indicates a path leading south through a shady stand of firs to the wilderness boundary, and then to a crossing of the South Fork Salmon River. Just before the creek, the Valley Loop Trail diverges to the south. Crossing the South Fork Salmon River shouldn't pose any problem (other than wet feet), but, like any stream crossing, use caution in early-season high water. If the creek is too high (or you prefer dry feet), you can avoid the crossing altogether by walking south on the dirt road you drove in on. This gated road leads to Josephine Creek Resort, a private inholding at the head of the drainage. The Tri-Forest Trail, your ticket to Kidd Creek, actually recrosses South Fork Salmon River and crosses the road 2.7 miles south. The trail is much prettier than the road, but the road is a fine option in high water (no other creek crossings on this route should give you any trouble).

Once across the creek, you find two trails on your right climbing the opposite bank. The first one (heading northwest) is the Old Caribou Trail. You want the unmarked "new" trail to the southwest. Take this path out of the streambed and head west across a parklike meadow to the junction with the Tri-Forest Peak Trail (9W11). Turn left (south) and proceed along the level, forested course of South Fork Salmon River. The pleasant streamside walk makes a nice excursion in its own right, meandering along the west side of the creek, through ferny glades and shady glens, before crossing back to the east bank and crossing the road, 2.7 miles from the trailhead (stay right at the signed fork 1.5 miles in, or you'll make a loop and end up back where you started).

At the road crossing, a trail sign indicates mileages to Kidd Creek, Ward Lake, and Swift Creek (all fairly accurate). Still on the Tri-Forest Trail, head southeast through dense fir forest, past some private cabins, and climb very gradually to cross Kidd Creek and arrive at the Ward Lake Trail junction. Turn left (east) to continue up the Kidd Creek drainage. (The Tri-Forest Trail continues south to cross Sawtooth Ridge, Hike 33)

The going gets steeper as you ascend along the side of Kidd Creek. As you climb, tree cover thins and you get glimpses of the view behind you (nice shot of Caribou Mountain) and the view ahead (sheer walls of the upper basin). Just over 5 miles from the trailhead, leave the trees behind and cross the wet meadows at the head of the drainage. Crystal clear snowmelt pools and gardens of summer wildflowers put the finishing touches on the idyllic scene. The only drawback is occasional cows—which also enjoy the pleasant valley (you can check with rangers to see if cattle are present, but in any case they don't cross the divide to Ward Lake).

The trail may fade in the meadow, but don't lose hope. It soon becomes distinct again on the west side of the rockslide above the meadows. If all else fails, just aim for the notch in the ridgeline directly south. You're sure to pick up the well-defined path on the west side of the narrowing gully. The final going is steep but short.

At 6.5 miles, top out on the saddle above Kidd Creek, just east of 8,038-foot Black Mountain. Take a rest and enjoy the view. To the south lies an array of peaks, including Gibson, Siligo, and Seven Up, plus all of the Swift Creek drainage at your feet. Should you find yourself here at sunrise someday, head out on the rocky ridgeline east of the saddle for a fine show.

South of the saddle, the trail descends steeply on switchbacks to cross a small grassy glade, then drops to the north shore of Ward Lake. (For a complete description of Ward and Horseshoe Lakes, see Hike 20.) Both lakes are best visited on day trips, as they get a lot of use, and much better camping is available along Swift Creek below.

The route down to Swift Creek, then on to the Landers Lake Trail is one of the prettiest sections of trail in the Alps. Descending from Ward Lake (pick up the path on the south side, at the outlet), the trail winds around to the southwest, traversing an open, ferny slope with expansive views of the valley below. It's all downhill, past the junction for Horseshoe Lake (the lake is 0.3 mile to the right; stay left for Swift Creek), down a rocky set of switchbacks, past flower gardens of columbines and shooting stars, then on down to the broad, level valley at the head of Swift Creek.

Proceed east along the Swift Creek Trail (8W15), through a chain of lush meadows with forests of corn lilies, yarrow, and cow parsnip. For a complete description of Swift Creek, see Hike 20, which describes this section in reverse.

At the Landers Lake Trail junction, 11.2 miles from the trailhead, turn left (north) and proceed 0.8 mile to the Sunrise Creek Trail junction. To return to the trailhead, turn left here and proceed 6.7 miles back to Big Flat on the Sunrise Creek and Yellow Rose Trails (this section is described in Hike 31). To pay a visit to Landers Lake, or hike off trail to the summit of Red Rock Mountain, refer to Hike 22.

Options: You can extend this hike by using the Union Creek and Dorleska Mine trails to return (described in Hike 31, in reverse). This adds another valley, several more lakes, and about 4 more miles to the itinerary. You can also make an off-trail hike to Salmon Lake from Horseshoe Lake. It's possible to make an alternate loop by descending from Salmon Lake to Tri-Forest Trail and returning to Big Flat, but it's steep with no trail. Only experienced hikers with good route-finding skills should attempt it.

33 Tri-Forest Peak–Deer Creek Loop

<table>
<tr><td align="right">Highlights:</td><td>This hike puts you right in the teeth of Sawtooth Ridge.</td></tr>
<tr><td align="right">Type of hike:</td><td>Day hike or backpack; out-and-back (day hike) or loop (backpack).</td></tr>
<tr><td align="right">Total distance:</td><td>13 miles (to Tri-Forest Peak); 26.9 miles (whole loop).</td></tr>
<tr><td align="right">Difficulty:</td><td>Moderate (Tri-Forest Peak); strenuous (whole loop).</td></tr>
<tr><td align="right">Elevation gain:</td><td>2,200 feet (to Tri-Forest Peak); 6,600 feet (whole loop).</td></tr>
<tr><td align="right">Maps:</td><td>USGS Caribou Lake, Covington Mill, Siligo Peak, and Ycatapom Peak quads; USDAFS Trinity Alps Wilderness map.</td></tr>
</table>

Finding the trailhead: From Weaverville, drive 40 miles north on California Highway 3 to Coffee Creek Road and go left (west). Follow this road 20 miles to an obvious fork (Coffee Creek Road is unpaved after first 5 miles). Go left (east) at the signed fork. The signed entrance to Big Flat Trailhead and campground is located 0.8 mile beyond the fork, on the right.

Parking and trailhead facilities: Ample parking at Big Flat Trailhead. The campground (no fee) is a popular but pleasant creekside camp. An outhouse is available, but no potable water.

Key points:
- 0.0   Trailhead.
- 0.3   Old Caribou Trail junction.
- 0.4   Tri-Forest Peak Trail junction.
- 1.5   Valley Loop junction.
- 2.7   Private road crossing.
- 3.6   Kidd Creek/Tri-Forest junction.
- 6.5   Tri-Forest saddle.
- 9.0   Deer Creek Trail junction.
- 10.5 Black Basin Trail.
- 12.0 Mumford Basin Trail.
- 17.0 Swift Creek Trail junction.
- 18.7 Landers Lake Trail junction.
- 19.5 Sunrise Creek Trail.
- 24.9 Yellow Rose Mine.
- 26.9 Trailhead.

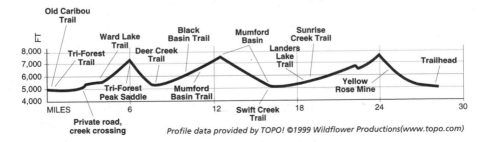

Profile data provided by TOPO! ©1999 Wildflower Productions(www.topo.com)

Tri-Forest Peak–Deer Creek Loop

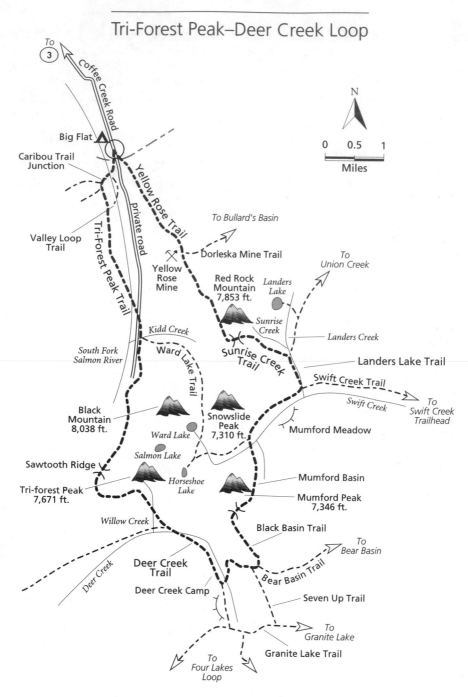

The hike: Of all the high places with a drop-dead view of the inner Trinity Alps, the jagged crest at the east end of Sawtooth Ridge may just be my favorite. Just 6.5 miles from Big Flat Trailhead, you top out on a 7,200-foot saddle, stroll a few hundred yards through a beautiful meadow, and take a seat among the teeth of Sawtooth Ridge. At your feet are Sapphire and

Emerald Lakes, as well as the entire Stuart Fork drainage, Sawtooth Mountain, and Thompson Peak. Just watch your footing, or you really will drop dead.

The Tri-Forest Trail (9W11) makes a fine day hike if you turn around at Sawtooth Ridge. Except for the last steep mile (1,200-foot rise), the route is a pleasant, level walk along the South Fork Salmon River. The only drawback is that you have to walk past Josephine Creek Resort, a private inholding that actually encompasses Josephine Lake.

For hikers looking for a longer backpack through some of the most beautiful corners of the Trinities, continue through Deer Creek, Swift Creek, and Sunrise Creek to make a 27-mile loop back to Big Flat. Either way, you will not be disappointed.

Start at the Big Flat trailhead and follow signs to the Kidd Creek and Caribou Lake Trails. Crossing the South Fork Salmon River shouldn't pose any problem, but use caution in early-season high water. If the creek is too high (or you prefer dry feet), avoid the crossing altogether by walking south on the dirt road on which you drove in. The Tri-Forest Trail crosses the road 2.7 miles south. The trail is much prettier than the road, but the road is a fine option in high water. See Hike 32 for a complete description of the first 3.6 miles to the Ward Lake–Tri-Forest junction. The scenic route, first on the west side of South Fork Salmon River, then on the east, is a mostly level, shady streamside hike. Follow signs for the Kidd Creek and Tri-Forest Trails.

At the Kidd Creek Trail junction (marked Ward Lake Trail on Forest Service map, but signed Kidd Creek), a left turn (east) leads to Ward Lake. Stay straight (south) on the Tri-Forest Trail. The next 1.5 miles skirts the eastern edge of the private property. Please respect the landowner's privacy as you pass. The trail meanders through mixed forest on a level, well-defined track. Occasionally the path climbs a short way above the valley bottom in order to clear the private property. Ignore trails or cow paths coming in from the west.

Soon you emerge from the trees and start ascending the east side of the valley. Views of Caribou Mountain, directly to the west, start out big and get bigger as you go. Look for a creek descending the east wall of the canyon 2 miles from the Ward Lake Trail junction. It's the last major tributary you encounter before starting up the steep switchbacks at the head of the drainage. Be sure to fill water bottles (purify all water).

The creek also marks the starting point for hikers looking to tackle the off-trail route to Salmon Lake. The pretty little lake, perched on a bench about 1,200 feet above the valley, is a worthwhile goal for those who like a tough scramble. The route is brushy and steep (detour north of the waterfall), but follows one of the prettiest, flower-filled gullies in all the Alps. Use a map and common sense. A longer but much easier route to Salmon, via the ridge above Horseshoe Lake, is described in Hike 20.

Past Salmon's outlet creek, the Tri-Forest Trail starts climbing more earnestly. Gradually at first, then more steeply, the trail ascends a well-defined track up the south wall of the drainage. Thoughtfully engineered switchbacks lead up the last steep mile, making the climb much easier than it appears to be from below.

Just over 6 miles from the trailhead, top out on the saddle directly west of 7,671-foot Tri-Forest Peak. The trail continues south, crossing the crest and

Sawtooth Ridge along Tri-Forest Peak–Deer Creek Loop.

plunging downhill along the headwaters of Willow Creek. But don't do that right away. First, hike up that meadow to the right (west) to aptly named Horse Heaven Peak, and take your well-earned seat among the teeth of Sawtooth Ridge. Get out your map and see how many peaks you can identify. Picture yourself diving into Emerald Lake from here.

When you've had enough of the view, either retrace your steps to the trailhead or continue on the loop by heading southwest, into the Willow Creek drainage. Beyond the saddle, you find the trail much less distinct, fading in and out of rocky slopes and meadows. Occasional cairns mark the path, but you don't have to work too hard to find it. The trail bends to the southwest, descending steeply into the canyon on rocky tread, then curves back to the southeast to follow the west bank of Willow Creek. This is wild terrain, rarely visited by humans. Great views of the Deer Creek drainage open up as you cross a meadow 1 mile below the saddle.

Descend through a dense stand of white firs and mixed pine after the meadow, making your way down to Willow Creek, where you cross the stream and continue on the east bank. The final steep descent brings you to a junction with the Deer Creek Trail (9W17). A right (west) turn here leads to Morris Meadow and the Stuart Fork Trail (Hike 11). It's possible to make a loop back to Big Flat by going that way and returning via Caribou Lake. That route, however, requires a tough, waterless, shadeless climb out of Stuart Fork. The view at the top is well worth the effort, but it's recommended only for hikers who like that sort of thing.

For the rest of us, a left turn (east) leads up the Deer Creek drainage. The forested valley is popular among deer hunters, who descend on Deer Creek Camp in the fall, but other than that most people only see the canyon while passing by one end or the other. The trail follows the north bank of Deer Creek, arriving at Deer Creek Camp and the Black Basin Trail junction in 2 gradually ascending miles.

The loop back to Big Flat goes up Black Basin Trail, but allow time for a day on the Four Lakes Loop, a spectacular route that circles Siligo Peak and four beautiful lakes (Hike 18). It starts at the end of Deer Creek Trail, 1 mile to the southeast.

To continue the loop, head east from Deer Creek Camp on the Black Basin Trail, which climbs northwest then southeast, through mixed conifers, on a steep, switchbacking ascent of Deer Creek canyon's east ridge. Nearly 1,000 feet up, after passing the ruins of Longs Cabin and a snowmelt pond, come to the first of two poorly marked junctions. The first path, on the right, is the Seven Up Trail (9W67), which connects with the Granite Lake Trail after a jaw-dropping traverse of the ridge beneath Seven Up Peak. The second path, also on the right, leads to the Bear Basin Trail (9W10). Both trails are described in Hike 21.

Stay left at both junctions, heading northwest on a long, gradual contour that brings you to a saddle on the ridge between Deer and Swift Creeks. Manzanita gets higher and trees more sparse as you climb. This section of trail is one of the least traveled paths in the Trinity Alps Wilderness, with signs that come and go and portions that have all but faded from view. If you prefer a well-maintained trail with dependable signs, stick to the Bear Basin or Granite Lake Trails.

Once you gain the saddle, the route down into Mumford Basin becomes more distinct. A steep descent on a well-defined trail leads to a high, wild-flower-dotted meadow at the heart of Mumford Basin, a secluded and wild canyon that hangs above Swift Creek. Despite constant traffic in Swift Creek far below, few people venture into Mumford Basin (coming from Swift Creek, the trail to Mumford Basin is hard to find). You'll likely have only bears and birds for company.

The final 2.5-mile descent to the floor of Swift Creek, through lush green glades, then lonely forests of white fir, ponderosa pine, and incense-cedar, is easy to follow. The trail stays on the west bank of the creek flowing out of Mumford Basin. It fades away again at the bottom, but cross Swift Creek and you run into the Swift Creek Trail (8W15). It's a regular highway compared to the trail you've been on. Turn right (northeast) to complete the loop; left (southwest) to reach Horseshoe and Ward Lakes (2 and 3 miles away, respectively).

For a complete description of the rest of the route back to Big Flat, along Swift Creek, Landers Creek, Sunrise Creek, and the Yellow Rose Mine Trail, see Hikes 31 and 32.

Options: Choose an alternate route back to Big Flat by using the Ward Lake Trail from Ward Lake (Hike 32 in reverse), or the Union Creek Trail to Bullards Basin (Hike 30 in reverse). Lakes within easy reach include Deer, Summit, Diamond, Luella, Granite, Horseshoe, Ward, and Landers. Good walk-up peaks are Siligo, Seven Up, and Red Rock Mountain.

34 Caribou Lakes

Highlights: A hike with a view around every corner; expect
company, but it's worth it.
Type of hike: Backpack; out-and-back (with optional "figure eight"
on Old Caribou Trail).
Total distance: 19 miles.
Difficulty: Moderate.
Elevation gain: 2,500 feet (add 1,000 feet for optional loop).
Maps: USGS Caribou Lake quad; USDAFS Trinity Alps
Wilderness map.

Finding the trailhead: From Weaverville, drive 40 miles north on California Highway 3 to Coffee Creek Road and go left (west). Follow this road 20
miles to an obvious fork (Coffee Creek Road is unpaved after first 5 miles).
Go left (east) at the signed fork. The signed entrance to Big Flat Trailhead
and campground is located 0.8 mile beyond the fork, on the right.

Parking and trailhead facilities: Ample parking at Big Flat Trailhead.
The campground (no fee) is a popular, pleasant, creekside camp. An outhouse is available, but no potable water.

Key points:

0.0   Big Flat Trailhead.
0.2   Valley Loop Trail and creek crossing.
0.3   Old Caribou Trail junction.
0.4   Tri-Forest Peak trail junction.
4.0   Caribou Meadow–Old Caribou Trail junction.
6.0   Browns Meadow.
8.5   Old Caribou Trail junction.
9.0   Lower Caribou, Snowslide, and Middle Caribou Lakes.
9.5   Caribou Lake.
10.5 Saddle between Caribou Basin and Stuart Fork (optional).

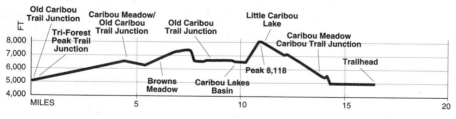

Profile data provided by TOPO! ©1999 Wildflower Productions(www.topo.com)

The hike: The most spectacular place in the Trinity Alps is a matter of
some debate among Alps aficionados. But no matter who's doing the talking, you can bet Caribou Basin will come up for consideration. At 72 acres,
Caribou Lake (or Big Caribou, as old-timers often call it) is by far the biggest

Caribou Lakes

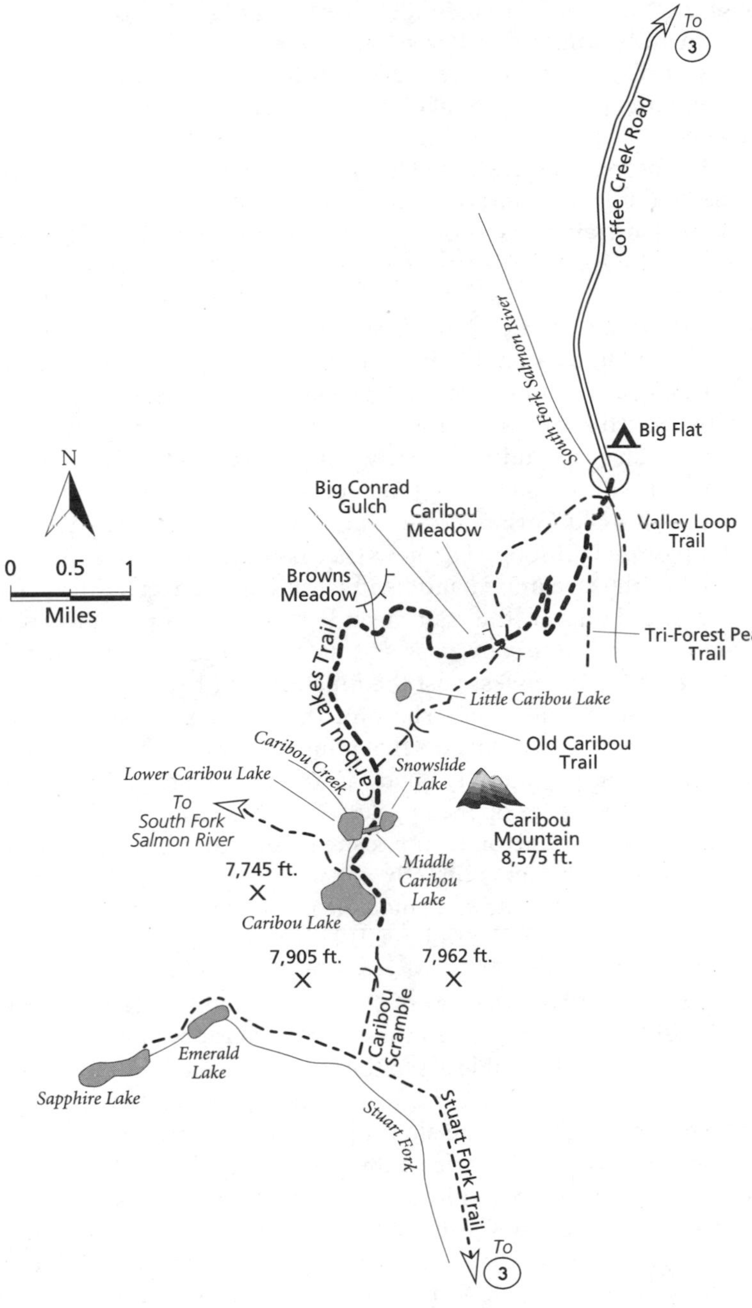

To
3

Coffee Creek Road

South Fork Salmon River

▲ Big Flat

Big Conrad
Gulch

Caribou
Meadow

Valley Loop
Trail

Browns
Meadow

Caribou Lakes Trail

Tri-Forest Peak
Trail

Little Caribou Lake

Old Caribou
Trail

Caribou Creek

*Snowslide
Lake*

Lower Caribou Lake

To
South Fork
Salmon River

Caribou
Mountain
8,575 ft.

7,745 ft.
✕

*Middle
Caribou
Lake*

Caribou Lake

7,905 ft.
✕

7,962 ft.
✕

Caribou
Scramble

*Emerald
Lake*

Sapphire Lake

Stuart Fork

Stuart Fork Trail

To
3

N

0   0.5   1
Miles

lake in the Trinity Alps. But size alone does not a beautiful basin make. Add
sweeping cliffs and wide benches of white granite, stunning meadows, three
more charming lakes, and endless views, and you begin to get a picture of
Caribou Basin. Of course, such beauty has not gone unnoticed. Expect plenty

of company here. An optional side trip (off trail) to Little Caribou Lake is the best place to find solitude in this region.

Though not difficult, the 9.5-mile hike to Caribou Lake can seem long and hot on a midsummer day. But you can take some consolation in the fact that the new trail goes around Caribou Mountain, not up and over its shoulder as the old trail does, which takes a considerable bite out of the steepness of the route. Just imagine slogging up and over this 8,118-foot sub-peak in each direction as the old-timers used to. History buffs, masochists, and seekers of solitude can create an interesting "figure-eight" route by using both the new trail and old trail (see optional side trip to Little Caribou Lake). Either way, there's not a lot of water en route, so be sure to refill when you have the opportunity.

From the trailhead, the path leads south through a shady stand of firs to the wilderness boundary and then to a crossing of the South Fork Salmon River. Just before the creek, the Valley Loop Trail diverges to the south. Crossing the South Fork Salmon River shouldn't pose any problem (other than wet feet), but use caution in early-season high water. Once across the creek, you find two trails climbing the opposite bank. The one to the right (northwest) is the Old Caribou Trail. This is the route you return on if you opt for the figure-eight loop. The new trail is on the left (southwest). Take this path out of the streambed and head west across a tree-dotted meadow.

After leaving the river, the trail meanders through a parklike setting of mixed conifers, and you soon pass the junction with the Tri-Forest Peak Trail (Hike 33). Continue west past the junction and begin climbing. . . and climbing. You ascend the lion's share of this route's elevation gain on a series of long, gradual switchbacks that climb the lower reaches of Caribou Mountain. The trail is generally shady in mixed forest, but look for great views when the tree cover opens up. Red Rock Mountain and Black Mountain dominate the ridgeline on the opposite side of the South Fork drainage, and Caribou Mountain looms directly ahead.

Top out in Caribou Meadow, a small clearing nestled on the shoulder of the mountain 4 miles from the trailhead. This is also the site of the junction with the Old Caribou Trail. It crosses your path from north to south, heading steeply uphill toward the top of Peak 8,118. Little Caribou Lake lies about 1,000 feet (and a couple of miles) above you in a basin on the north side of the mountain. No trail leads to the secluded lake, but the easiest way to get there is to take the Old Caribou Trail to a point level with the basin, then strike off across the granite slopes (the route to Little Caribou Lake is described in the optional side trip at the end of this chapter).

To continue on the new and improved trail, head west as the path contours around the shoulder of Caribou Mountain. The route around the mountain is longer, but a whole lot easier than going up and over. The trail is mostly level all the way around, passing through mixed forest and along a sunny bench literally carved into the mountain's sweeping granite flank. You'll find the first dependable water sources since the South Fork along this section of exposed granite, where little streams collect and drain into Big Conrad Gulch. All water along the route should be purified.

Caribou Basin from the Caribou Lakes Trail.

Look for big views to the west as you round the shoulder of Caribou Mountain and head slightly downhill to reach Browns Meadow, 6 miles from the trailhead. If you're going to spend a night along the trail, this is the place to do it. Browns Meadow is a wide, sloping meadow stocked with a few granite boulders, an alder-choked stream, a rusty wheelbarrow, and an assortment of summer wildflowers—pussy toes, corn lilies, Shasta daisies, etc. A spring crosses the trail just after the meadow.

From Browns Meadow, ascend moderate switchbacks to an obvious notch in the ridgeline. Here, you emerge onto the west side of Caribou Mountain and get your first view of what all the fuss is about. Thompson Peak and its permanent snowfields dominate the skyline, and the whole of Caribou Basin soon comes into view as the trail contours along through the granite. Snowslide and Lower Caribou are the first lakes you see, with the huge bowl containing Caribou looming above them. Easy hiking, ever-increasing views, and a rainbow's worth of wildflowers dominate the last few miles of the trail.

Just past the second junction with the Old Caribou Trail, 8.5 miles from the trailhead, the path follows a series of moderate switchbacks downhill into the basin. Cross a small meadow before arriving at the granite dike separating Snowslide and Lower Caribou Lakes, then choose any one of the meandering trails that crisscross the heavily used area. More people choose to stay in this area than at Caribou proper, probably because the lower basin is more protected from wind, and because these campsites are the first you encounter—hence the first place to put down that heavy pack. Avoid using campsites too close to the water.

To reach Caribou Lake, follow cairns on either side of the dike (both trails lead up to the lake). The path on the left (southeast) is the most direct, while the path on the right (which goes around the northwest side of Middle Caribou Lake) meanders up the outlet stream. Middle Caribou Lake is really just a pond sandwiched between Snowslide and Lower Caribou Lakes.

At 72 acres and 72 feet deep, Caribou dwarfs all other lakes in the Alps, and the setting is equal to the lake. Caribou simply sweeps you up in a smorgasbord of alpine delights: sparkling ponds and hanging gardens with late summer gentians, primroses, and monkeyflowers cluster around the lake's southern shore. The western shore is steep and rocky, but a delightful series of meadows on the southwest side of the lake make for one of the most beautiful sights in the Alps (look at, but definitely don't camp in, this fragile environment).

The deep blue water is ideal for long swims; the possibilities for exploration endless. The only hike you should feel obligated to do while at Caribou is a short jaunt to the saddle between this basin and Stuart Fork. An obvious use trail leads up the south wall of the cirque to the low point on the ridgeline. The switchbacks get steeper and steeper as you rise 700 feet in just under a mile to the gap. Once on top, behold one of the most spectacular vistas in all the Alps. Sawtooth Ridge is so close on your left it seems like you must be sitting right in the granite maw. In front and far below stretch Stuart Fork and beautiful Morris Meadow, and on your right are Emerald and Sapphire Lakes in their sheer-sided granite trough. You can also see every major peak in the Alps; Sawtooth, Siligo, Granite, Wedding Cake, and Thompson Peak all seem close enough to touch. Caribou Basin is spread beneath your feet. For the best view of all this alpine finery, wander a short way west up the ridgeline for an unobstructed vista.

Of course, you might also consider hiking down to Stuart Fork, but think before you hike. Called the Caribou Scramble, the trail ahead plummets nearly 2,500 feet straight down to the canyon bottom, and every foot is in the sun. Endless switchbacks and no shade or water make this one of the most arduous sections of trail in the Alps. You can use this trail to make a longer loop back to Big Flat by connecting the Stuart Fork, Deer Creek, and Tri-Forest Trails.

For the return back to the trailhead you have two choices: return the way you came or go up and over Peak 8118 on the Old Caribou Trail.

Old Caribou Trail: To return via the Old Caribou Trail and make an elegant figure-eight loop, hike back to the junction in the trees half a mile before Snowslide–Lower Caribou. Take the obvious trail going east up Caribou Mountain. It's a steep 1,200-foot haul to the top of Peak 8118. At the top, a short ramble to the north of the saddle yields a view of Little Caribou Lake, tucked into a rocky bowl 1,000 feet below. Don't be tempted to head straight down to the lake from here. A much better route is to follow the trail down the northeast slope of the mountain. A mile below the saddle, take a line across the open granite slope and shoot for the obvious basin to the west. Rock cairns may lead the way.

Little Caribou Lake is a secluded body of water at 7,150 feet. The 10-acre lake gets very few visitors. Swim out to the lake's small granite islands, relax in the sun, and imagine what it was like when Caribou Basin had solitude like this.

After returning to the trail from Little Caribou Lake, it's a steep descent to Caribou Meadow on rough tread, then more steep hiking down Caribou Gulch before finally winding back around to the crossing at the South Fork Salmon River near the trailhead. In Caribou Meadow you can pick up the new trail again if you want a quicker return.

Options: Create a longer loop back to Big Flat by descending into Stuart Fork on the Caribou Scramble, then returning via the Tri-Forest Trail (Hike 33), Ward Lake Trail (Hike 32) or Yellow Rose Trail (Hike 31).

35 Adams Lake

Highlights:	An easy hike to a glorified frog pond well worth visiting as an easy day trip in early or late season, or as a backpack for families with young kids or beginners.
Type of hike:	Day hike or backpack (one night); out-and-back.
Total distance:	5.2 miles.
Difficulty:	Easy.
Elevation gain:	1,400 feet.
Maps:	USGS Caribou Lake quad; USDAFS Trinity Alps Wilderness map.

Finding the trailhead: From Weaverville, drive 40 miles north on California Highway 3 to Coffee Creek Road and go left (west). Follow this road 16 miles to the signed trailhead on the right (Coffee Creek Road is unpaved after first 5 miles). The trailhead is small and easy to miss. Look for an old jeep track on the right, several feet higher than Coffee Creek Road.

Parking and trailhead facilities: A small pullout is the only parking (there's more parking available along Coffee Creek Road in both directions); no facilities. The closest campgrounds are Goldfield and Big Flat.

Key points:
    0.0   Trailhead.
    2.1   Adams Creek crossing.
    2.6   Adams Lake.

The hike: The short route to little Adams Lake makes for a pleasant and easy day trip. It's also a nice overnight destination for families with young children. My parents started taking my sister and me here about the time we learned to walk.

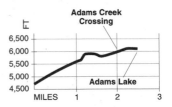

Profile data provided by TOPO!
©1999 Wildflower Productions
(www.topo.com)

Adams Lake

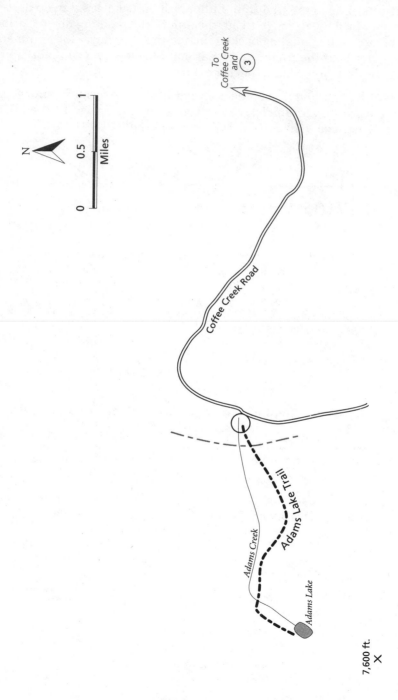

Adams Lake along Adams Lake Trail.

A Forest Service gate and information sign are located at the beginning of the trailhead, but there may or may not be a sign for Adams Lake (it comes and goes). The old jeep road switchbacks uphill to the northeast, then turns on itself to climb moderately but steadily southwest up the ridgeline. Look for the remnants of an old mining ditch near the turn.

Continue up the ridgeline in mixed forest of large fir and pine, and don't be tempted to take any of the faint jeep tracks diverging from the main road. The trees thin out 0.5 mile up the ridgeline as the trail contours around the hill in front of you.

A brief downhill is followed by more moderate climbing through shady stands of fir, pine, incense-cedar, and manzanita, then easy walking alongside Adams Creek. The rest of the hike is along the alder-choked creek, making for a pleasant grade and plenty of greenery. A gap in the alders opens up about 2.1 miles in, and you cross the creek to finish the hike on the west bank. A few hundred yards uphill from the crossing you pass through a small meadow, skirt a few large granite outcroppings, and then arrive at the lake itself.

The 1-acre lake is bordered by talus slopes and a steep granite wall on the south, and willows, alders, and grassy shores on the other sides. A cattail pond thrives at the outlet. The last time I visited Adams Lake was on a misty, drizzly day in late September. The scenic little pond was as quiet as any place I've ever been in the Alps—not a soul was around and even the frogs were silent—and I would have sworn I was 20 miles deep in the wilderness, not 2.

36 South Fork Coffee Creek Loop

Highlights:	An off-the-beaten track hike through several scenic drainages, with a couple of on-the-beaten track lakes en route.
Type of hike:	Backpack; loop.
Total distance:	16.8 miles.
Difficulty:	Moderate.
Elevation gain:	4,000 feet.
Maps:	USGS Deadman Peak quad; USDAFS Trinity Alps Wilderness map.

Finding the trailhead: From Weaverville, drive 40 miles north on California Highway 3 to Coffee Creek Road and go left (west). Follow this road 15 miles to the signed trailhead on the right (Coffee Creek Road is unpaved after first 5 miles). The trailhead is 0.5 mile past the South Fork bridge.

Parking and trailhead facilities: Parking area is in a little clearing a few rough yards off the main road; no water or other facilities. The closest campgrounds are Goldfield and Big Flat.

Key points:
0.0	Trailhead.
2.3	Steveale Creek Trail junction.
5.4	Long Gulch Trail junction.
6.4	Long Gulch Lake.
10.3	Trail Gulch Lake.
10.9	North Fork Coffee Creek Trail junction.
12.2	Steveale Creek Trail junction.
14.5	South Fork Coffee Creek Trail junction.
16.8	Trailhead.

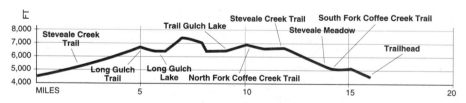

Profile data provided by TOPO! ©1999 Wildflower Productions (www.topo.com)

The hike: Much has been made about South Fork Coffee Creek's location—it's entirely north of Coffee Creek. Still, the water flows south, so I suppose that's something (though so does the water in the North and East Forks). In any event, whoever named the tributaries sure wasn't holding a compass.

Directional problems aside, this is a splendid hike through little-traveled drainages with lush meadows, incredible views, and a couple of good swimming lakes. Solitude is always a good bet (except at the lakes), and peak baggers will pass within easy reach of 7,617-foot Deadman Peak.

South Fork Coffee Creek Loop

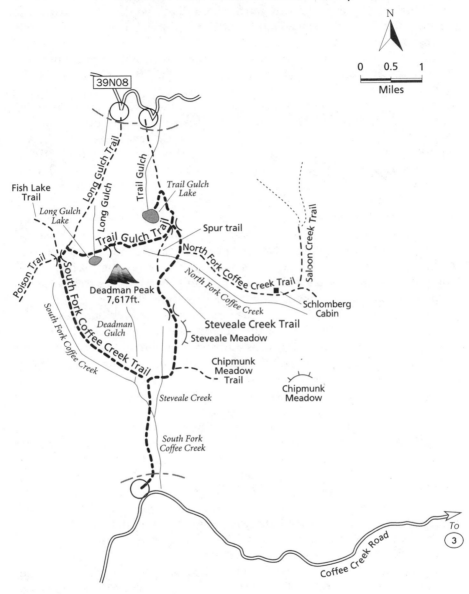

Hiking north from the trailhead, you immediately pass a metal Forest Service gate (closed to keep vehicles off the old jeep track). Past the gate, the track starts climbing up a gully, then switchbacks moderately up a hillside thick with Douglas-fir and ponderosa pine. A more gentle grade leads northeast, to a point high above South Fork Coffee Creek, where you round the shoulder of the ridge and continue north along the course of the creek. The going is shady and level, even slightly downhill as you make your way up the drainage.

Just over 1 mile from the trailhead, pass an old, overgrown jeep track that veers to the right (east), toward the creek. Don't take it. A trail sign for the South Fork Trail points the way north on the path you're on. Pass a cabin site just after the trail sign. Debris indicates the cabin was of relatively recent vintage.

The trail bisects a couple of small meadows lined with mature incense-cedar, some of the biggest cedar trees in the Alps. After the meadows, descend to a crossing of the South Fork, 2 miles from the trailhead. On the east bank now, climb moderately just under 0.5 mile to a junction with the Steveale Creek Trail (9W61). To the right (east) the sign indicates connections with Chipmunk Meadow and North Fork Coffee Creek trails. That's the way you return. To the left (northwest), the South Fork Trail (9W04) continues up the drainage. A sign points the way to Taylor Creek (which is true, but it's a rather obscure destination to get a sign all to itself).

Stay left on the South Fork Trail and make your way northwest through the wide, very gently sloping valley. Mixed forest and ferny meadows alternate for the next 2 miles, with only one thing to mar the scenery: occasional cow pies and cattle-trampled grass (you can check with rangers on current grazing conditions, but this is one of the few drainages south of the Scott Mountains divide that has had grazing in recent years). Cattle trails obscure the path somewhat in a few places, but cairns show the way.

Fill water bottles from the South Fork or one of its tributaries before starting the ascent at the head of the canyon. Be sure to purify all water. A half-mile climb through mixed forest ends at a saddle on the Salmon–Scott Mountains Divide, where a few battered and broken signs mark a three-way junction. The Poison Canyon Trail goes left (west), the Fish Lake Trail goes north (see Hike 50), and the Long Gulch Trail goes right (northeast), plunging over the ridgeline and down to Long Gulch Lake. Both Long Gulch Lake and Trail Gulch Lake are accessible via relatively easy trails (3.5 and 2.5 miles, respectively) on the north side of the divide. See Hike 49 for a complete description of these trails and the two lakes.

To continue the loop, head downhill on the Long Gulch Trail, switchbacking to the bottom of the drainage and another junction. A left (south) turn leads to the Long Gulch Trailhead on Forest Road 39N08. Turn right (east) on Trail Gulch Trail and walk slightly uphill over rocky tread to Long Gulch Lake. The 12-acre, deep blue lake is great for swimming. Repeatedly. You can do laps around the island.

At the outlet on the northeast side of the lake, near an overused campsite, pick up the trail as it crosses the creek to the east. Look up. Your challenge is to climb to the ridgeline on the east side of the cirque. It's a steep haul, so tank up on water before you start the ascent.

Less than a mile from the lake, top out on the crest and enjoy the view. It's fantastic—especially the granite-rimmed blue gem at your feet. Also at your feet is another trail junction. Ignore it. The trail going straight downhill is the old path, which descends steeply toward the North Fork Coffee Creek, then climbs back up toward Trail Gulch Lake. A new trail, shown on the 1998 Forest Service Wilderness map but not on the USGS quad, avoids that elevation loss by cutting across the ridgeline to the saddle above Trail Gulch Lake. (Note: The names of Long and Trail Gulch lakes are reversed on the USGS quad; see Hike 49 for an explanation of the name game.)

Go left (east) on the newer trail, and arrive at the saddle in an easy downhill mile. The stroll is shaded by mature firs and accompanied by excellent views of the North Fork Coffee Creek drainage. (Note: If you're contemplating climbing Deadman Peak, this is as fine a place as any to leave the trail.)

At the saddle above Trail Gulch Lake, a well-signed trail junction provides several options. Turn left (north) to descend 0.8 mile to the lake. To start the return portion of the loop, take either the North Fork Coffee Creek or Steveale Creek Trails (you end up in the same place). They both lead downhill (south) from the crest. Both paths can be difficult to follow as you descend into the forested drainage. I recommend the North Fork Coffee Creek Trail, which is a bit more distinct and a bit more scenic. Once you descend into the large, lush meadow at the head of North Fork Coffee Creek, you should have no trouble identifying a signed junction at the bottom of the glade. (Even if you lose the trail on the way down, you're sure to end up in the meadow.)

At the junction, the North Fork Trail (9W02) continues east, across the creek, to Saloon Creek, Schlomberg Cabin and the heart of the North Fork Coffee Creek drainage (see Hike 37). To the right (southwest), a spur trail, signed Steveale Creek, leads to the Steveale Creek Trail (9W61). Pass through a cool, lush thicket of alders as you cross the wet drainage bottom, than ascend moderately through shady fir forest to a junction with the Steveale Creek Trail proper (0.7 mile from the last junction). This is where you end up if you take the other trail from the saddle above Trail Gulch Lake. A sign

Steveale Meadow.

indicates Trail Gulch is to the right (north) and Steveale Meadow is to the left (south). Go south.

The next stretch contours pleasantly along a slope high above the North Fork Coffee Creek drainage. Wildflowers appear in little bunches where granite gives way to grass. On the horizon, Mount Shasta's white summit pierces the sky above the distant ridges. The short traverse leads to the divide above Steveale Creek, where you descend to a saddle at the head of a steeply sloping meadow.

The path descends the east side of the meadow. Alder thickets line the canyon bottom, and Caribou Mountain looms directly ahead on the horizon. A half-mile descent leads to an old cow camp at the bottom of Steveale Meadow ("Camp Siberia," says an old hand-carved sign). Just beyond the camp is an unmarked junction. The trail back to South Fork Coffee Creek crosses to the west bank of Steveale Creek. On the east bank, the little-used Chipmunk Trail bends away from the creek and climbs west to wild and empty Chipmunk Meadow. An old mine is just a few hundred yards up the path.

On the west bank, the Steveale Creek Trail enters the shady forest and veers southwest, away from the deepening canyon, and descends in less than a mile to a junction with South Fork Coffee Creek Trail. Turn left (south) and retrace your steps 2.3 miles to the trailhead.

Options: Explore the upper North Fork Coffee Creek drainage (down to Schlomberg Cabin, Saloon Creek, and Hodges Cabin; see Hike 37).

37 North Fork Coffee Creek

Highlights:	Rugged canyon scenery, cascading rivers, and numerous historic cabins.
Type of hike:	Day hike or backpack; out-and-back.
Total distance:	13 miles.
Difficulty:	Easy to moderate.
Elevation gain:	1,750 feet (to Schlomberg Cabin).
Maps:	USGS Billys Peak and Deadman Peak quads; USDAFS Trinity Alps Wilderness map.

Finding the trailhead: From Weaverville, drive 40 miles north on California Highway 3 to Coffee Creek Road and go left (west). Follow this road 9 miles to the signed trailhead on the right (Coffee Creek Road is unpaved after first 5 miles). The trailhead is just before the North Fork bridge.

Parking and trailhead facilities: Adequate parking, but don't be surprised to find numerous cars here on summer weekends; no facilities. The closest campgrounds are Goldfield and Big Flat.

North Fork Coffee Creek

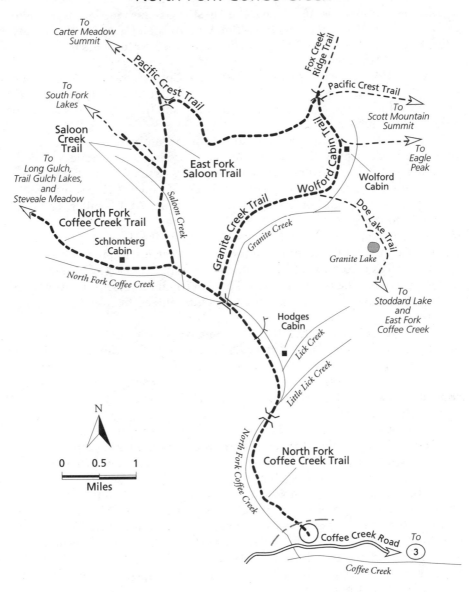

Key points:

  0.0 Trailhead.

  3.5 Hodges Cabin.

  4.5 Granite Creek Trail.

  6.5 Schlomberg Cabin.

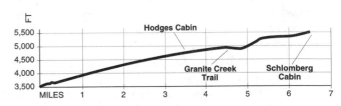

Profile data provided by TOPO! ©1999 Wildflower Productions (www.topo.com)

The hike: Most people use the North Fork Coffee Creek Trail (9W02) to stroll 3.5 miles to historic Hodges Cabin, spend the day poking around the idyllic site, eat a picnic lunch, sign the guest register, then skip back down the trail at the end of the day. It's a fine way to spend a day in the Trinity Alps. But to sample some of the most rugged, lonely wilderness in the Alps, don't stop at Hodges Cabin.

Beyond Hodges, you can use North Fork Coffee Creek Trail to reach Schlomberg Cabin, a dilapidated old miner's shelter in a pretty green glade above the North Fork, as well as Wolford Cabin and the headwaters of North Fork Coffee Creek.

The trail starts with a quick climb to gain a line high above the creek. After the initial ascent, the path assumes a more moderate grade as it contours northwest and then north, following the course of North Fork Coffee Creek. Oaks, Douglas-fir, and several varieties of pine provide some shade, but expect sunny and hot hiking in the first mile. At 1.5 miles, the trail descends to creek level just before a bridge (and near an old cabin site, minus the cabin). Crossing to the west bank, you hike the rest of the way to Hodges Cabin on a meandering path that wanders up and down along the creek, through mixed forest dominated by fir and incense-cedar and punctuated by lovely little flower gardens. Fly fishermen beware: you pass within casting distance of several sparkling holes guaranteed to contain trout. Allow time.

At Hodges Cabin, a makeshift bridge on a tree trunk permits a dry crossing of the now wide and placid river. The two-story structure, with assorted outbuildings, was restored by the US Forest Service in 1987. It's now inhabited by caretakers in the summer, who will be happy to show you around and tell you about the history of the site. The original cabin was built by Walter Hodges in the early 1920s. The southern California businessman wanted a vacation home in his beloved Trinity Alps, and constructed a 2,000-square-foot house in the remote valley. It was once a bustling little outpost, with its own hydroelectric plant and telephone. Be sure to fill water bottles at the cabin's sweet tasting spring.

Another historic site, unknown to many visitors, lies 0.5 mile downstream above the confluence of the North Fork and Lick Creek. Though little remains at the site, a seasonal Native American village was once located in a meadow neatly hidden in the forest above the confluence. To reach it, follow an unmaintained path south of Hodges Cabin, on the east side of the North Fork, and make your way up to the hidden plateau, passing some old mining relics on the way.

North of Hodges Cabin, the canyon of the North Fork widens into a broad valley where forest and meadow alternate regularly along the drainage, and sandy streamside beaches invite a lazy afternoon in the sun. An easy mile of near-level walking brings you to another steel bridge over the North Fork, where you cross back to the east side. Look for (and sniff for) a remarkably fragrant stand of azaleas at the crossing (best in early season). Just across the bridge, 4.5 miles from the trailhead, arrive at the Granite Creek Trail junction (8W09). Signs indicate that Wolford Cabin, Granite Lake, and the

Hodges Cabin.

Doe Lake Trail (8W05) lie to the right (northeast). Turn here if you want to reach Wolford Cabin in the most direct way (check with rangers on current conditions, however; hundreds of downed trees made some trails in this area, including Granite Creek and East Fork Coffee Creek, nearly impassable in recent years).

To reach Schlomberg Cabin and the headwaters of North Fork Coffee Creek, continue northwest on the North Fork Trail. The path crosses Saloon Creek (no more bridges) and ascends to a signed junction with the Saloon Creek Trail. Another historic cabin, this one unnamed but still standing (and strangely made out of stucco), is located on a flat that you pass just after crossing the creek. It reportedly belonged to Hodges's carpenter.

At the Saloon Creek Trail junction, stay left (west) on the North Fork Trail to reach Schlomberg Cabin (the junction is signed "South Fork Lakes" to the right; "Long Gulch Lake–Steveale Meadow" to the left). A mile west of the junction you emerge into an open meadow; the historic cabin is located in a forest-fringed clearing just below. Schlomberg is the most deteriorated of the cabins still standing in this corner of the Alps.

Options: Two miles beyond Schlomberg Cabin the trail connects with the Steveale Creek Trail and Trail Gulch and Long Gulch Lakes (Hikes 36 and 49). For a scenic loop route, take the Saloon Creek Trail and East Fork Saloon Trail to the Pacific Crest Trail, then make a loop back by way of Wolford Cabin and the Granite Creek Trail (adds about 10 miles, partially described in Hike 46). Granite Lake and Doe Lake are also within striking distance (not described here; check with rangers on current condition of trail). The loop can also be extended by using East Fork Coffee Creek Trail and walking back to the trailhead on Coffee Creek Road.

38 Billys Peak Lookout

Highlights:	A steep but relatively short hike to an old fire lookout site; great view.
Type of hike:	Day hike; out-and-back.
Total distance:	6 miles.
Difficulty:	Moderate.
Elevation gain:	2,900 feet.
Maps:	USGS Carrville quad; USDAFS Trinity Alps Wilderness map.

Finding the trailhead: From Weaverville, drive 42 miles north on California Highway 3 (past Coffee Creek) and turn left (west) on Forest Road 38N34 (signed Billys Peak Trailhead). The access road is closed October 30 to May 1. Trailhead signs point the way where logging roads merge with the main road. At 4.6 miles park at a wide landing. Billys Peak Trail starts on the uphill (north) side of the clearing.

Parking and trailhead facilities: No facilities or drinking water. The nearest Forest Service developed campground is Trinity River 1 mile away on CA 3, immediately south of FR 38N34.

Key points:

    0.0   Trailhead.
    3.0   Billys Peak Lookout.

The hike: The Billys Peak Trail (7W08) is the path to take if you're a fan of big views and you want instant gratification. It's a stairway hike straight to the top of a 7,000-foot granite perch on the very edge of the Trinity Alps Wilderness. The 360-degree view from the summit takes in Mount Shasta, Lassen Peak, the Coffee Creek drainage, and a host of peaks in the inner Alps. Despite the name, the summit

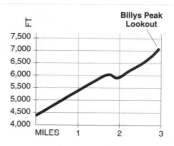

Profile data provided by TOPO!
©1999 Wildflower Productions
(www.topo.com)

is not really Billys Peak, but an unnamed island of rock where the fire lookout was built (the real Billys Peak is slightly higher and lies to the northwest).

The trail rises steeply at first, but soon settles into a more moderate grade on shady switchbacks that leads northwest under a canopy of mixed fir and pine. In less than a mile you gain the ridgeline and continue to climb moderately, with ever better views of Coffee Creek as you ascend. The forest cover gets more sparse and the trail more rocky as you climb. The upper portion of this hike is very hot and sunny in the summer time.

A long contour to the southwest leads to the final assault on the peak, where a series of steep, rocky, and exposed switchbacks leads to the summit. In the middle of this steep section, which will certainly be strenuous on a hot day, someone has painted this message on a boulder: "The spirit

Billys Peak Lookout

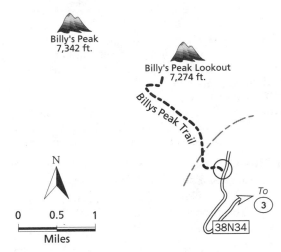

indeed is willing, but the flesh is weak." While I can't condone the graffiti, it's an appropriate sentiment on a hot day.

The last few steps are in a rock gully, then you pop up on top—nothing but air and horizon in every direction. Mount Shasta is so close it looks like you can reach out and touch it. The only remains of the fire lookout are the foundation and a few rusted old cans, but it's enough to make you wonder about the fortunate few who used to spend their summers up here. Return the way you came.

Billys Peak Lookout.

39 Stoddard Lake

Highlights: A short hike to a big lake, pretty meadows, thick forests, and plenty of company.
Type of hike: Day hike or backpack; out-and-back or optional loop.
Total distance: 6.4 miles.
Difficulty: Easy.
Elevation gain: 750 feet (add 300 feet for optional loop).
Maps: USGS Billys Peak and Tangle Blue Lake quads; USDAFS Trinity Alps Wilderness map.

Finding the trailhead: From Weaverville, drive 43 miles north on California 3 to the signed turn for Eagle Creek–Horse Flat (3 miles north of Coffee Creek). Turn left (west) on County Road 135 and proceed 1.2 miles to the signed left turn for the Stoddard Lake Trailhead (on Forest Road 38N22). The unpaved road is easy to follow (stay left at 5.4 miles) to the junction with Forest Road 38N27 at 5.8 miles. Go left (west) and continue to the trailhead at 8.7 miles.

Parking and trailhead facilities: Ample parking but no facilities. Horse Flat, Eagle Creek, and Trinity River Campgrounds are within a few miles of the trailhead.

Key points:
0.0 Trailhead.
0.4 Old Stoddard Trail junction.
2.3 East Fork Coffee Creek Trail junction–Stoddard Cabin site.
3.5 Stoddard Lake.
3.6 Old Stoddard Trail.
6.4 Trailhead.

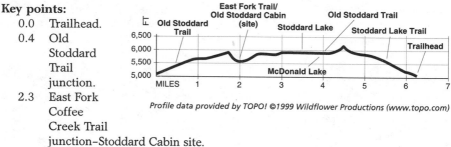

Profile data provided by TOPO! ©1999 Wildflower Productions (www.topo.com)

The hike: The Stoddard Lake basin's attractions are easy to list: good swimming, fishing, and camping an hour and a half from the trailhead, which account for its main detraction—summer crowds that rival any other popular Trinity destination. Add swarms of early-season mosquitoes, a herd of grazing cattle, and frequent horseback riders from nearby dude ranches, and you might want to give Stoddard Lake a wide berth if it's a quiet wilderness experience you're after.

Of course, there's usually a good reason for a crowd, and Stoddard is no exception. At just under 6,000 feet elevation, the lake warms up early in the summer and offers a great basecamp from which to explore the area. Stoddard and neighbor McDonald Lake are both deep blue lakes in the protected shelter of a low-lying basin. Each lake is rimmed by thick forests of mixed

Stoddard Lake

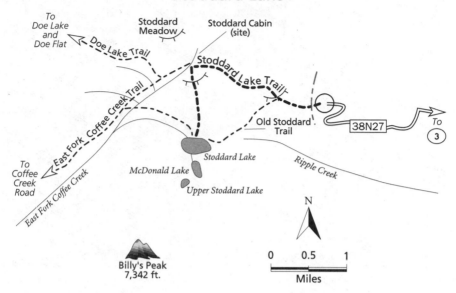

conifers, with plenty of elbowroom to absorb the crowds. With lots of opportunities for exploring the surrounding area (both on and off trail), there should be little surprise that Stoddard is a popular destination. It's a great place for families with young children, as the hike in is very gentle.

The Stoddard Lake Trail (7W06) starts uphill, heading west on a wide path through a forest of Douglas-fir, incense-cedar, and ponderosa pine. The trail soon levels out and climbs gently to a meadow 0.4 mile from the trailhead. The main trail veers right (northwest) through the meadow, while an unmarked and subtle path forks left (southwest). This unmarked path is the Old Stoddard Lake Trail, which climbs steeply over a ridgeline and into the lake basin by the most direct route. While shorter than the new trail by about a mile, the old trail is considerably steeper and unmaintained (it's not even on the new Forest Service wilderness map). It is a pretty route, however, and I recommend taking it on the way back.

To continue on the new trail, stay right and ascend moderately through the shady forest. Look for views of Mount Shasta to the east as you climb. The route is easy the rest of the way. Pass flower-filled meadows and a little creek that feeds a glade full of California pitcher plants.

After crossing aster-filled Stoddard Meadow, arrive at the junction with East Fork Coffee Creek Trail in a flat next to the old Stoddard Cabin site (there's not much left of the historic cabin, which, like the lake and meadow, was named after nineteenth-century rancher John Stoddard). The junction is signed Doe Flat to the right (west), Stoddard Lake to the left (south). The junction is just over 2 miles from the trailhead.

The last mile to the lake rises moderately to the south, arriving abruptly at the shoreline in a shady stand of fir and lodgepole pine. McDonald Lake is located immediately south of Stoddard, behind a screen of mixed conifers.

McDonald and Stoddard Lakes.

McDonald is simply a smaller version of Stoddard. Farther to the southwest and 450 feet higher is Upper Stoddard Lake, a little pond tucked into the granite shelf at the head of the basin. No trail leads to Upper Stoddard, but you can pick your way up the rocky outlet without much difficulty (stay north to avoid the steepest sections). The lake is a 0.5 mile scramble from McDonald Lake.

To return to the trailhead, you can either retrace your steps or create a loop by using the unmaintained Old Stoddard Trail. At the northeast side of Stoddard Lake, where the new trail ends, find the path leading northeast. The sometimes-obscure path leads uphill to the crest of a ridge, then plunges a mile to a junction with the new trail. Look for great views of Mount Shasta from the ridgetop. The route is generally easy to follow (if somewhat overgrown). Arrive at the junction in the first meadow you passed on the way in. Turn right (east) and proceed 0.4 mile to the trailhead.

Options: The East Fork Coffee Creek Trail (8W06) connects to Doe and Granite Lakes (Doe Lake Trail, 8W05) and Coffee Creek Road. The Stoddard spur trail (8W24), located on the northwest side of Stoddard Lake, also leads to the East Fork Trail.

40 Bear Lakes

Highlights:	Classic Trinity Alps setting: granite cirques, great views, and sparkling lakes.
Type of hike:	Day hike or overnight; out-and-back.
Total distance:	11.2 miles.
Difficulty:	Moderate.
Elevation gain:	3,200 feet.
Maps:	USGS Tangle Blue Lake quad; USDAFS Trinity Alps Wilderness map.

Finding the trailhead: From Weaverville, drive 48 miles north on California Highway 3 to the signed turn for Bear Lake Trailhead on County Road 137 (8 miles north of Coffee Creek). If the first Bear Lake Road access is closed (as it was in recent years), proceed another 2 miles to the second entrance (the road makes a loop with two ends on CA 3). Turn left (west) at either entrance and proceed just over a mile to the signed trailhead at Bear Creek. A bridge over the creek is closed to vehicles so you'll have to park on the north side of stream (if you come from that end) and walk across the bridge to the trailhead.

Parking and trailhead facilities: Limited parking and no facilities (more than a few cars here is a good indication to go elsewhere, as there is nowhere else to go and you'll likely find all their occupants at Bear Lake). A few undeveloped campsites are available, but the closest developed campgrounds are at Eagle Creek and Trinity River, a few miles south on CA 3.

Key points:

0.0	Trailhead.
1.0	Bear Creek bridge.
4.6	Big Bear Lake.
5.6	Little and Wee Bear Lakes (off-trail).

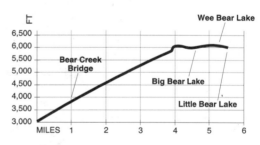

Profile data provided by TOPO!
©1999 Wildflower Productions (www.topo.com)

The hike: The Bear Lakes basin presents the classic crowd problem caused by too much beautiful scenery too close to the trailhead. Here the problem is exacerbated by the basin's limited camping opportunities and lack of alternative trail systems (the hike is a dead-end). Come here on a busy summer weekend, when the trailhead parking is full, and it'll be hard to find a place to pitch a tent. That said, the Bear Lakes basin is still not as heavily used as many other easy-to-reach destinations in the Alps, and it's not uncommon to find solitude here on weekdays and out-of-season. I've been here in the fall and not seen another soul.

The Trinity Alps' easternmost lakes (if you examine the map you'll see it took a creative eastward jog of the wilderness boundary to include the Bear

Bear Lakes

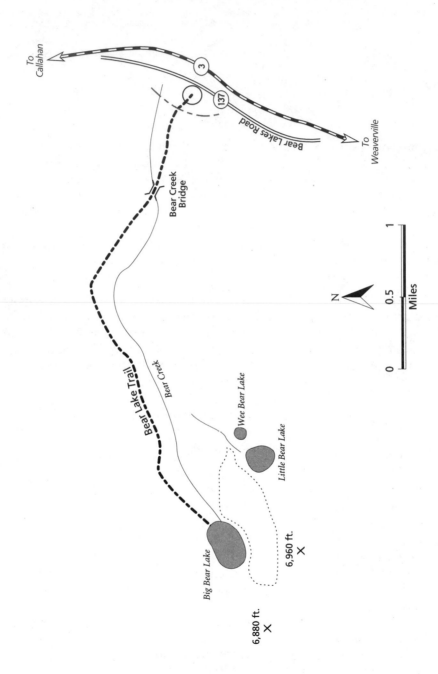

Lakes basin) are set in a northeast-facing cirque at a relatively low elevation of 6,000 feet. But the northern exposure, granite surroundings, and impressive view of Mount Shasta create a slice of alpine wonder equal to many higher, more remote settings. Good swimming, fishing, and exploring abound.

The Bear Lake Trail (7W03) starts at a signed trailhead on the south side of Bear Creek and climbs steeply up a set of switchbacks, through mixed forest of fir, cedar, and scattered oaks. After the initial ascent, the trail contours more moderately up the drainage. A mile from the trailhead, cross Bear Creek on a new wood-and-steel bridge (within sight of the old crossing), then continue climbing on the north side of the creek.

The trail ascends through open hillsides of oak and manzanita on the ridgeline high above Bear Creek. Over the next couple of miles you continue to climb in a westerly direction, steeply at times, up the drainage. Pine, fir, and incense-cedar dominate the forest as you ascend. Look for an emerald green fern meadow just over halfway to Big Bear Lake, and an obvious avalanche path shortly after that. The broken trees and other winter wreckage are an impressive sight.

Just over 4 miles in, the trail breaks out into the open, rocky upper drainage, where cairns lead the way up beautiful granite slabs. Across Bear Creek, the notch in the ridge to the south marks the entrance to Little and Wee Bear Lakes (there's no trail to the gap, but you can get there from Big Bear without much difficulty). At 4.6 miles, the path crosses the outlet stream and deposits you at the edge of Big Bear Lake. Tucked into a rugged granite cirque and surrounded by bare rock with a few stunted stands of western white pine and mountain hemlock, the 28-acre lake is one of the largest in the Alps. There are great views of Mount Shasta from the basin's eastern edge and, in the summer, little gardens of wildflowers fill the cracks in the granite slabs.

Little and Wee Bear Lakes are directly to the southeast, on the other side of an unnamed peak (just shy of 7,000 feet) that sits between the two cirques. You can get there by going around the east side of the peak and following cairns on a moderate traverse to the notch that leads to Little and Wee Bears. No trail is established, but the 1-mile route is not difficult. Once through the gap, you come first to pond-size Wee Bear, then to medium-size Little Bear (a smaller version of its big brother, but with more elbowroom and more trees). The Little–Wee Bear basin is a great place to visit should you find Big Bear crowded.

You can return to Big Bear Lake the way you came or, to make a loop, go over the saddle west of Little Bear Lake. On the other side, you find yourself in the upper end of the basin above Big Bear. It's a beautiful setting with great views, wildflowers, and sublime snowmelt pools. Once Big Bear is in sight, it's a simple matter to pick your way down to the lake. Simple, at least, in terms of route-finding. No trail leads the way, so expect some serious bushwhacking to get through the underbrush between you and the outlet. This second route is steeper, longer, and more difficult than the first, but it's certainly beautiful. From Big Bear, return to the trailhead the way you came.

41 Tangle Blue Lake

Highlights:	An easy hike to a lake that lives up to its pretty name.
Type of hike:	Day hike or backpack; out-and-back.
Total distance:	7.6 miles.
Difficulty:	Easy.
Elevation gain:	1,100 feet.
Maps:	USGS Tangle Blue Lake quad; USDAFS Trinity Alps Wilderness map.

Finding the trailhead: From Weaverville, drive 53 miles north on California Highway 3 (13.3 miles past Coffee Creek) to the signed left turn (west) onto Forest Road 39N20. The turn is in the middle of a sharp right-hand curve, 0.8 mile after starting uphill toward Scott Mountain Summit. Trailers are not advisable on the narrow road, but passenger cars should be fine (though this road can be impassable after a heavy rain). Stay left at the fork at 2 miles, and straight at 3 miles. The trailhead is 3.8 miles from the highway. A locked timber company gate bars the trail.

Parking and trailhead facilities: Ample parking but no facilities or potable water. The nearest campgrounds are on CA 3 (several along the road toward Coffee Creek).

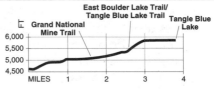

Profile data provided by TOPO!
©1999 Wildflower Productions (www.topo.com)

Key points:

0.0   Trailhead.
1.7   Grand National Mine spur trail.
2.7   East Boulder Lake Trail.
3.8   Tangle Blue Lake.

The hike: If lakes were judged on name alone, Tangle Blue Lake would be my second favorite in the Alps (Billy-be-Damned takes first, but just barely). Local legend attributes the name to a bad hangover. Tangle Blue is a pretty lake with a beautiful meadow on one side, plush campsites, and plenty of exploring potential. The hike is ideal for families or anyone looking for a gentle route. The only drawback is cows, which also appreciate the lakeside meadow and fine views. Though infrequent, they do visit.

From the trailhead parking area, head right (west) on the Grand National Trail (8W23), past the timber company gate and along an old dirt road to a bridge across Tangle Blue Creek. The single-lane bridge spans Tangle Blue just upstream from the confluence with Horse Creek. After crossing the bridge, stay right as the road climbs westward along the banks of Tangle Blue Creek. The road to the left leads to Horse Creek, and a trail marker signals the way if there's any confusion.

Tangle Blue Creek lives up to the allure of its name as much as the lake itself. The stream cascades and tumbles through a rugged canyon, with many clear deep pools and small pour-offs. The moderate grade and wide roadbed make for easy hiking, with a lot of elbowroom for a side-by-side walk with friends. The banks of the creek are lined with

Tangle Blue Lake

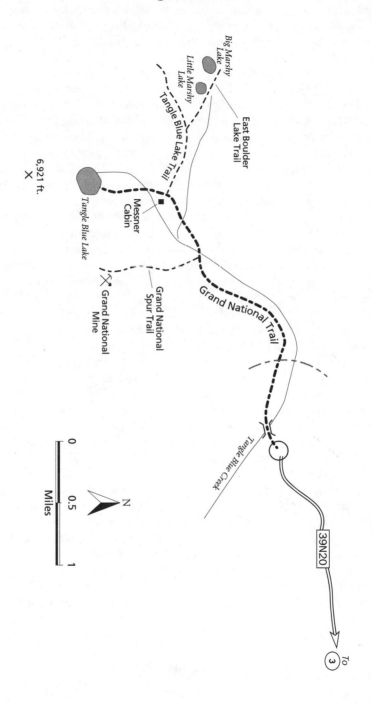

dense stands of incense-cedar, fir, and pine, with a lush understory of thick ferns.

The trail remains above the creek as it climbs gradually higher. After about 0.5 mile there are dense stands of manzanita on both sides of the trail—anyone who has ever fought through the thick, thorny bushes will appreciate the wide track between them.

Arrive at an old trailhead and Forest Service gate 1.5 miles from the trailhead (the hike used to be shorter), then walk through a majestic grove of enormous incense-cedar trees a quarter mile past the gate. The trees, ferns, and meadow offer an attractive spot to put up your feet for awhile. Moss on the cedars here is so bright green it seems to glow on a gray day. A brief walk uphill from the glowing moss (just under 2 miles from the trailhead) brings you to a junction with the spur trail to the historic Grand National Mine. Go left (south) to explore the ruins of the old mine and right (west) to continue toward Tangle Blue Lake. An obscure trail sign on a cedar tree indicates the direction. Descend slightly to a creek crossing, which should pose no problems except for at the peak of high water. Purify all water in the Trinity Alps.

Continue on actual trail (not old jeep track) for the first time since starting. The path continues for all of a quarter mile, then crosses the outlet from Little Marshy Lake. This creek may actually appear to be two creeks late in the year. After the crossing, the trail resumes on an old dirt road again.

Hike up the wide, rocky roadbed to a signed trail junction just under 2.7 miles from the trailhead. The sign indicates Tangle Blue Lake is to the left (south) and Marshy Lake is to the right (west). Use the right fork to reach the Pacific Crest Trail.

Take the left fork toward Tangle Blue Lake and immediately pass a huge double incense-cedar at the head of a beautiful meadow. Look up to the left and catch your first glimpse of the granite walls looming over the head of the Tangle Blue basin. Just before the end of the meadow, jog left and cross Tangle Blue Creek for the final time. Pass the remains of the old Messner Cabin site, then ascend moderately alongside the creek for the final 0.5 mile to the lake. Little creeklets flow through lush stands of willow, alder, and fern.

Emerge from the willow wonderland at the edge of a large meadow at the north end of Tangle Blue Lake. You may have to share the fine views with a few cows, but until grazing laws change, there's nothing you can do about it.

The 12-acre lake is set in a picture-perfect setting, with towering granite peaks overlooking the southern shores and easy walking all the way around the perimeter. Several campsites here are some of the few in the Alps that still have old Forest Service stoves in place.

Cattails, unusual in the Alps, thrive here on the east and north shores. There's also a nice little beach with accompanying meadow at the south end. The unnamed 6,900-foot peak above Tangle Blue Lake makes a fine scramble, with even finer views, but use caution on loose rock. An unmaintained use trail leads up the lake's inlet. The slightly higher (by a few hundred feet) peak on the east side of the lake also offers good scrambling potential. Return by the same route.

Options: The East Boulder Lake Trail leads to Marshy Lakes, then connects with the Pacific Crest Trail (Hike 46), just 3 miles away. From there a number of destinations along the Scott Mountains divide are easily accessible.

Hikes From
Forest Highway 93
(Callahan–Cecilville Road)

42 Mill Creek Lake and Washbasin Lake

     Highlights: A little-used trail to a little lake with an optional off-trail trek to Washbasin Lake; big views of Scott Valley.
     Type of hike: Day hike or backpack; out-and-back.
     Total distance: 8.2 miles.
     Difficulty: Easy (except off-trail segment to Washbasin Lake).
     Elevation gain: 1,000 feet (add 800 feet for off-trail segment).
     Maps: USGS Billys Peak and Callahan quad; USDAFS Trinity Alps Wilderness map.

Finding the trailhead: From Callahan (on California Highway 3, approximately 65 miles north of Weaverville), drive west on South Fork Road to the junction with Forest Roads 40N17 and 40N16 (you can also take South Fork Road from Forest Highway 93 to reach the same junction). Turn left (southeast) on FR 40N16 and proceed 4.5 miles to the trailhead at road's end (very rough going the last 100 yards).

Parking and trailhead facilities: Ample parking but no water or other facilities. The nearest Forest Service campgrounds are Scott Mountain, Hidden Horse, and Trail Creek.

Key points:
    0.0   Trailhead.
    3.0   Mill Creek Lake.
    3.3   Klatt Mine.
    4.1   Washbasin Lake.

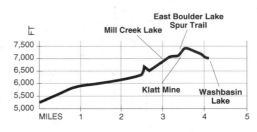

Profile data provided by TOPO!
©1999 Wildflower Productions (www.topo.com)

The hike: Mill Creek Lake is a pretty little backcountry pond that seems to go unnoticed—and unvisited—by most Trinity Alps hikers. The 3-acre lake is neatly hidden in a cleft gouged into a granite cirque 3 miles up the Little Mill Trail. You won't miss the lake if you approach from below, but hikers coming over the ridge from East Boulder Lake (Hike 43) may mistake an unnamed pond high in the Little Mill Creek drainage for the lake itself, and never actually descend far enough to see Mill Creek Lake. Even more rarely seen is

Mill Creek Lake and Washbasin Lake
East Boulder and Upper Boulder Lakes
Middle Boulder and Telephone Lakes Loop

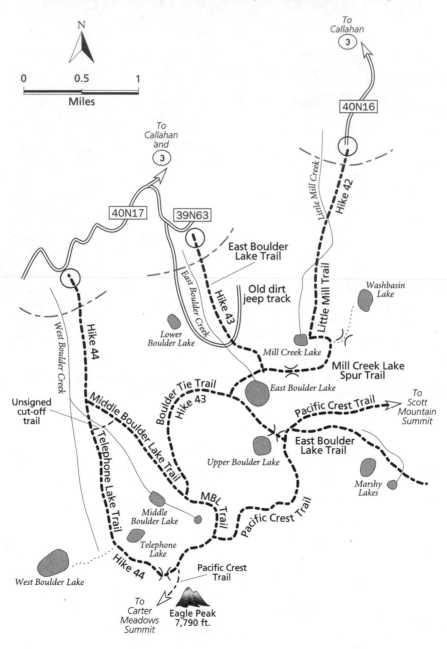

N

0   0.5   1
Miles

To Callahan
3

40N16

To Callahan and
3

40N17   39N63

East Boulder Lake Trail

Old dirt jeep track

Little Mill Creek

Little Mill Trail

Hike 42

Washbasin Lake

East Boulder Creek

Hike 43

Lower Boulder Lake

Mill Creek Lake

Mill Creek Lake Spur Trail

West Boulder Creek

Hike 44

Boulder Tie Trail

Hike 43

East Boulder Lake

Pacific Crest Trail

To Scott Mountain Summit

Unsigned cut-off trail

Middle Boulder Lake Trail

East Boulder Lake Trail

Telephone Lake Trail

Upper Boulder Lake

MBL Trail

Pacific Crest Trail

Marshy Lakes

Middle Boulder Lake

Telephone Lake

Hike 44

West Boulder Lake

Pacific Crest Trail

To Carter Meadows Summit

Eagle Peak 7,790 ft.

Washbasin Lake.

Washbasin Lake, a larger body of water located one drainage to the east. No trail leads to Washbasin, and it remains well off the beaten track for most Alps hikers.

A high subalpine meadow, just under the crest of the Scott Mountains, hangs over the cirque. Snowmelt ponds, wildflowers, views of Scott Valley, and fascinating old mine relics make the upper basin a wonderful place to spend a day or two exploring. Though Little Mill is quite close to the popular East Boulder basin, it gets far fewer visitors.

Start hiking south from the trailhead on a wide track in the shade of a dense white fir forest. The Little Mill Trail (8W01) follows the course of the Little Mill Creek 3 miles to the lake, passing in and out of forest cover and through several scenic meadows on the way. The meadows here (at least in the lower drainage), like the others on the north side of the Scott Mountains, have been heavily grazed by cattle. Watch your step and purify all water.

Less than 0.5 mile from the trailhead, the old jeep track peters out and the rest of the hike is on trail. After crossing from the west to the east side of Little Mill Creek, ascend through a series of meadows with alder thickets lining the stream. Cow paths can make the trail somewhat confusing, but cairns generally lead the way (don't get confused at an unmarked fork just over a mile in; both branches meet again further upcanyon).

Good views of the granite headwall above Mill Creek Lake appear as you climb higher. The ascent is extremely easy going for most of the way, but steepens considerably after the third meadow. Switchbacks lead up the east side of the drainage, and before you know it the trail pops out on a grassy bench just under 3 miles from the trailhead. Rock-lined Mill Creek Lake is just over the granite dike directly ahead.

To reach Washbasin Lake and the trail to East Boulder Lake, head east from Mill Creek Lake and pick up Little Mill Trail, which climbs the steep, grassy east wall of the basin. The trail passes within 50 yards of a tailings pile from the old Klatt Mine. The historic site, complete with old ore cart, is worth a look. On the north side of the mine, the trail continues switchbacking east up the slope to a wide, grassy bench with more mining relics. Here the trail forks south and north.

Go right (south) along the bench to reach East Boulder Lake. The trail skirts the pretty upper basin meadows and a scenic pond, then bends around to the west and drops over the ridge to East Boulder Lake (1 mile away).

To follow the off-trail route to Washbasin Lake, turn left (north) and shoot for the saddle on the ridge to the northeast. The trail soon disappears in a maze of old, faint paths, but the route is easy to pick out in the open, nearly treeless terrain. Just angle up to the low gap, 0.5 mile away, and you soon hit the crest of the ridge above Washbasin. From here it's an easy descent through a sparse forest of foxtail and lodgepole pine to the edge of the lake, 0.3 mile east of the ridge. Cairns lead through the forest, but you can't miss it if you walk east from the crest.

Washbasin Lake, as its name implies, sits in a deep, rocky bowl. Red meta-igneous rocks and royal blue water lend a dash of color to the rugged cirque. The 10-acre lake is very clear, its shoreline very rocky, and its number of visitors very low. Enjoy.

Options: Take the spur trail over the ridge to East Boulder Lake (Hike 43). The large lake makes a nice contrast to Little Mill Creek Lake.

---

43 East Boulder and Upper Boulder Lakes

See Map on Page 194

Highlights:	A short hike to a beautiful, sprawling basin dotted with sparkling lakes, open meadows, and commanding views.
Type of hike:	Day hike or overnight; out-and-back (with optional loop).
Total distance:	10 miles (includes optional side trips).
Difficulty:	Easy to moderate.
Elevation gain:	1,600 feet (800 feet to East Boulder Lake).
Maps:	USGS Billys Peak quad; USDAFS Trinity Alps Wilderness map.

Finding the trailhead: From Callahan (on California Highway 3, approximately 65 miles north of Weaverville), drive west on South Fork Road to the junction with Forest Roads 40N17 and 40N16 (you can also take South Fork Road from Forest Highway 93 to reach the same junction). Go straight (southwest) at the signed junction and follow unpaved FR 40N17 past McKeen

Divide. Continue 5 miles to the signed turn for East Boulder Trailhead. Turn left (east) on FR 39N63 and follow signs to the trailhead at road's end (9 miles from Callahan).

Parking and trailhead facilities: Ample parking but no water or other facilities. The nearest Forest Service campgrounds are Scott Mountain, Hidden Horse, and Trail Creek.

Key points:

0.0	Trailhead.
2.0	East Boulder Lake.
2.1	Mill Creek Lake spur trail.
2.2	Boulder Tie Trail.
2.6	Upper Boulder Lake.
3.1	Pacific Crest Trail.
5.6	Middle Boulder Trail.
6.3	Boulder Tie Trail.
8.0	East Boulder Lake.
10.0	Trailhead.

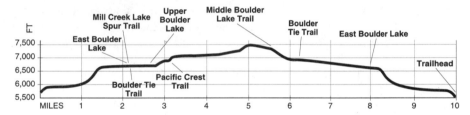

Profile data provided by TOPO! ©1999 Wildflower Productions (www.topo.com)

The hike: How many Boulder lakes can one wilderness have? This group of Boulders (which includes East, Upper, Middle, West, and Lower) is not to be confused with Big and Little Boulder (near Coffee Creek) or Boulder Creek Lakes (off Canyon Creek). Now that's cleared up, this particular set of Boulder lakes (East and Upper) occupies one of the most distinctive cirques in this corner of the Trinity Alps.

The wide and open East Boulder basin is dominated by steep headwalls of red peridotite rock, crystal clear water, and sprawling meadows as smooth and flat as a putting green. A few stands of stunted trees, including white firs and several pine species (lodgepole, western white, etc.), provide shade on a hot day. The basin also harbors a surprising amount of sage, which looks decidedly out of place up here in a subalpine environment (cows probably brought sage seeds up from their winter home in Scott Valley).

A listing of the basin's attributes would not differ remarkably from a description of Middle Boulder (one drainage to the west, Hike 44), but the rocks, meadows, peaks, trees, and lakes of the East Boulder basin seem to have been assembled with an artist's touch. Everything is in perfect proportion, everything in its place. Upper Boulder Lake and its two companion ponds, perched on a terrace at the head of the basin, are a delightful surprise hidden just under the crest of the Scott Mountains.

The only downside to this hike is the fact that, like other destinations on the north side of the Scott Mountains, you may encounter cows here during the summer and early fall. The other drawback (which may actually be a plus, depending on your point of view) is that the road comes within 2 easy miles of the lake, which means you probably won't be alone here unless you come out of season or midweek. Water is plentiful, but be sure to purify everything you drink.

From the trailhead, the path climbs south along the course of East Boulder Creek (on the east side of the stream; an old dirt track, closed to vehicles, runs along the west side of the creek). The initial climb is in the shade of mixed fir, pine, and a few incense-cedar, ascending gradually through forest intermixed with grassy glades. The trail passes through private property, so please be respectful.

At 1.6 miles from the trailhead, the path crosses an old road (shown on the USGS topo, but not on the Forest Service wilderness map) and starts climbing more steeply toward the basin above. Just below the lake, East Boulder Creek cascades down a picturesque waterfall surrounded by colorful gardens of summer wildflowers. The trail ascends a series of moderate switchbacks up the east side of this headwall. At the top, the basin is laid out at your feet. The 32-acre lake is one of the biggest in the wilderness.

Two trails branch off from the north side of East Boulder Lake. To the east lies a spur trail that hops over the ridge to Mill Creek Lake (Hike 42). The unnamed path starts on the hillside at the northeast corner of East Boulder, ascends a series of well-defined switchbacks to the ridgeline, then

East Boulder Lake and Meadow.

plunges down into the Mill Creek drainage. The lake is about 1.5 miles away (don't mistake the pond at the head of Mill Creek for the lake, which is hidden in a granite slot below).

The other trail junction lies on the west side of East Boulder Lake. If the sign has fallen down, look for a path heading west through the shoreline grass. This is the Boulder Tie Trail, which leads around the shoulder of the ridge to the west and over to Middle Boulder Lake. This is the way you return if you follow the hike in the direction described. (It makes no difference which direction you hike the loop.)

To continue to Upper Boulder Lake, follow the East Boulder Lake Trail south and climb the low dike to the terrace in the upper basin. Here you find three teardrop ponds with emerald shores, a few stunted shade trees, and a commanding view of Scott Valley and points north. Steep walls of red rock lend a fortresslike effect to the upper basin. Be sure to fill water bottles before leaving Upper Boulder, as tributaries along the next 3 miles aren't always dependable.

Beyond the uppermost pond, the trail ascends steep switchbacks to reach the jagged crest of the Scott Mountains. Here you're treated to a bird's eye view of the inner Alps, the granite peaks above Bear Lakes, and a stunning view of Mount Shasta (allow time for a long rest; the vista is incredible).

Once over the divide, descend a few hundred yards to a junction with the Pacific Crest Trail. A left (east) turn leads along the PCT to Scott Mountain Summit (see Hike 46 for a description of the PCT), while going straight (south) you continue on the East Boulder Lake Trail, also called the Marshy Lakes Trail on this side of the divide. Marshy Lakes Trail descends 1.5 miles to Big and Little Marshy Lakes. Big and Little Marshy Lakes are a pretty pair of lakes you can see in the drainage below. The trail down is a straightforward descent, steep at first, then turning into an idyllic stroll through meadows and along a sparkling stream.

To continue on the loop, turn right (west) on the PCT and follow it 2.5 miles along the crest to the Middle Boulder Lake Trail. This section of the PCT, above treeline and nearly level for most of the way, with a constant supply of spectacular views and incredible scenery, is one of the most stunning walks in the Trinity Alps.

At the signed Middle Boulder Lake Trail junction, turn right (north) and descend on steep switchbacks into the basin below. Like the East Boulder basin, Middle Boulder also has two ponds nestled onto a green terrace, high above the larger lake below. After passing the ponds, but before descending all the way to Middle Boulder Lake, look for the Boulder Tie Trail veering off to the right (north). The little-used, unsigned path may be hard to see; it's a faint line that traverses the hillside on a nearly level contour. The trail becomes more distinct as you proceed north, bending around the shoulder of the ridge and heading back toward East Boulder Lake. The trail starts on an open, exposed slope of short grasses and brush, but soon becomes more forested as you make your way around the ridge. Arrive back at the western edge of East Boulder Lake. Return to the trailhead the way you came.

Options: Extend your hike west along the Pacific Crest Trail for up to 12 more miles (described in Hike 46). You can also climb to the summit of 7,790-foot Eagle Peak on an off-trail walk-up located west of the PCT–Middle Boulder Lake Trail junction. For an easier side trip, take the Mill Creek Lake spur trail (at the north end of East Boulder Lake) and explore the secluded basin east of East Boulder Lake (Hike 42).

44 Middle Boulder and Telephone Lakes Loop

See Map on Page 194

Highlights:	A short loop with varied terrain, several lakes, and great views.
Type of hike:	Day hike or backpack (1–2 nights); semi-loop.
Total distance:	9.2 miles.
Difficulty:	Moderate.
Elevation gain:	2,400 feet.
Maps:	USGS Billys Peak quad; USDAFS Trinity Alps Wilderness map.

Finding the trailhead: From Callahan (on California Highway 3, approximately 65 miles north of Weaverville), drive west on South Fork Road to the junction with Forest Roads 40N17 and 40N16 (you can also take South Fork Road from Forest Highway 93 to reach the same junction). Go straight at the signed junction and follow unpaved FR 40N17 past McKeen Divide. Continue 5.5 miles to the signed trailhead at a turnout next to West Boulder Creek (6 miles from Callahan).

Parking and trailhead facilities: Horse corral and room for a few cars, but no other facilities. Scott Mountain and Trail Creek Campgrounds are nearby.

Key points:
- 0.0 Trailhead.
- 1.6 Middle Boulder Lake and Telephone Lake Trail junction.
- 3.5 Middle Boulder Lake.
- 3.8 Boulder Tie Trail.
- 4.3 Pacific Crest Trail.
- 4.9 Telephone Lake Trail.
- 5.8 Telephone Lake.
- 7.6 Middle Boulder Lake and Telephone Lake Trail junction.
- 9.2 Trailhead.

The hike: If you're determined to see all of the Boulder Lakes in the Trinity Alps (one map lists seven), then you'll pass this way eventually. Your time won't be wasted. Like most of the hikes on the north side of the Scott Mountains, this route serves up a gentle hike along meadow-lined creeks, past

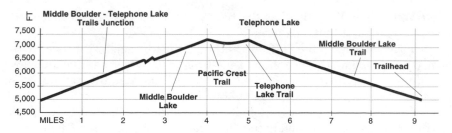

Profile data provided by TOPO! ©1999 Wildflower Productions (www.topo.com)

forest-fringed lakes, and along the Pacific Crest Trail. But be forewarned: you have to share the lovely scenery with cows, or at least the results of cows passing through.

The trail starts with a moderate ascent as it climbs south along the course of West Boulder Creek. Climb on switchbacks through the shade of mixed fir and pine forest, then level out and contour gently uphill, parallel to and above the creek. Small tributaries cross the trail frequently, but they may dry up in late season (the main creek is never far away). Be sure to purify water from all sources.

After skirting the edge of a meadow, enter a stand of mature incense-cedars and start climbing farther above the creek. At 1.6 miles from the trailhead, arrive at a signed junction. Middle Boulder Lake Trail is to the left (southeast); West Boulder Lake, Telephone Lake, and Eagle Creek Trail are all to the right (southwest). The loop is described here in a clockwise direction (returning via Telephone Lake), though you could just as easily do it the other way.

The 1.5 miles from the junction to Middle Boulder Lake is a pleasant stroll along the forested canyon bottom, following Middle Boulder's outlet as the drainage rises gently toward the forested upper basin. Pass in and out of streamside meadows along the way (plenty of camping opportunities in the forest fringes), and cross an open, grassy glade just before arriving at Middle Boulder's northeast corner. The shallow lake is backed by a rocky headwall to the south, where the terrain suddenly steepens to reach the crest of the Scott Mountains, and by red fir and pines on the north. To the east an open, verdant basin slopes upward to the divide between Middle Boulder and East Boulder Lakes. Two more little pools are perched on a bench 800 feet higher, just below the crest.

The trail (marked by cairns where the meadow engulfs it) leads southeast toward the obvious gap on the ridgeline. Halfway up is the not-so-obvious junction with the spur trail over to East Boulder Lake. If you have extra time, you can use this route to make a loop through the East Boulder drainage (combine the spur trail, the East Boulder Lake Trail, and the PCT; see Hike 43).

To continue on the Middle Boulder–Telephone Loop, climb steeply to the junction with the PCT atop the divide, 4.3 miles from the trailhead. The views get better and better with every step as you climb out of the basin and onto the open ridgeline. Once you gain the divide you can see the heart of the Trinity Alps to the southwest and, back the way you came, the sprawling

Scott Valley. The PCT also has the best view of Mount Shasta that you'll ever see without climbing a peak.

Turn right (west) on the PCT and hike 0.6 mile through forest cover to the signed junction with the Telephone Lake Trail on the edge of a small meadow. The junction is at the base of Eagle Peak, a 7,790-foot summit that makes for a nice off-trail ascent. To reach Telephone Lake, turn right (north) and climb 0.3 mile to recross the divide. Then it's all downhill as the trail switchbacks north, crosses a pretty hanging meadow, then plunges down to the edge of little Telephone Lake. The lake's rocky shore is fringed by dense stands of red fir, hemlock, and pine, and a small granite peak hangs above the southern edge. There's no permanent inlet or outlet, so the water level in the lake fluctuates dramatically each summer.

West Boulder Lake (the last of the Boulders) is just under 2 miles due west of Telephone Lake. No trail leads to it, but enough people have made the cross-country trek that a line of cairns helps point the way.

Finish the loop by following the trail north from Telephone Lake. The path descends gradually through forest cover, with good views across the alder-thick meadows of West Boulder Creek. Arrive at the junction with the Middle Boulder Trail 1.8 miles from Telephone Lake. Just before the signed junction, you might see a faint trail leading east. It's an unmaintained cutoff that leads over to the Middle Boulder Trail (don't take it unless you plan to do the loop again). From the signed junction, retrace your footsteps to the trailhead.

Options: Eagle Peak, located near the Telephone Lake–PCT junction, makes for a nice summit without straying too far away. You can also make a nice little loop connecting the Wolford Cabin Trail and PCT for a day hike that takes in great scenery and an historic cabin.

45 Fox Creek Lake and Mavis Lake

Highlights:	A pleasant hike to a forested basin with four small lakes to explore.
Type of hike:	Day hike or backpack; out-and-back.
Total distance:	8 miles.
Difficulty:	Easy.
Elevation gain:	1,200 feet.
Maps:	USGS Billys Peak quad; USDAFS Trinity Alps Wilderness map.

Finding the trailhead: From Callahan (on California Highway 3, approximately 65 miles north of Weaverville), take South Fork Road on the south side of town. Head west through a small residential neighborhood as the road becomes Forest Road 40N17. Follow this unpaved road past McKeen Divide and continue 7.5 miles to the signed Fox Creek Ridge Trailhead. You

Fox Creek Lake and Mavis Lake

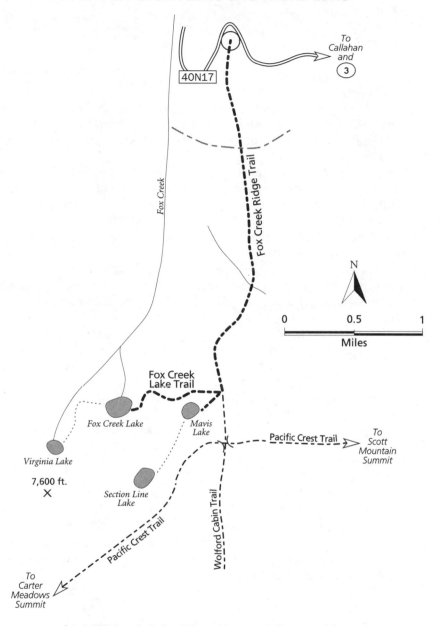

pass turns for Mill Creek Lake (FR 40N16) and East Boulder Lake (FR 39N63) on the way.

Parking and trailhead facilities: Ample parking in a wide turnout where the road rounds the point of a ridge; no camping or water. The nearest Forest Service campgrounds are Scott Mountain and Trail Creek (on CA 3 and Forest Highway 93, respectively).

Key points:

- 0.0   Trailhead.
- 3.0   Spur trail to Pacific Crest Trail.
- 3.2   Mavis Lake.
- 4.0   Fox Creek Lake.

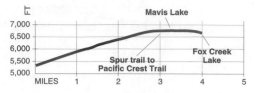

Profile data provided by TOPO!
©1999 Wildflower Productions (www.topo.com)

The hike: The Fox Creek Ridge Trail is the shortest and easiest way to reach Mavis and Fox Creek Lakes, two small lakes in a forested basin on the north side of the Scott Mountain divide (the basin can also be accessed via the Pacific Crest Trail). Each lake has a companion pond, reachable by relatively easy off-trail routes that add to the exploring opportunities.

Unlike the other trails on this side of the Scott Mountain divide, which tend to follow canyon bottoms, the Fox Creek Ridge Trail does just what the name implies—follows the spine of a ridge. As such, the forested route has far less cow sign than most other hikes on this side of the divide.

The trail starts across the road from the parking area. The path heads south, beginning with a steep, exposed ascent on a rocky backbone of manzanita-covered ridge. Fortunately, this attention-grabbing climb is extremely short. You soon reach a shady, mixed-conifer forest, where you continue climbing more gradually along the ridgeline. Look for mature incense-cedars and an impressive stand of white firs.

A mile from the trailhead cross a forested flat where late starters could make a camp (there's water in a nearby creek). Pass another small tributary a mile later, after an alder-lined meadow, then continue the pleasant forest walk to an unmarked trail junction 3 miles from the trailhead. The left fork climbs up to the Pacific Crest Trail (Hike 46), atop the divide; the right fork is the Fox Creek Lake Trail to Mavis and Fox Creek Lakes.

Turn right (west) and follow the level, rocky tread as it bends around into the basin. Another unmarked junction appears after 200 yards (a sign may be on the ground). In any case, Mavis Lake is to the left (south) and Fox Creek Lake is to the right (west).

The path to Mavis climbs over a granite moraine and arrives at the edge of the 3.5-acre lake after skirting a little pond on Mavis's northeast side. Mavis is small and shallow, but it's set in a pretty little bowl surrounded by a dense forest of red fir and hemlock. Section Line Lake, its companion, is a mile to the south (and slightly west). No trail leads to Section Line, but you should have no problem following ducks to the lake.

To reach Fox Creek Lake, continue west from the junction and follow the rocky trail as it winds around a spur ridge and drops down into the Fox Creek basin. Arrive at the lake a mile from the last junction, 4 miles from the trailhead.

At 9 acres, Fox Creek Lake is by far the largest in this four-lake basin. Grassy fringes, lilypad-lined shores, and spacious campsites make it an extremely pleasant place to spend a few days. The rocky west shore is best for fishing (no lilypads) and the forested edges on the north and east have numerous campsites.

Though no maintained trail leads from here to Virginia Lake, an obvious use trail (look for cairns) has been established. Pick it up at the northwest corner of the lake and follow it over a rocky ridge to the southwest. On the other side of the dike is the outlet creek flowing from Virginia Lake. Stay on the east side of the creek and follow it 0.75 mile to the lake.

Virginia Lake's clear water is cupped in a rocky cirque just beneath the crest of the Scott Mountains. The pretty setting is punctuated by an idyllic meadow near the outlet and almost guaranteed solitude.

Options: The Pacific Crest Trail is right next door (less than 1 mile from the junction before Mavis Lake). You can follow it to a number of other lakes along the Scott Mountains divide. At the PCT junction, another trail leads down to Wolford Cabin and destinations on the south side of the divide (see Hike 37).

46 Pacific Crest Trail (PCT)

Highlights:	The Pacific Crest Trail (PCT) hugs the spine of the Scott Mountains divide, serving up endless views and access to a string of lakes.
Type of hike:	Backpack; out-and back (or shuttle).
Total distance:	24 miles (at recommended turnaround).
Difficulty:	Moderate.
Elevation gain:	1,600 feet.
Maps:	USGS Deadman Peak, Billys Peak, Tangle Blue Lake, and Scott Mountain quads; USDAFS Trinity Alps Wilderness map.

Finding the trailhead: From the junction of California Highway 3 and Forest Highway 93 just north of Callahan, go west on FH 93 toward Cecilville. Proceed 12 miles to the signed Carter Meadows Summit–PCT trailhead on the left (south) side of the highway. If you pass the entrance to Carter Meadows you've gone too far. For car shuttles (or for PCT hikers who want to go in the "right" direction), the other trailhead is at Scott Mountain Summit, 55 miles north of Weaverville on CA 3. The signed PCT Trailhead is on the west side of the highway. To get a head start, you can drive to the edge of the Wilderness Area boundary by taking the dirt road that leads right (northwest) from the Scott Mountain trailhead. Follow the road 2.5 miles to a locked gate and park. This is Marshy Lakes Road (described at the end of this chapter). This road provides access to a youth camp and private property at the Marshy Lakes. Take care to avoid blocking the road or gate.

Parking and trailhead facilities: Ample parking at both trailheads. No water or other facilities are available at Carter Meadows Summit. Hidden Horse campground (a Forest Service site with toilets and water) is located a

Pacific Crest Trail (PCT)

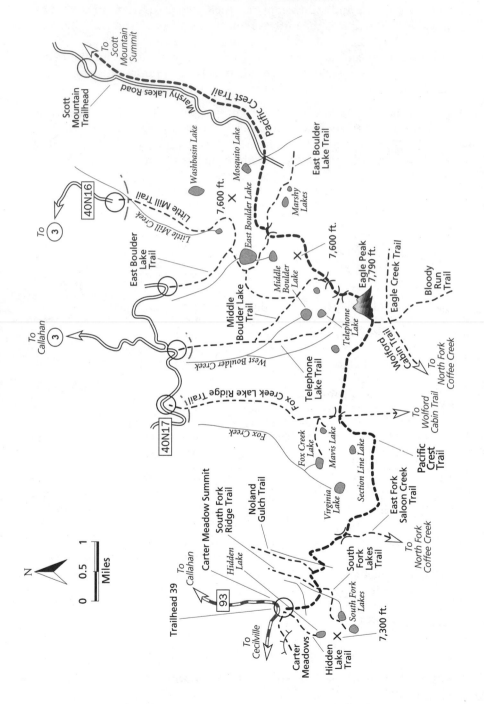

Scott Mountain Trailhead

To Scott Mountain Summit

Marshy Lakes Road

Pacific Crest Trail

Washbasin Lake

Mosquito Lake

7,600 ft.

East Boulder Lake

East Boulder Lake Trail

Marshy Lakes

40N16

Little Mill Trail

Little Mill Creek

To 3

East Boulder Lake Trail

East Boulder Lake

Middle Boulder Lake

7,600 ft.

Eagle Peak 7,790 ft.

Eagle Creek Trail

Bloody Run Trail

To Callahan

3

Middle Boulder Lake Trail

Telephone Lake

Wolford Cabin Trail

To North Fork Coffee Creek

West Boulder Creek

Telephone Lake Trail

To Wolford Cabin Trail

Fox Creek Lake Ridge Trail

40N17

Fox Creek

Fox Creek Lake

Mavis Lake

Section Line Lake

Pacific Crest Trail

East Fork Saloon Creek Trail

Virginia Lake

Carter Meadow Summit

South Fork Ridge Trail

Noland Gulch Trail

South Fork Lakes Trail

To North Fork Coffee Creek

N

0 0.5 1
Miles

Trailhead 39

To Callahan

Hidden Lake

93

To Ceciliville

Carter Meadows

Hidden Lake Trail

South Fork Lakes

7,300 ft.

mile away in Carter Meadows. A Forest Service campground is located next to the Scott Mountain Trailhead (no water).

Key points:
- 0.0 Trailhead.
- 1.4 South Fork Lakes Trail junction.
- 2.8 Noland Gulch Trail junction.
- 3.1 Scott Mountain crest–East Fork Saloon Creek Trail junction.
- 6.1 Mavis Lake–Wolford Cabin Trail junction.
- 8.3 Eagle Creek–Bloody Run Trail junction.
- 9.0 Telephone Lake Trail junction.
- 9.5 Middle Boulder Lake Trail junction.
- 12.0 East Boulder–Marshy Lakes Trail junction.
- 13.8 Marshy Lakes Road crossing.
- 15.7 Scott Mountain crest.
- 18.9 Scott Mountain Summit Trailhead.

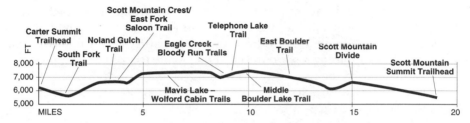

Profile data provided by TOPO! ©1999 Wildflower Productions (www.topo.com)

The hike: The Pacific Crest Trail runs for more than 2,500 miles from Mexico to the Canadian border. Only 18.9 of those miles cross the Trinity Alps Wilderness, but what a stretch it is! The PCT slices across the wilderness along the spine of the Scott Mountains, passing within a stone's throw of more than a dozen lakes, serving up one stunning view after another, and traversing some of the least-crowded areas of the Alps. Only diehard PCT through-hikers make it to this remote section of the path, while most Trinity Alps hikers stick to the better-known routes in the inner Alps, which leaves an uncrowded, glorious trail for those willing to seek it out.

The PCT lies between Scott Mountain summit on the east end and Carter Meadows Summit on the west. It makes for an easy through-hike if you can arrange a car shuttle, or an excellent out-and-back trip, with numerous opportunities for taking side trips along the way. And since it's built to PCT specifications (no more than a 5 percent grade), the trail delivers incredible scenery without exacting an exorbitant price in sweat and sore legs.

This description starts from Carter Meadows Summit. It's a longer drive, but I like going this direction because you hike toward Mount Shasta on the way out. The spectacular peak often looks so close you think you can step right off the trail and onto its snowcapped summit. And if you're hiking out and back (instead of arranging a car shuttle), walking this direction allows you the option of shortening the route by several miles without missing anything noteworthy.

At the Carter Meadows Summit Trailhead there's a three-way junction. To the right (west) a spur trail descends 0.2 mile to Carter Meadows proper (more parking and a toilet), and the path in the middle heads south, uphill, to Hidden Lake (see Hike 48). To the left (southeast) the PCT immediately crosses the wilderness boundary and starts a moderate descent on a shady, well-maintained path.

Follow the PCT downhill through mixed conifers, with good views across the South Fork Lakes basin between the branches. The trail crosses several small creeks on the gentle descent and passes a number of fern and alder thickets. After 1.4 miles, arrive at the junction with the South Fork Lakes Trail (Hike 47). The trail to the left (north) drops to the South Fork Trailhead, while the path to the right (south) climbs very steeply to South Fork Lakes in less than a mile.

The PCT continues straight (east), climbing moderately out of the drainage and around a spur ridge. Look for good views across the basin and along the divide above you. An impressive, unnamed peak hangs over the head of the drainage behind you, on the crest of the Scott Mountains. In the next drainage, 2.8 miles from the trailhead, climb gently south to the junction with the Noland Gulch Trail (it drops down to a little-used trailhead). The PCT continues climbing toward the crest on a wide track. The first pass is a false summit, with the real thing a few hundred yards farther along. Catch your breath and admire the view: the stunning granite heart of the Trinity Alps lies directly to the southwest.

From the top of the divide, the PCT heads east along the ridgeline, while the East Fork Saloon Creek Trail plunges south to connect with Saloon Creek and eventually the North Fork Coffee Creek Trail. From here, you can take advantage of a seldom-used loop connecting Saloon Creek with South Fork Lakes, then returning to the trailhead via the PCT. There is also an unmaintained and unnamed trace of a trail that heads west along the ridge and soon peters out.

To continue on the PCT, head east and follow the easy grade through shady fir forests, fern-covered hillsides, and countless vistas of Sawtooth Mountain and other peaks. Take advantage of water crossings to refill your bottles, as creeks are less frequent along the next few miles of the PCT. From the Saloon Creek junction to the Fox Creek–Wolford Cabin junction, you traverse 3 miles of PCT bliss. Gentle hiking and great views on both sides of the divide punctuate the trail as you contour along the crest. Just before the Fox Creek–Wolford Cabin junction, a duck marks a little-used cross-country route to Section Line Lake, which is immediately below the divide to the north. At the Fox Creek–Wolford Cabin junction, 6.1 miles from the trailhead, you can make excursions on both sides of the divide. To the north lie Mavis and Fox Creek Lakes (Hike 45), and to the south are historic Wolford Cabin and connections to a network of trails on the north side of Coffee Creek.

The PCT continues east, contouring around the south side of the crest. Less than a mile from the Fox Creek junction, the trail skirts the top of a drainage that drops steeply away on the north side of the divide. No trail

The Pacific Crest Trail with Mount Shasta in the background.

leads down the hill, but West Boulder Lake is tucked away in the canyon below. Most West Boulder visitors reach the lake via a cross-country route from nearby Telephone Lake.

A moderate ascent leads around the prow of a ridge, alternating between stunted tree cover and wide open views of the wild terrain spread out below, and soon you arrive at the next trail junction (just over 2 miles from the last one). A sign points the way right (south) to the Bloody Run–Eagle Creek Trails. Just downhill from the PCT is a three-way junction with routes leading south, east, and west. The PCT continues its level contour to the left (northeast), bending around the base of Eagle Peak.

Shortly after the Bloody Run junction, you pass an old miner's camp decorated with an antique wheelbarrow, where a nearby spring flows through a metal pipe (purify all water to be safe). Another 0.5 mile of parklike walking brings you to the junction with the Telephone Lake Trail. Telephone Lake, yet another pleasant little lake on the north side of the divide, lies less than a mile away to the left (northwest). An easy ramble along the crest quickly brings you to the junction with the Middle Boulder Lake Trail, 0.5 mile farther along. From this ridgetop junction you can see Middle Boulder Lake and two companion ponds nestled in the basin below (see Hike 44 for a description of Middle Boulder and Telephone Lakes).

The next 2.5 miles comprises one of the prettiest sections of trail in the whole Trinity Alps Wilderness. The rocky tread winds around the south side of a spur ridge, commanding one endless view after another, with pyramid-shaped Mount Shasta dominating the skyline ahead. Wildflower gardens grow in grassy pockets below the trail where water seeps through the rocks, nourishing little explosions of colorful blooms.

At the East Boulder Lake junction, 12 miles from the trailhead, you again have the option of exploring beautiful drainages on both sides of the divide. East Boulder is in an open, grassy basin on the north side of the crest, with several companion ponds that make for an idyllic setting (see Hike 43). Below you to the south lies little Marshy Lakes basin, with lush meadows, two small lakes (with marshy shorelines), and great views of nearby granite crags. Both destinations are just a mile away from the PCT.

If you haven't dropped a car or arranged a ride at the Scott Mountain end of the trail, 6.9 miles further east, you may want to consider turning around here. The rest of the route is less spectacular than the section you've just hiked, and there are fewer opportunities for camping and exploring. The trail parallels a dirt road part of the way and passes an area used by a children's summer camp.

To continue to Scott Mountain, follow the PCT east on a gentle contour around the head of the basin, then descend through mixed forest to a crossing of Marshy Lakes Road (just after crossing the outlet from Mosquito Lake). This dirt road, closed to the public, is used by nearby Camp Unalayee and other owners of private inholdings. A spur road, located a few hundred yards east of the PCT crossing, leads uphill to the camp and Mosquito Lake. (If you run into a group of kids, that's where they're probably from.)

From the Marshy Lakes Road crossing you have two options. The PCT continues east, parallel to and slightly below the road for nearly 2 miles. At that point, the road and trail almost touch again, at a pass atop the divide, then the trail veers away into the forest and traverses the last 3.5 miles to the Scott Mountain Summit Trailhead. Alternatively, the road leads an easy 1.5 miles to a locked gate, where you can leave a car shuttle. The road or trail are both good options from here, depending on your inclination.

Options: The PCT passes many trail junctions with options for short and long itineraries (get out the map and use your imagination). The best peak ascent en route is Eagle Peak (7,790 feet). For a good historic side trip, take the Wolford Cabin Trail and visit several old cabin sites in the North Fork Coffee Creek drainage (Hike 37).

47 South Fork Lakes

Highlights:	A short but steep hike to a beautiful, secluded cirque with two pleasant lakes and plenty of off-trail opportunities.
Type of hike:	Day hike or overnight; out-and-back.
Total distance:	5 miles (with optional 10-mile side trip).
Difficulty:	Moderate.
Elevation gain:	900 feet.
Maps:	USGS Deadman Peak quad; USDAFS Trinity Alps Wilderness map.

South Fork Lakes • Hidden Lake

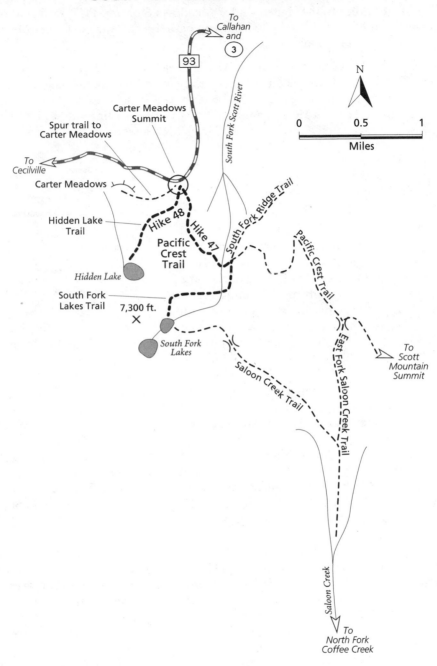

To Callahan and ③

93

Carter Meadows Summit

Spur trail to Carter Meadows

To Cecilville

Carter Meadows

South Fork Scott River

Hidden Lake Trail

Hike 48

Hike 47

South Fork Ridge Trail

Pacific Crest Trail

Hidden Lake

South Fork Lakes Trail

7,300 ft.
✕

South Fork Lakes

Pacific Crest Trail

East Fork Saloon Creek Trail

To Scott Mountain Summit

Saloon Creek Trail

Saloon Creek

To North Fork Coffee Creek

N

0   0.5   1
Miles

Finding the trailhead: From the junction of California Highway 3 and Forest Highway 93 just north of Callahan, go west on FH 93 toward Cecilville. Proceed 12 miles to the signed Carter Meadows Summit–PCT Trailhead on the left (south) side of the highway. If you pass the entrance to Carter Meadows you've gone too far.

Parking and trailhead facilities: Ample parking, though you may have to resort to Carter Meadows on particularly crowded weekends (a short spur trail links the two parking areas). No water or other facilities at Carter Meadows Summit. Hidden Horse campground, a Forest Service site with toilets and water, is located a mile away in Carter Meadows.

Key points:
  0.0   Trailhead.
  1.4   South Fork Lakes trail junction.
  2.5   South Fork Lakes.

Profile data provided by TOPO!
©1999 Wildflower Productions
(www.topo.com)

The hike: Despite the short distance to South Fork Lakes, an extremely steep section of trail makes it feel like you're really going somewhere. And thanks to the beauty of the large, rugged basin, you really are. The cirque serves up an equal mix of shady woods; emerald, grass-fringed shoreline; and rocky, imposing cliffs. Good views of the South Fork Scott River drainage can be seen from the east side of the lower lake.

From the trailhead, follow the signed Pacific Crest Trail southeast as it descends through fir and hemlock into the South Fork drainage (see Hike 46 for complete description of the PCT). After a gradual descent that crosses a number of small creeks, the path fords South Fork Scott Creek in the lush canyon bottom where alders, ferns, and willows create a minigarden with a tropical feel.

After crossing the South Fork, ascend to the junction with the South Fork Lakes Trail, 1.4 miles from the trailhead. The junction has not been signed in recent years, but the well-used trail should be obvious. Turn right (south) to reach South Fork Lakes. A left (north) turn leads downhill to the South Fork Trailhead (Carter Meadows Summit is a better starting point). The PCT continues straight (east).

Soon after turning onto the South Fork Lakes Trail, you learn why the Forest Service warns equestrians to use extreme caution on this route: it's short but very steep. A moderate ascent leads to the bottom of a wide, grassy valley that holds the main stem of South Fork Lakes' outlet stream. A quick look around, however, reveals this is not the cirque that holds South Fork Lakes. The cirque you're after lies another 800 feet above you, atop that vertical headwall to the west. The trail winds through a stand of fir, then climbs the steep canyon wall in a series of switchbacks. The grueling ascent is balanced by good views and summer wildflowers fed by a number of little creeklets and seeps that make it seem as if the mountain itself is leaking.

Once you reach the top, it's a short walk across near-level terrain to the lower of the two South Fork Lakes. The upper lake is just a quarter mile southwest of the lower lake (a use trail leads along the west side of the lower lake, then follows the inlet stream to the upper). A thick forest of pine and fir separates the two bodies of water. The lakes are 4 and 6 acres, respectively, and have remarkably different settings. The 7,794-foot peak to the south of Upper South Fork Lake is an easy off-trail summit with a great view. Return the way you came, or see the optional side trip below.

Options: You can make a longer loop (add 10 miles) by taking the Saloon Creek and East Fork Saloon Creek Trails back to the PCT. From the south side of Lower South Fork Lake, find the Saloon Creek Trail (9W01) and head southeast, over the Scott Mountain divide and down to the junction with the East Fork Saloon Creek Trail (9W03). Turn left (north) and follow it back to a junction with the PCT atop the divide. Turn left (northwest) and return to the trailhead. Longer options are possible on the PCT (Hike 46) and North Fork Coffee Creek (Hike 37).

48 Hidden Lake

See Map on Page 211

Highlights:	A short hike to a pretty little lake on the north side of the Scott Mountains divide.
Type of hike:	Day hike or overnight; out-and-back.
Total distance:	2 miles.
Difficulty:	Easy.
Elevation gain:	500 feet.
Maps:	USGS Deadman Peak quad; USDAFS Trinity Alps Wilderness map.

Finding the trailhead: From the junction of California Highway 3 and Forest Highway 93 just north of Callahan, go west on FH 93 toward Cecilville. Proceed 12 miles to the signed Carter Meadows Summit–PCT Trailhead on the left (south) side of the highway. If you pass the entrance to Carter Meadows you've gone too far.

Parking and trailhead facilities: Ample parking is available, though you may have to resort to Carter Meadows on particularly crowded weekends (a short spur trail links the two parking areas). No water or other facilities are available at Carter Meadows Summit. Hidden Horse campground, a Forest Service site with toilets and water, is located a mile away in Carter Meadows.

Key points:
    0.0 Trailhead.
    1.0 Hidden Lake.

The hike: With a name like Hidden Lake, you might expect this to be a difficult hike into a remote, hard-to-find basin. Don't come here if that's

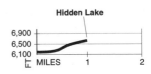

Profile data provided by TOPO!
©1999 Wildflower Productions
(www.topo.com)

Hidden Lake.

what you're after. In reality, Hidden Lake is one of the most accessible, easy-to-reach bodies of water in the Trinity Alps. It's a pretty little 3-acre lake in a rugged cirque gouged into the north side of the Scott Mountains— a good destination for a short day hike (when a picnic is the priority), or even an overnight trip for families with small children.

The Hidden Lake Trail starts at Carter Meadows Summit, heading south up a ridge that splits two other trails. To the left (southeast), the Pacific Crest Trail starts its 18-mile run through the Trinity Alps Wilderness, and a spur trail to Carter Meadows veers right (southwest).

Ascend moderately up the rocky ridgeline through red fir and mountain hemlock. Soon, emerge into open, brushy terrain with good views over the South Fork Scott River and the wild country along the divide. Once over the crest of the ridge, the trail winds through forest cover again and abruptly ends at the edge of Hidden Lake, 1 mile from the trailhead.

The clear water serves up good swimming, fishing, and simple afternoon daydreaming (not necessarily in that order). The impressive cliff rising from the lake's south shore makes for a spectacular backdrop, and summer wild-flowers sprinkle the hills that rise more gently. There's plenty of shady elbowroom to wile away an afternoon. Return the way you came.

49 Trail Gulch–Long Gulch Loop

Highlights: A hike with great swimming, fishing, and ridgetop views.
Type of hike: Day hike or backpack; loop.
Total distance: 9 miles.
Difficulty: Moderate.
Elevation gain: 1,950 feet.
Maps: USGS Deadman Peak quad; USDAFS Trinity Alps Wilderness map.

Finding the trailhead: From the junction of California Highway 3 and Forest Highway 93 just north of Callahan, go west on FH 93 toward Cecilville. Proceed 12.5 miles to the signed Carter Meadows access road (Forest Road 39N08), on the left (south) side of the highway. Proceed 2.5 miles to the signed trailhead for Trail Gulch Lake (on the left). Long Gulch Trailhead is 0.8 mile farther.

Parking and trailhead facilities: Parking at both trailheads; no facilities. Hidden Horse Campground, a Forest Service site with toilets and water, is located a mile away in Carter Meadows and Trail Creek Campground is 5 miles west, where FR 39N08 rejoins FH 93.

Key points:

0.0	Trailhead.
2.0	Trail Gulch Trail junction.
2.5	Trail Gulch Lake.
3.0	Steveale Creek–North Fork Coffee Creek junction.
4.6	Long Gulch Lake.
4.8	Long Gulch Trail.
8.2	Long Gulch Trailhead.
9.0	Trailhead.

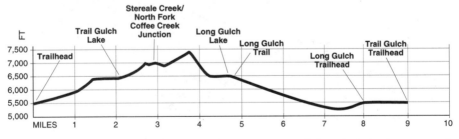

Profile data provided by TOPO! ©1999 Wildflower Productions (www.topo.com)

The hike: This short loop makes a nice day hike or a good overnight (especially if you have little kids in tow). The two lakes en route, Trail Gulch and Long Gulch, are deep and blue and tucked into nearly identical, deep-set granite cirques. They aren't quite as spectacular as the Alps' more famous

Trail Gulch–Long Gulch Loop
Twin Lakes and Fish Lake

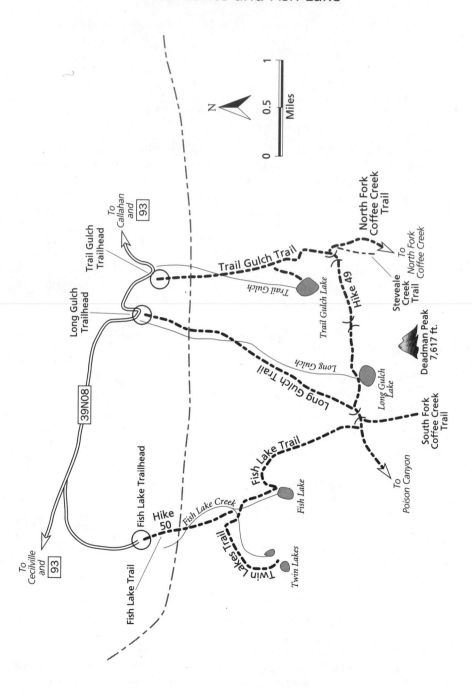

N

0   0.5   1
Miles

To Callahan and [93]

Trail Gulch Trailhead

Trail Gulch Trail

Trail Gulch

Trail Gulch Lake

North Fork Coffee Creek Trail

To North Fork Coffee Creek

Steveale Creek Trail

Hike 49

Deadman Peak 7,617 ft.

Long Gulch Trailhead

Long Gulch Trail

Long Gulch

Long Gulch Lake

South Fork Coffee Creek Trail

To Poison Canyon

39N08

Fish Lake Trailhead

Fish Lake Trail

Fish Lake Creek

Fish Lake

Fish Lake Trail

Hike 50

Twin Lakes Trail

Twin Lakes

To Cecilville and [93]

lakes (like Caribou and Sapphire), but they're a lot easier to reach, and they get a mere fraction of the visitors the more popular lakes get. Still, the trails on the north side of the Scott Mountains have been "discovered" in recent years, so visitors are more numerous than they used to be.

There's some confusion over the names of these lakes. Decades ago, mapmakers reversed the names of Trail Gulch and Long Gulch Lakes, causing considerable consternation among old-timers who remembered the lakes' correct names. But once a mistake is committed to paper, it's difficult to change. While producing the 1998 Forest Service wilderness map, officials decided to correct the situation. In 1999, the Forest Service changed trail signs to agree with the new map (which places Long Gulch to the west, Trail Gulch to the east). The confusion has not been totally laid to rest, however; the USGS quad still shows the lakes in reverse.

Whatever you call these lovely lakes, they both merit a long swim on a hot summer afternoon. To avoid further confusion, this text refers to the lakes as they appear on the 1998 Forest Service wilderness map. To do the loop, park at the Trail Gulch Trailhead and start hiking south on the Trail Gulch Trail (9W15). Traveling in the other direction is equally good.

The trail climbs steadily along the outlet creek. First on the west bank, then on the east, you follow the little stream through mixed fir and mountain hemlock, alder thickets, and meadow grass. This drainage and Long Gulch show the effects of cattle grazing. Be sure to purify all water and carry plenty to drink on the ridgetop trail between lakes, as no water is available.

After 2 easy miles (a couple of steep pitches, but nothing to cause concern), arrive at the spur trail that leads to Trail Gulch Lake. Turn right (southwest) to reach the lake in just under 0.5 mile. To continue the loop, go straight and make a steep, switchbacking ascent to the ridgeline above. On top of the ridge, at nearly 7,000 feet, get a bird's eye view of the lake and a sea of peaks in every direction. The Marble Mountains dominate the horizon to the north.

A three-way trail junction is just a few yards down the other side of the ridge. The North Fork Coffee Creek and Steveale Creek Trails head downhill to the south (see Hikes 36 and 37). Until the early 1990s, you had to hike down into the basin, then all the way back up again to reach Long Gulch Lake. New trail construction, however, has created a welcome path that cuts across the top of the drainage, saving you all the hard-earned elevation you just gained. Turn right (west) on this signed trail and stroll through open forest to the saddle above Long Gulch Lake. There you find the old trail from Steveale Creek coming up from the southeast. (The new trail is shown on the 1998 Forest Service wilderness map, but not the USGS quad.)

The view from this saddle is even better than the last, with all of the Long Gulch basin laid out beneath your feet. Deadman Peak towers to 7,617 feet directly south along the ridgeline. After you've had enough of the vista, head over the side and plunge down on a descent that varies from steep to steeper. Switchbacks ease the impact on the knees.

Long Gulch Lake.

At the bottom, the trail crosses the outlet creek near a much-used campsite, then meanders along the forested north shore of Long Gulch Lake. On a hot day, the island out in the middle of the blue water demands a long visit.

On the west side of the lake, follow the trail 0.3 mile west over level, rocky terrain to a junction with the Long Gulch Trail (9W14). A left turn (southwest) leads up to the ridgeline and a three-way trail junction, where the South Fork Coffee Creek Trail heads south (Hike 36).

The route back to the trailhead lies to the right (north), down the Long Gulch Trail. The next 3 miles are much like the approach up the Trail Gulch drainage: a gently descending path through forest and cow-trampled meadow, and a crossing from the west to east bank of the stream before arriving at the trailhead. Trail Gulch Trailhead lies 0.8 mile to the east along FR 39N08.

Options: This hike can be extended on both the South Fork Coffee Creek and North Fork Coffee Creek Trails (Hikes 36 and 37). Schlomberg Cabin, a historic site at the head of the North Fork Coffee Creek drainage, is an easy side trip.

50 Twin Lakes and Fish Lake

See Map on Page 216

Highlights: A short hike to a tranquil pond
that stretches the definition of lake.
Type of hike: Day hike or overnight; out-and-back.
Total distance: 3.8 miles.
Difficulty: Easy.
Elevation gain: 900 feet (plus 400 feet for Twin Lakes).
Maps: USGS Deadman Peak quad; USDAFS Trinity Alps
Wilderness map.

Finding the trailhead: From the junction of California Highway 3 and Forest Highway 93 just north of Callahan, go west on FH 93 toward Cecilville. Proceed 17 miles to the signed turn for Trail Creek Campground–Forest Road 39N08. Turn left (south) and proceed 1 mile on FR 39N08 to the signed turn (right) for Fish Lake Trailhead. Continue 2 miles on this dirt road to the trailhead.

Parking and trailhead facilities: Ample parking; no water or other facilities. Trail Creek Campground (a Forest Service site with toilets and water) is the closest developed site.

Key points:
0.0   Trailhead.
1.2   Twin Lakes–Fish Lake Trail junction.
1.9   Twin Lakes.
1.9   Fish Lake.

Profile data provided by TOPO!
©1999 Wildflower Productions
(www.topo.com)

The hike: Twin Lakes and Fish Lake are shallow little ponds that sit in an isolated drainage northwest of Deadman Peak. Neither big, nor deep, nor very well known, the lakes don't attract much attention, which makes them eminently suitable for a quiet picnic or overnight if you're looking to avoid the more popular destinations nearby. Like the other drainages on the north side of the Scott Mountain divide, however, this one is subject to cattle grazing in the summer.

Fish Lake is still a nice place to visit in the early season (cows usually don't arrive until after the Fourth of July). The 3-acre pond is in a gentle setting of meadows and shady forest glades, the whole tucked into a glacial basin under the 7,500-foot crest of the Scott Mountains. Brook trout fishing, as indicated by the lake's name, is usually good.

The trail climbs south from the parking area, paralleling Fish Lake Creek on a 1.9-mile, 900-foot climb to the lake. The route virtually follows the course of the creek the entire way (crossing the stream twice en route). Ascend through mixed forest of fir and pine, eventually crossing a number of grassy benches before reaching the lake. The open grassland offers good views across the headwaters of the South Fork Salmon River.

Just over midway, at 1.2 miles, arrive at a junction with the Twin Lakes Trail. A right (west) turn here leads 0.7 mile to Twin Lakes, a pair of ponds that match Fish Lake (though smaller). To reach Fish Lake, continue south at the junction and climb moderately to the sheltered basin. Return the way you came.

Options: The Fish Lake Trail continues southeast from the lake, ascending to a three-way trail junction atop the divide below Deadman Peak. The Long Gulch Trail (Hike 49) descends to Long Gulch Lake and offers a possible loop if you return to the trailhead on Forest Road 39N08. The South Fork Coffee Creek Trail (Hike 36) continues south to Coffee Creek Road. And the Poison Trail (more commonly known as the Taylor Creek Trail) heads west along the crest and then down to Taylor Creek and the little-used Poison Trailhead (not to be confused with the Poison Canyon along North Fork Swift Creek, Hike 23).

51 China Spring Trail to Grizzly Lake

Highlights:	The quickest route to Grizzly Lake—hence the quickest way to heaven.
Type of hike:	Backpack; out-and-back.
Total distance:	13.4 miles.
Difficulty:	Strenuous.
Elevation gain:	5,400 feet.
Maps:	USGS Thompson Peak quad; USDAFS Trinity Alps Wilderness map.

Finding the trailhead: From Cecilville (30 miles west of Callahan on Forest Highway 93), drive 3 miles east on FH 93 to the signed turn for East Fork campground–Petersburg Ranger Station (County Road 003). Turn right (south) and drive 5 miles, past the ranger station, to a signed fork just after the road becomes unpaved (and just after crossing a bridge over the South Fork Salmon River). Take the right fork, signed China Spring Trailhead, and follow Forest Road 37N07 the rest of the way to the trailhead. FR 37N07 winds uphill for just under 6 miles to the signed trailhead on the right.

Parking and trailhead facilities: Roadside parking, but no facilities or water. The closest camping is at East Fork Campground.

Key points:
- 0.0 Trailhead.
- 1.2 Hunters Camp/China Spring.
- 2.5 North Fork Trail junction.
- 6.0 Grizzly Meadows.
- 6.7 Grizzly Lake.

China Spring Trail to Grizzly Lake

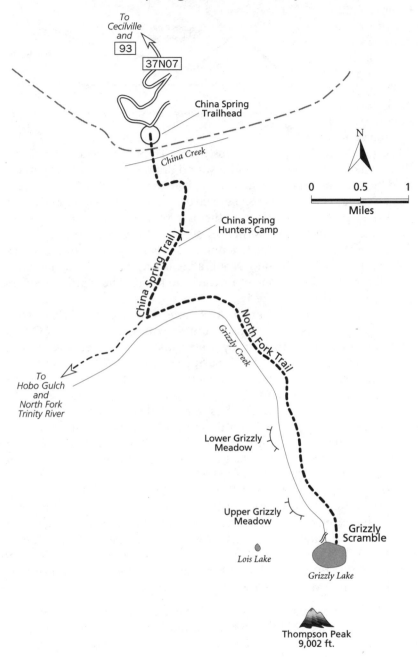

To Cecilville and 93

37N07

China Spring Trailhead

China Creek

N

0   0.5   1
Miles

China Spring Hunters Camp

China Spring Trail

North Fork Trail

Grizzly Creek

To Hobo Gulch and North Fork Trinity River

Lower Grizzly Meadow

Upper Grizzly Meadow

Grizzly Scramble

Lois Lake

Grizzly Lake

Thompson Peak 9,002 ft.

The hike: If Grizzly Lake is your idea of heaven, then the China Spring Trail is where you want to be on Judgement Day. A steep 6.7-mile hike will get you in before the gates close. Grizzly Lake, perched on a

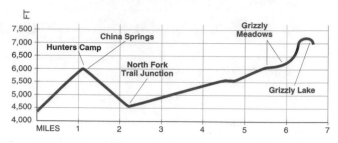

Profile data provided by TOPO! ©1999 Wildflower Productions (www.topo.com)

castle-like granite shelf at 7,100 feet, crowned by Thompson Peak and a glacieret, guarded by a clifflike approach and a waterfall pouring off its ramparts, and buffered by a sublime meadow at its base, is heaven on earth for anyone who appreciates mountain scenery. Since construction of the China Spring Trail, you can expect plenty of company. In the past, part of Grizzly's appeal was the long, glorious hike along the North Fork Trinity River to get there. The 18.5-mile route (one way) kept traffic to a minimum. For anyone with the time and inclination, the North Fork route is still a great way to go (it's hands down a prettier hike, and definitely one of my favorite trails). The North Fork Trinity River route is described in Hike 1.

For hikers with a limited amount of time, China Spring is the trail of choice. Driving time is a little longer (unless you're coming from Oregon), but you can dive into Grizzly's icy water just hours after you leave the trailhead. From the trailhead, the China Spring Trail (11W08) contours south, across China Creek, to begin a steep, waterless ascent to the Salmon River divide. The Douglas-fir and ponderosa pine forest gives way to red fir as you climb. On the way up, the stiff climb is somewhat compensated by the ever-increasing views across the Salmon River drainage. It takes just over 1 mile and a considerable amount of sweat to gain 1,600 feet and the top of the divide. Catch your breath and take the plunge over the other side, descending another 1.3 miles, through the shade of mature Douglas-fir and pine, to the junction with the North Fork Trail (12W01).

You can find cold, clear, and much appreciated water in a stream just west of the junction, down the North Fork Trail. Now that you've lost all the elevation you just gained, it's time to earn it back—and then some. The North Fork Trail climbs more than 2,000 feet over the next 4.2 miles, most of it in one final steep scramble at the end. For a complete description of this section of the trail and Grizzly Lake, see Hike 1.

Options: Experienced navigators can make several off-trail hikes from Grizzly Lake. Besides Thompson Peak, other destinations in the area include Lois Lake, Little South Fork Lake, and Mirror Lake. Use the map and good judgement. Trail options include the North Fork (Hike 1), Bobs Farm (Hike 3), and Rattlesnake Creek (Hike 2).

Appendix A: Contact Information

WILDERNESS PERMITS

All overnight visitors to the Trinity Alps Wilderness must obtain a wilderness permit before entering the backcountry. Permits are free and are available without reservation. Simply call ahead or stop by one of the ranger stations on the way to the trailhead (see contact information below) and pick one up. If you arrive after hours you can fill out a permit form at self-registration boxes located outside the stations. The Weaverville Ranger Station unveiled a slick computerized registration system in 1999. The system allows you to get your permit and current information on the route (including the number of people who are already there). Campfire permits are also required, and you should always check to see if any special fire hazards or restrictions are in effect.

FOR MORE INFORMATION

Klamath National Forest
Petersburg Ranger Station
2405 Caribou Rd.
Cecilville, CA 96031
(530) 462-4683

Klamath National Forest
Scott and Salmon River Ranger
   District
11263 N. Highway 3
Ft. Jones, CA 96032
(530) 468-5351

Shasta–Trinity National Forest
Big Bar Ranger District
Star Route 1, Box 10
Big Bar, CA 96010
(530) 623-6106

Shasta–Trinity National Forest
Coffee Creek Ranger Station
Star Route 2, Box 4630
Trinity Center, CA 96091
(530) 266-3211

Shasta–Trinity National Forest
Weaverville Ranger District
P.O. Box 1190
Weaverville, CA 96093
(530) 623-2121

Six Rivers National Forest
Lower Trinity Ranger District
P.O. Box 68
Willow Creek, CA 95573
(530) 629-2118

Six Rivers National Forest
Orleans Ranger District
Drawer B
Orleans, CA 95556
(530) 627-3291

Trinity County Chamber of
   Commerce
P.O. Box 517
Weaverville, CA 96093
(530) 623-6101
www.trinitycounty.com

USGS Map Distribution
P.O. Box 25286
Federal Center
Denver, CO 80225
(888) ASK-USGS

Appendix B: Further Reading

Harmon, Will. *Leave No Trace.* Helena, Mont.: Falcon Publishing, 1997.

——. *Wild Country Companion.* Helena, Mont.: Falcon Publishing, 1994.

Jones, Alice Goen. *Flowers and Trees of the Trinity Alps.* Weaverville, Calif.: The Trinity County Historical Society, 1986.

——, ed. *Trinity County Historic Sites.* Weaverville, Calif.: The Trinity County Historical Society, 1981.

Jorstad, W.O. *"George." Behind the Wild River.* Lewiston, Calif.: Trinity, 1995.

Knudtson, Peter M. *The Wintun Indians of California and their Neighbors.* Happy Camp, Calif.: Naturegraph Publishers, Inc., 1977.

Little, Elbert L. *National Audobon Society Field Guide to North American Trees— Western Region.* New York: Knopf, 1994.

Peterson, Roger Tory. *A Field Guide to Western Birds.* The Peterson Field Guide Series. Boston: Houghton Mifflin, 1990.

Schneider, Bill. *Bear Aware.* Helena, Mont.: Falcon Publishing, 1996.

Wallace, David Rains. *The Klamath Knot.* San Francisco: Sierra Club Books, 1983

Appendix C: Hiker's Checklist

Always make and check your own checklist!

If you've ever hiked into the backcountry and discovered that you've forgotton an essential, you know that it's a good idea to make a checklist and check the items off as you pack so that you won't forget the things you want and need. Here are some ideas:

Clothing
- [ ] Dependable rain parka
- [ ] Rain pants
- [ ] Windbreaker
- [ ] Thermal underwear
- [ ] Shorts
- [ ] Long pants or sweatpants
- [ ] Wool cap or balaclava
- [ ] Hat
- [ ] Wool shirt or sweater
- [ ] Jacket or parka
- [ ] Extra socks
- [ ] Underwear
- [ ] Lightweight shirts
- [ ] T-shirts
- [ ] Bandanna(s)
- [ ] Mittens or gloves
- [ ] Belt

Footwear
- [ ] Sturdy, comfortable boots
- [ ] Lightweight camp shoes

Bedding
- [ ] Sleeping bag
- [ ] Foam pad or air mattress
- [ ] Ground sheet (plastic or nylon)
- [ ] Dependable tent

Hauling
- [ ] Backpack and/or day pack

Cooking
- [ ] 1-quart container (plastic)
- [ ] 1-gallon water container for camp use (collapsible)
- [ ] Backpack stove and extra fuel
- [ ] Funnel
- [ ] Aluminum foil
- [ ] Cooking pots
- [ ] Bowls/plates
- [ ] Utensils (spoons, forks, small spatula, knife)
- [ ] Pot scrubber
- [ ] Matches in waterproof container

Food and Drink
- [ ] Cereal
- [ ] Bread
- [ ] Crackers
- [ ] Cheese
- [ ] Trail mix
- [ ] Margarine
- [ ] Powdered soups
- [ ] Salt/pepper
- [ ] Main course meals
- [ ] Snacks
- [ ] Hot chocolate
- [ ] Tea
- [ ] Powered milk
- [ ] Drink mixes

Photography
- [ ] Camera and film
- [ ] Filters
- [ ] Lens brush/paper

Miscellaneous
- [ ] Sunglasses
- [ ] Map and a compass
- [ ] Toilet paper
- [ ] Pocketknife
- [ ] Sunscreen
- [ ] Good insect repellent
- [ ] Lip balm
- [ ] Flashlight with good batteries and a spare bulb
- [ ] Candle(s)
- [ ] First-aid kit
- [ ] Your FalconGuide
- [ ] Survival kit
- [ ] Small garden trowel or shovel
- [ ] Water filter or purification tablets
- [ ] Plastic bags (for trash)
- [ ] Soap
- [ ] Towel
- [ ] Toothbrush
- [ ] Fishing license
- [ ] Fishing rod, reel, lures, flies, etc.
- [ ] Binoculars
- [ ] Waterproof covering for pack
- [ ] Watch
- [ ] Sewing kit

Index

Page numbers in *italics* refer to photographs.

About the Author

Northern California native Dennis Lewon is the founder of Packrats Wilderness Travel, a backpacking and wilderness education program for youth. He leads trips in the Trinity Alps, Yosemite National Park, and Point Reyes National Seashore. As a freelance writer, Lewon has contributed to publications including *Backpacker, Escape, Travelocity,* and *Islands* magazines. As a contributing editor to *Escape,* he has hiked trails throughout Glacier National Park, in the Highlands of Scotland, and among the volcanoes of the South Pacific.

Elevation profile data compiled from TOPO!, a registered trademark of Wildflower Productions. For more information on available products or to order TOPO! interactive maps on CD-ROM, contact

Wildflower Productions
375 Alabama Street, Suite 400
San Francisco, CA 94110

tel: 415-558-8700
fax: 415-558-9700
info@topo.com

or visit www.topo.com.

The Wilderness Society

THE WILDERNESS SOCIETY'S ROOTS

When their car came to a screeching halt somewhere outside of Knoxville, Tennessee, the passengers were in hot debate over plans for a new conservation group. The men got out of the car and climbed an embankment where they sat and argued over the philosophy and definition of the new organization.

Three months later, in January 1935, the group met again in Washington, D. C. Participants in the meeting included Robert Sterling Yard, publicist for the National Park Service; Benton MacKaye, the "Father of the Appalachian Trail"; and Robert Marshall, chief of recreation and lands for the USDA Forest Service. "All we desire to save from invasion," they declared, "is that extremely minor fraction of outdoor America which yet remains free from mechanical sights and sounds and smells." For a name, they finally settled on The Wilderness Society.

Among the co-founders was Aldo Leopold, a wildlife ecologist at the University of Wisconsin. In Leopold's view, The Wilderness Society would help form the cornerstone of a movement needed to save America's vanishing wilderness. It took nearly 30 years, but President Lyndon B. Johnson finally signed The Wilderness Act of 1964 into law September 3rd, in the rose garden of the White House.

THE WILDERNESS SOCIETY TODAY

The founders called the organization The Wilderness Society, and they put out an urgent call, as we do today, for "spirited people who will fight for the freedom of the wilderness." Today, Americans enjoy some 104 million acres of protected wilderness, due in large part to the efforts of The Wilderness Society. The Wilderness Society is a nonprofit organization devoted to protecting America's wilderness and developing a nation-wide network of wild lands through public education, scientific analysis and activism. The organization's goal is to ensure that future generations will enjoy the clean air and water, wildlife, beauty and opportunity for renewal provided by pristine forests, mountains, rivers and deserts. You can help protect American wildlands by becoming a Wilderness Society Member. Here are three ways you can join: **Telephone: 1-800-THE-WILD; E-mail: member@tws.org or visit the website at www.wilderness.org; Write: The Wilderness Society, Attention: Membership, 900 17th Street Northwest, Washington, D.C. 20006.**

FALCON GUIDES ®Leading the way™

FalconGuides® are available for where-to-go hiking, mountain biking, rock climbing, walking, scenic driving, fishing, rockhounding, paddling, birding, wildlife viewing, and camping. We also have FalconGuides on essential outdoor skills and subjects and field identification. The following titles are currently available, but this list grows every year. For a free catalog with a complete list of titles, call FALCON toll-free at 1-800-582-2665.

BIRDING GUIDES
Birding Georgia
Birding Illinois
Birding Minnesota
Birding Montana
Birding Northern California
Birding Texas
Birding Utah

PADDLING GUIDES
Paddling Minnesota
Paddling Montana
Paddling Okefenokee
Paddling Oregon
Paddling Yellowstone & Grand
  Teton National Parks

WALKING
Walking Colorado Springs
Walking Denver
Walking Portland
Walking Seattle
Walking St. Louis
Walking San Francisco
Walking Virginia Beach

CAMPING GUIDES
Camping Arizona
Camping California's
  National Forests
Camping Colorado
Camping Oregon
Camping Southern California
Camping Washington
Recreation Guide to Washington
  National Forests

FIELD GUIDES
Bitterroot: Montana State Flower
Canyon Country Wildflowers
Central Rocky Mountain
  Wildflowers
Chihuahuan Desert Wildflowers
Great Lakes Berry Book
New England Berry Book
Ozark Wildflowers
Pacific Northwest Berry Book
Plants of Arizona
Rare Plants of Colorado
Rocky Mountain Berry Book
Scats & Tracks of the Pacific
  Coast States
Scats & Tracks of the Rocky Mtns.
Sierra Nevada Wildflowers
Southern Rocky Mountain
  Wildflowers
Tallgrass Prairie Wildflowers
Western Trees

ROCKHOUNDING GUIDES
Rockhounding Arizona
Rockhounding California
Rockhounding Colorado
Rockhounding Montana
Rockhounding Nevada
Rockhounding New Mexico
Rockhounding Texas
Rockhounding Utah
Rockhounding Wyoming

HOW-TO GUIDES
Avalanche Aware
Backpacking Tips
Bear Aware
Desert Hiking Tips
Hiking with Dogs
Hiking with Kids
Mountain Lion Alert
Reading Weather
Route Finding
Using GPS
Wild Country Companion
Wilderness First Aid
Wilderness Survival

MORE GUIDEBOOKS
Backcountry Horseman's
  Guide to Washington
Family Fun in Montana
Family Fun in Yellowstone
Exploring Canyonlands & Arches
  National Parks
Exploring Hawaii's Parklands
Exploring Mount Helena
Exploring Southern California
  Beaches
Hiking Hot Springs of the Pacific
  Northwest
Touring Arizona Hot Springs
Touring California & Nevada
  Hot Springs
Touring Colorado Hot Springs
Touring Montana and Wyoming
  Hot Springs
Trail Riding Western Montana
Wilderness Directory
Wild Montana
Wild Utah
Wild Virginia

■ *To order any of these books, check with your local bookseller*
*or call FALCON ® at **1-800-582-2665**.*
Visit us on the world wide web at:
www.Falcon.com

FALCON®